palgrave macmillan law masters

intellectual property law

Series editor: **Marise Cremona**

palgrave macmillan law masters

intellectual property law

tina hart
Principal Lecturer in Law at the University of Huddersfield

linda fazzani
Formerly Consultant at Berwin Leighton Paisner law firm, London

simon clark
Partner at Berwin Leighton Paisner law firm, London

Fourth edition

Series editor: Marise Cremona
Professor of European Law
European University Institute
Florence
Italy

This edition first published 2006 by
PALGRAVE MACMILLAN
Houndmills, Basingstoke, Hampshire RG21 6XS and
175 Fifth Avenue, New York, N.Y. 10010
Companies and representatives throughout the world

PALGRAVE MACMILLAN is the global academic imprint of the Palgrave
Macmillan division of St. Martin's Press, LLC and of Palgrave Macmillan Ltd.
Macmillan® is a registered trademark in the United States, United Kingdom
and other countries. Palgrave is a registered trademark in the European
Union and other countries.

ISBN-13: 0–230–00633–1
ISBN-10: 0–230–00633–7

This book is printed on paper suitable for recycling and
made from fully managed and sustained forest sources.

A catalogue record for this book is available from the British Library.

10	9	8	7	6	5	4	3	2	1
15	14	13	12	11	10	09	08	07	06

Printed and bound in Great Britain by
The Cromwell Press, Trowbridge, Wiltshire.

Contents

Preface to Fourth Edition

This fourth edition includes three completely new chapters, which cover in detail the design law regime applicable in the UK following the introduction of the registered and unregistered Community designs and the amendments to the UK registered design laws.

The implementation of the Copyright and Related Rights Regulations 2003, SI 2003/2498 (referred to in this book as the 'New Copyright Regulations') has led to substantial amendments to the copyright chapters.

Chapter 18 covers the new Artist's Resale Right, also known as '*droit de suite*', which introduces an entitlement for artists to be paid royalties on the resale of their artistic works. The chapter on performance rights has been substantially amended to cover the Performances (Moral Rights, etc) Regulations 2006, which created moral rights for performers, as well as covering the changes brought in by the New Copyright Regulations.

The chapters on patents reflect some of the amendments made to the Patents Act 1977 by the Patents Act 2004. In particular section 70 which deals with groundless threats of infringement and effectively overrules the decision in *Cavity Trays Ltd* v. *RMC Panel Products Ltd* [1996] RPC 361. There are also adjustments made to the provisions concerning employee-inventor compensation. The definition of 'enabling disclosure' continues to attract refinement as demonstrated by the House of Lords' decision in *Synthon BV* v. *SmithKlineBeecham plc* [2005] UKHL 59.

All the chapters have been updated to cover the latest cases as at May 2006. We have also included Hot Topics in most chapters which highlight recent developments of particular interest.

Once more, we would like to thank the various people who have helped us in the production of this edition.

Tina would like to pay tribute to the students she has taught for the last fourteen years at the University of Derby. Their thought-provoking questions and comments on the areas of patent and trade mark law have certainly added to her enthusiasm for the subject as she looks forward to teaching a new group of students at the University of Huddersfield. She would also like to thank her children Martyn junior and Josephine for their continued love and patience with their mother, when yet again she cannot take them to the park.

Simon would like to thank the members of Berwin Leighton Paisner's Intellectual Property and Business & Technology Services departments for producing the first drafts of their respective chapters, namely Caroline Barber (Copyright), Gavin Llewellyn (Designs), Tamara Quinn (Database Rights), Toby Headdon (Performance Rights), Warsha Kale and Talya Morris (Competition), Navene Alim (Internet), and to thank Michael Hagi-Savva and Louisa Duffield-Harding for compiling the source materials and producing some of the text, and Emma Rumens for ensuring that it all stayed in the correct order!

Table of Cases

Table of Statutes

Table of Statutory Instruments

Table of European and International Legislation

Chapter 1

Introduction

Key words

- **Exclusive right** – only the owner of the intellectual property has the right to deal in it.
- **Intellectual property** – an example of intangible personal property. It is a collection of ideas and information in a broadly commercial context that the law recognises as having a value by providing protection.
- **Monopoly** – the statutory right to keep others out of the market (granted as a patent).

1.1 The Subject Matter

The aim of this book is to thoroughly ground you in Intellectual Property Law. It is worth starting off with a brief overview of the central concepts and terms. This will give you an indication of the areas that the book will cover and help you fit them all together as you continue through the book.

Patents

A patent is a monopoly right granted by the Government through the Patent Office to an individual who has invented a product or process. The basic objectives for granting this right are: to inform the public through publication of details from the application of the latest technological advances; to provide an incentive for innovation and thereby stimulate economic activity; and to provide a reward for creative and innovative effort.

Copyright

This is an exclusive right to deal with original literary, dramatic, artistic and musical works. As well as protecting the fruits of creative effort, the legislation also protects those who have invested in those efforts by providing protection for sound recordings, films and published editions of literary work.

Database right

Information arranged in a methodical and systematic way, usually accessible by electronic means such as databases, was originally protected under copyright law. However, with the implementation of the EU Directive on the legal protection of databases by the Copyright and Rights in Databases Regulations 1997, a new database right was created.

Performers' rights

These are linked with copyright but are aimed at providing protection for the actual performance of copyright works as distinct from the copyright works themselves.

Trade marks

Trade marks are words or symbols used in relation to goods and services that distinguish the owner's goods and services from those of another. Current legislation allows for the possibility of distinctive smells and sounds also attracting protection. The law in this area restrains others from applying the owner's brand to their goods and services. The trade mark owner's rights are protected by statute, if registered, or by common law, where the rights in the trade mark are based on use and goodwill.

Designs

Designs that give visual appeal to mass produced goods may be protected as registered designs, whereas designs that are merely functional are protected as unregistered designs. A child's toothbrush in the shape of a dinosaur is an example of the former, whereas an item of garden equipment is an example of the latter.

Confidential information

Equitable remedies are available to restrain the use of trade secrets and other confidential information without the owner's authority.

1.2 The Protection Provided

Legal recognition of intellectual property is provided by a negative form of protection. The legislation will usually describe the owner's right as 'exclusive', thus, by implication, giving the owner the right to restrain others from using his intellectual property without authority.

It can be argued that the protection given is purely economic as the intellectual property owner is being provided with the exclusive right to exploit that property. However, since 1988, there is also a recognition of moral rights under the Copyright, Designs and Patents Act 1988. The author of a work can, among other things, protect the integrity of the work using his right to object to derogatory treatment of the work under s.80. By its very nature intellectual property requires protection on an international level. For example, the author Alice Walker is an American national whose work is produced in the United States of America. Her work is also popular in the United Kingdom and other countries. Thus to afford her protection in the United States alone would be of little benefit. There have been a number of international agreements in existence since the nineteenth century to protect intellectual property owners internationally but on the whole their purpose was to harmonise and regularise the criteria for protection, as well as to provide for reciprocity. Intellectual property owners must still enforce their rights through national courts and thus rely on the differing methods of protection each domestic court may utilise. Added to this, intellectual property owners may be operating in jurisdictions where the system of intellectual property protection is less than they would enjoy at home. Concerns about the lack of intellectual property protection in certain states led to the Agreement on Trade Related Aspects of Intellectual Property Rights (the TRIPs Agreement, 1994), one of the multilateral agreements signed to establish the World Trade Organisation.

The Agreement is based on three principles. First, to establish minimum standards for the protection and enforcement of intellectual rights in all Member States. Second, each country must protect the nationals of other Member States by granting the rights set out in the Agreement. Third, members are required to provide the nationals of other states with protection that is 'no less favourable' than that provided to their own nationals. Added to this is the 'Most Favoured Nation Principle'. This is stipulated in Article 4(1), which states:

> 'With regard to the protection of intellectual property, any advantage, favour, privilege or immunity granted by a Member to the nationals of any other country shall be accorded immediately and unconditionally to the nationals of all other Members.'

The Agreement is administered by the World Trade Organisation. It is sovereign states rather than individual intellectual property owners who will make use of the WTO's Dispute Settlement Body, to complain about the lack of intellectual property protection.

1.3　Justification

It would appear that the protection of intellectual property rights conflicts with policies in the European Economic Area (EEA) to maintain free competition. However, it can be argued that the market economy is stimulated by the fact that consumers are assisted in making choices from a selection of goods by the use of trade marks, for example, that distinguish one trader's goods from those of another. Further, because the trade mark informs the consumer about the quality of the owner's goods, there is an element of consumer protection. Granting patents encourages innovation so more goods are available on the market.

Competition within the European Economic Area is protected by Articles 28–30 of the Treaty of Rome, which provide for the free movement of goods, and Articles 81–6, which legislate for free competition within the European Economic Area.

Nationally, the abuse of intellectual property is checked using a variety of means, for example licences of right for patents are provided during the last four years of the 20-year term, and compulsory licences are also available for unreasonable underuse of the patent by the patentee. Section 144 of the Copyright, Designs and Patents Act restrains anti-competitive licensing in relation to copyright and s.238 does the same in relation to unregistered design rights.

1.4 Sources of Law

Intellectual property law is mainly codified. Each of the main subjects of intellectual property is governed by statute and supported by delegated legislation. The following are the main statutory sources of law:

Registered Designs Act 1949 (as amended);
Patents Act 1977 (as amended);
Copyright, Designs and Patents Act 1988;
Trade Marks Act 1994;
Copyright and Rights in Databases Regulations 1997;
Council Regulation of 12 December 2001 on Community Designs; and
Patents Act 2004.

Confidential information and passing off are creatures of common law. Intellectual property cannot be protected on a mere national level and international influences can be found within the above legislation, most of which was passed to enforce the international obligations of the United Kingdom as well as to update the law. For example, one of the objectives of the Trade Marks Act 1994 was to implement Council Directive 89/104/EEC of 21 December 1988 to approximate the laws of the Member States relating to trade marks, and the Patents Act 1977 was passed, among other things, to give effect to provisions in the European Patent Convention.

More recent changes which have been made include Commission Regulation of 21 October 2002 implementing Council Regulation (EC) No. 6/2002 on Community Designs (2245/2002/EC), and the changes made to the Copyright, Designs and Patents Act 1988 by the New

Copyright Regulations, to implement the Directive of the European Parliament and the Council of the European Union 2001/29/EC on the harmonisation of certain aspects of copyright and related rights in the information society.

A body of case law has developed on the interpretation of the above provisions by national courts and international bodies such as the European Patent Office. Common law also has a part to play in the areas of passing off and the law of confidence.

Intellectual property law is administered in the Chancery Division of the High Court, with appeals to the Court of Appeal and House of Lords. The Patents Court is also part of the Chancery Division and will hear cases regarding patents and registered designs. Since the passing of the Copyright, Designs and Patents Act 1988, there is also a Patents County Court.

As we have already indicated, the nature of the protection given for intellectual property is negative. The owners will usually go to court to restrain unauthorised use of their property by others. In some cases, the remedy sought is the interlocutory injunction. An interlocutory injunction is an order sought by the intellectual property owner as a first step in proceedings before the substantive issues regarding ownership and infringement are considered. As a result, some of the case law that has developed has done so mainly from trial judges making a decision as to whether they are satisfied the claimant has at least an arguable case, because that is all a claimant needs to show at the stage of seeking an interlocutory injunction.

Cases on intellectual property law are reported in specialist law reports as well as the standard reports. Students of intellectual property law can, therefore, also consult the *Reports of Patent, Design and Trade Mark Cases* (RPC) published by the Patent Office and the *Fleet Street Reports* (FSR) published by Sweet & Maxwell. *Cases of the European Board of Appeal* (EPOR) report on decisions concerning European patents. The *European Intellectual Property Review* (EIPR) is the main journal where academic work on the subject can be found.

1.5 Useful Websites

There is a wealth of materials on intellectual property (as on other subjects) to be found on the Internet. Below are a list of useful website addresses for those interested in pursuing the topics raised in this book in further detail:

www.intellectual-property.gov.uk (Government-backed IP site)
www.intelproplaw.com (The Intellectual Property Law Server)
www.ipo.org (Intellectual Property Owners Association)

www.aipla.org (American Intellectual Property Law Association)
www.nominet.org.uk (Nominet)
www.icann.org (Internet Corporation for Assigned Names and Numbers)
www.inta.org (International Trademark Association)
www.cla.co.uk (Copyright Licensing Agency)
www.oami.eu.int (Office of the European Union)
www.curia.eu.int (European Community Cases)
www.wipo.org (World Intellectual Property Organisation)
www.wto.org (World Trade Organisation)
www.patent.gov.uk (UK Patent Office)

Summary

1.1 Intellectual property is a form of personal intangible property. The subject includes copyright, database right, registered and unregistered trade marks, patents, registered and unregistered designs as well as the law of confidence.

1.2 The legal protection is negative in the sense that the law can be used to stop others exploiting the intellectual property owner's property.

1.3 The market economy is arguably stimulated by this legal incentive to create, and competition law exists in the European Union and United Kingdom to discourage abuse of the rights granted to those who create.

1.4 Intellectual property law is mainly a creature of statute but has also developed through common law and equity.

Part I

Patents and Confidential Information

Chapter 2

Patents

Key words

- **Claims** – the monopoly claimed by the applicant. It will contain details of what is new and inventive about the subject matter.
- **Priority date** – the date on which the application is received. If the patent is granted it takes effect from that date.
- **Specification** – a description of the invented product or process with details of how it works.

2.1 What is a Patent?

Ibrufen, DVDs, Cats' Eyes and bagless vacuum cleaners are examples of well-known inventions. In return for sharing the information about their ideas, the inventors of these products have been rewarded with patents by the state.

A patent gives the owner (the patentee) the exclusive right to exploit the invention. For up to 20 years (25 in the case of pharmaceutical patents), the patentee has the legal right to stop others producing the patented goods or applying the patented process by suing for infringement. This means that, for the duration of the patent, others cannot produce the patented product or use the patented process without the patentee's permission, and this is so even if a third party has come upon the patented product or process completely independently. The grant of a patent is, therefore, the grant of a monopoly right for a specified period.

2.2 Historical Background

Patents were originally granted by the Crown exercising its Royal Prerogative. Letters Patent were a royal proclamation that the bearer had the Crown's authority to do whatever had been authorised within the Letters.

The earliest record of a granted patent dates from 1331, to a Flemish weaver who wanted to practise his trade in England. Most of the patents granted at this time were to encourage trade in general rather than for new inventions. In many cases, the grant of a patent was the Crown's method of controlling trade, and towards the end of Elizabeth I's reign there were many abuses of the system. In *Darcy* v. *Thomas Allen* (1602) Co Rep 84b, a monopoly granted to a merchant exclusively to import, make and sell playing cards was held to be void because it was contrary to the common law.

The Statute of Monopolies 1623 was passed to control or limit these abuses. Monopolies *per se* were excluded unless they came within the exception in s.6. Under s.6, a 14-year monopoly could be granted for any 'manner of new manufacture'. Whereas the section allowed for the grant of patents, the actual application procedure and enforcement of the monopoly right were still governed by the common law. The Patents Act 1835 was passed to deal with disclaimers and prolongations of claim, but the first comprehensive statute on the subject was the Patent Law Amendment Act 1852, which set up the Patent Office and Registrar of Patents. The Act also introduced the requirement that a 'specification' be filed with any application for a patent describing the nature of the invention.

In 1883, the Patents, Designs and Trade Marks Act was passed to enable the United Kingdom to satisfy its obligations of reciprocity under the Paris Convention for the Protection of Industrial Property. This Act required a full specification including detailed claims to be completed by the applicant and examined by the Patent Office before a patent would be granted. The case of *Nobel's Explosive Company Ltd* v. *Anderson* (1894) 11 RPC 115 established that it was no longer possible to claim that the patent extended to matter contained in the specification where such matter was not in the 'claim'. This highlighted the use of claims to mark the legal boundaries of the patent.

At this point, the United Kingdom patent system was purely a deposit system, where applications were checked simply to make sure that they had been completed correctly. The need to prove that an invention was really 'new' did not come until the Patents Act 1907, which introduced the practice of checking applications for 'novelty', with searches being extended to cover patents granted over the previous 50 years. The grounds for declaring a patent invalid were codified in the 1907 Patents Act. In the 1919 Patents Act it was stated that invalid claims within an application would not invalidate the whole application.

The entire patent system was overhauled by the Patents Act 1949. The modern law on patents is set down in the Patents Act 1977 which was passed to satisfy the United Kingdom's obligations under the European Patent Convention 1973, the Community Patent Convention 1975 and the Patent Co-operation Treaty 1970. It contains sections outlining the procedures followed in the European Patent Office and plans for the Community Patent. The 1949 Act was not completely repealed by the 1977 Act; only the parts that were in conflict with the European Patent Convention. The unaffected provisions now form part of the 1977 Act which itself has been amended by EC legislation and the TRIPs Agreement. In 2004, further amendments were added by the Patents Act 2004. This was passed to implement changes agreed by the Diplomatic Conference to the European Patent Convention in 2000 and to introduce measures designed to assist with the enforcement of patent rights and the resolution of disputes.

2.3 Why are Patents Granted?

The ability to stop others using or manufacturing the patented product or process effectively stops competition for the 20-year period. One might ask: how can this be justified? First of all, in obtaining a patent, the patentee has publicised the invention. While others cannot use the patent during the patent period, they can certainly look at the details and learn from the technological advances made. The grant of the patent is the reward for sharing knowledge regarding new inventions. Second, the inventor who is rewarded in this way may be encouraged to make other useful inventions. The patent is thus an incentive to be more creative. A third possible justification for patents is that, as new products are invented, this stimulates the economy as there are more products for consumers to buy.

The patentee will have often spent a great deal of money on research and development of the product in question. Having the monopoly for a limited period allows that investment to be recouped before others come onto the market to compete. Further, without the grant of a patent, others who have not had to invest in research and development would be able to copy the invention, produce it more cheaply and still make a profit, thereby depriving the inventor of the ability to recoup the investment. To ensure that the patentee uses the monopoly only for the legitimate purpose of recouping the investment, and not for the purpose of purely blocking out competition, there is provision for compulsory licences to be granted if the patentee has not commercially exploited the patent after a certain period. This is looked at in more detail in Chapter 5.

2.4 The Patent System

The application

There are two methods of obtaining a patent in the United Kingdom. An applicant can apply for a domestic patent from the Patent Office at either the main office in Gwent or the branch office in London. Alternatively an application can be made at the European Patent Office (EPO) in Munich, and originally the applicant would designate the United Kingdom (as well as other Member Countries) as countries where registration was desired. Under the European Patent Convention (EPC) 2000, which amends the original Convention, all of the signatories to the EPC are automatically treated as designated. Thus a Contracting State, such as the United Kingdom, is automatically designated. If the EPO application is successful in respect of the United Kingdom, the patent in the United Kingdom will be governed by the 1977 Act.

The date on which an application is filed is called the 'priority date' and the duration of the patent is calculated from that date. Establishing the priority date is important for two reasons. Novelty is judged by considering the state of the art at that date. So the invention must not have been anticipated at that date. Further, any person who in good faith had prior to that date been committing what would otherwise be an infringing act may continue to engage in those activities after the patent has been granted, although it is likely that such prior use would invalidate the patent application (see Chapter 3).

Under s.14, the application should be in the prescribed form and filed in the prescribed manner, accompanied by the prescribed fee. The application must include a 'specification', a 'claim' or 'claims' and any drawings that are referred to. The application should also include an abstract. It is possible, when filing an application, to claim as the priority date the date of an earlier application made within the previous 12 months; but only if the earlier application consists of or contains matter in support of the later application. Under s.16, the application will be published in the official journal of the Patent Office (unless the application is withdrawn) and it is only at this stage that the application is available to the public.

Within a year of the date of filing the application (the priority date), s.17 allows for the applicant to request a preliminary examination and search. This will be carried out by an official at the Patent Office, to make sure that the legal requirements have been complied with. There will also be a search of the prior art. A report of the search will then be sent to the applicant. The applicant will then request a substantial examination within six months. If the application succeeds, the patent will be granted, a notice will be published and the grant will take effect from the date of publication, although the duration of the patent runs from the date of the application.

A patent application may be amended after filing but before grant, either to correct any deficiencies in the application that are identified by the Patent Office or at the applicant's choice following receipt of the results of either the preliminary or the substantive search. It is a condition of these amendments that they do not result in any 'added matter' being included.

The specification

The specification is essentially a description of the invention and the best method of performing it. It should include drawings graphically representing the invention and how it is proposed to work. A good specification will describe the invention comprehensively, as any omissions will reduce the effectiveness of the patent. The specification must disclose enough detail so that a 'person skilled in the art' could perform or make the invention. If it does not, the patent could be subject to revocation.

The claims

The claims form part of the specification. These are the legal parts of the application which a court will look at to determine whether there has been infringement. Section 14(5) states that the claims should: 'define the matter for which the applicant seeks protection; be clear and concise; be supported by the description; and relate to one invention or to a group of inventions which are so linked as to form a single inventive concept.' A failure to indicate fully all the invention's features will make it easier for third parties to engage in activities that fall outside the claims of a valid patent and thus avoid an action for infringement. On the other hand, a patent can be invalidated if the claims overstate the abilities of the invention. The claims will define and set out what is 'novel' and 'inventive' about the invention. These should act as boundaries to the patentee's property over which others should not trespass.

The abstract

The abstract is the part of the document that is directed to the technician. It will contain sufficient technical information for a skilled person in that area to study the science to see whether it goes beyond what already exists in the field.

2.5 The International Patent System

The grant of a patent in the United Kingdom does not automatically provide international protection. However, whereas there is still no such thing as a worldwide patent, there are a number of international arrangements that make it possible to obtain protection in other jurisdictions.

Paris Convention for the Protection of Industrial Property 1883

Two basic principles emerge from the Paris Convention: the principle of reciprocity and the system of priority. Under the principle of reciprocity, nationals of any one of the Member States are to be accorded the same rights in another Member State as nationals of that second Member State. The system of priority allows an application to be made in one Member State claiming an earlier date of application, if the earlier application was made in another Member State within the previous 12 months. The priority system also means that the earlier application will not defeat the second application for want of novelty.

Patent Co-operation Treaty 1970

The Patent Co-operation Treaty (PCT) is administered by the World Intellectual Property Organisation (WIPO) in Geneva. The objective behind the system is to eliminate the need to make applications in a number of countries. A national of a Member State can file an 'International Patent Application' in a given patent office (known as the 'Receiving Office'), designating the countries in which registration is being sought. This has the effect of filing the application in both the first country and also in the designated countries. The application is then transmitted to an International Searching Authority which will do the prior art search and transmit the results to the individual patent offices of the designated states. From that stage, the further prosecution in each country is dealt with by the local patent office in accordance with its normal procedure. Recent Regulations under the PCT came into force on 1 January 2004 and the UK Patent Act 2004 has made minor changes to the 1977 Act to clarify the relationship between domestic patent law and the PCT.

European Patent Convention 1973

The principles behind the European Patent Convention (EPC) are similar to those of the Patent Co-operation Treaty in that the applicant makes a single application designating particular European countries.

All the Member States of the European Union are signatories of the Convention plus other countries such as Switzerland. The Convention is administered by the European Patent Office, with questions of interpretation being handled by the Boards of Appeal. In *Merrill Dow* v. *Norton* [1996] RPC 76, the House of Lords said that courts in the United Kingdom must consider the decisions of the European Patent Office on the interpretation of the Convention. By implication this means that the approach of the EPO should be followed when interpreting sections of the Patent Act 1977. The European Patent Convention was revised in 2000, following agreement by the Diplomatic Conference in November 2000.

Community Patent Convention 1975

Member States of what was then the European Economic Community (now the European Union) established the Community Patent Convention, in order to set up a system where a single community-wide patent could be granted. The plans are that this system will also be administered by the

European Patent Office in Munich. There is now a draft Directive to introduce a community patent. It is hoped that there will be a Community-wide patent by 2012.

The Future of Patents

The patent system was the first of the intellectual property systems to legislate for a truly harmonised and community-wide system. The advances in patent law that are on the horizon relate not so much to harmonisation but on how the system is to address the advances in biotechnology, genetic engineering and computing.

Hot Topic . . .

ACCESS TO DRUGS! DO INTERNATIONAL AGREEMENTS TO ENFORCE PATENTS HARM THE SICK IN DEVELOPING COUNTRIES?

Since the creation of the World Trade Organisation (WTO), there has been an ongoing debate about the extent to which the trade rules are fair to consumers in the developing and least developed countries. In relation to the enforcement of patents through Article 27 of the Agreement on Trade Related Aspects of Intellectual Property Rights – the TRIPs Agreement (passed as one of the WTO Agreements and referred to in Chapter 1), the thrust of the debate has been whether it is fair for wealthy multinational pharmaceutical companies to expect poorer countries to abide by patent rules which would result in expensive medicine. The first question to ask is whether there is really a link between having a patent in force and the cost of the drug in question. The price of medicine will inevitably reflect the cost of taking out a licence for its production. According to Raghaven (Raghaven, *Recolonization GATT, the Uruguay Round and the Third World*, Third World Network, 1991), before Italy started allowing patents for drugs, Hoffman La Roche was selling Librium and Valium (two drugs patented in the United Kingdom) to the National Health Service in the United Kingdom at forty times their price in Italy. When countries liberalise their patent laws in such a way as to allow local industries to produce their own generic versions of patented drugs, the result has been better access to essential drugs for the local people, improvement in the research expertise of the local pharmacists and an improvement in the country's balance of payments as other developing countries purchase their medical requirements there in preference to the more expensive multinational pharmaceutical companies (see for example the India Patents Act 1970). The problem for drug companies is that a great deal of investment is expended on research and development into new drugs. Although expensive and time consuming to develop, once a new drug has been invented it is easy to copy through reverse engineering. Developing countries were given more time to make their intellectual property systems TRIPs compliant. The least developed countries were given even more time. The WTO, Declaration on the TRIPs Agreement and Public Health Ministerial Conference, held in Doha in 2001, has responded to some of the concerns in relation to the implementation of intellectual property rights in the field of health but there is no doubt that the debate will continue.

Summary

2.1 A patent is a monopoly granted to the owner by the state in return for disclosing information about the invention.

2.2 Regulation of the patent system dates back to the Statute of Monopolies 1623. The modern statute on patents is the Patents Act 1977.

2.3 Patents are granted in return for information about technological advances. The monopoly is also justified as it allows the owner to recoup the investment in research and development before others can enter the market.

2.4 The main part of the application is the specification that will include claims and an abstract.

2.5 The United Kingdom's membership of a number of reciprocal international conventions has influenced the law on patents.

2.6 The patent system will need to adapt to address advances in biotechnology and genetic engineering.

Exercises

2.1 What exactly does the owner of a patent obtain from the state?

2.2 Why should anyone be allowed to keep their competitors out of the market for up to 20 years?

2.3 Your client has developed a chemical compound to produce a fat busting drug. She would like to apply for a patent. Advise her of the procedure.

2.4 What is the best way to achieve international protection for a patent?

Further reading

Agreement on Trade-Related Aspects of Intellectual Property Rights, Including Rights including Trade in Counterfeit Goods (1994) ILM 33, 81.

Henderson, *TRIPs and the Third World: the Example of Patents in India* [1997] EIPR 11, 651.

McGrath, *The Patent Provisions in TRIPs: Protecting Reasonable Remunerations for Services Rendered – or the Latest Development in Western Colonialism?* [1996] EIPR 7, 398.

WTO, *Declaration on the TRIPs Agreement and Public Health Ministerial Conference*, WTO Doc. WT/MIN(01)/DEC/2 (2001).

Chapter 3

Patentability (1)

Key words

- **Anticipated** – details of the invented product or process were in the public domain prior to the date of the application.
- **Availability to the public** – the subject matter of the patent application was in the public domain prior to the date of the application.
- **Enabling disclosure** – there is sufficient information concerning the invented product or process for a skilled person to make it work.

3.1 Introduction

Patent protection is available for products and processes that satisfy four basic requirements of patentability.

Patentability under the 1977 Act is based on Articles 52–7 of the European Patent Convention, and it is the practice of English courts to take into account the spirit and purpose of that Convention in settling disputes that arise either on application or after a patent has been granted.

Section 1(1) of the 1977 Act states that a patent may only be granted if the invention in question:

(a) is new (or novel);
(b) involves an inventive step;
(c) is capable of industrial application; and
(d) is not excluded under s.1(2) or (3).

Before considering questions of novelty, inventive step and industrial application, one should make sure that the subject of an application does not fall within one of the exclusions.

3.2 Exclusions from Patentability

If the subject of the application falls under one of the exclusions, there is no need to go any further. The exclusions are in ss.1(2) and (3) of the Patents Act. Section 1(2) states:

'It is hereby declared that the following (among other things) are not inventions for the purposes of this Act, that is to say, anything which consists of:

(a) a discovery, scientific theory or mathematical method;
(b) a literary, dramatic, musical or artistic work or any other aesthetic creation whatsoever;
(c) a scheme, rule or method for performing a mental act, playing a game or doing business, or a program for a computer;
(d) the presentation of information

but the foregoing provision shall prevent anything from being treated as an invention for the purposes of this Act only to the extent that a patent or application for a patent relates to that thing as such.'

Discoveries are not patentable under paragraph (a). However, if they lead to something tangible, they may be able to attract patent protection. For example penicillin, a naturally occurring medicine, which was discovered in 1928, could not be the subject of a patent. However, 12 years on, drugs produced from it were patented. The importance of the last two words of s.1(2) ('as such') is illustrated by cases such as *Genentech Incorporation's Application* [1989] RPC 147. In that case, one of the questions the court had to consider was whether the invention in question (a process for the production of human growth hormone in bacteria that would result in an enzyme capable of dissolving fibrin in blood clots) was excluded from patentability because it related to a discovery. It was stated that where an invention consists of more than excluded subject matter, the application should be looked at as a whole. In other words, if the application contains excluded subject matter, it should not be rejected simply on that basis. If an application consists of excluded subject matter, then the suggestion is that it does not contain any other subject matter. However, an application containing excluded subject matter can also contain other, 'included', subject matter. Thus whereas it is not permissible to patent a discovery, it is possible to patent an invention that embodies that discovery.

Computer-implemented inventions

The subject matter excluded from patentability by paragraph (b) is already capable of being protected under the law of copyright. The exclusion of computer programs, under paragraph (c), has been a source of frustration for the software industry. Although copyright is available to protect computer programs, as we shall see later, copyright, in comparison to patents, is not a monopoly right. The cases in this area either concern computer programs themselves or inventions that include a computer program. *Gale's Application* [1991] RPC 305, is an example of the former. The applicant discovered an improved method of calculating square root numbers using a computer. Instructions were placed into the electronic circuitry of a read-only memory unit (ROM). However, outside the computer, the instructions did not represent a technical process nor did they provide solutions to technical problems within the computer. The Court of Appeal was of the view that the subject of *Gale's Application* was essentially a computer program and, therefore, excluded from patentability. The fact that the invention was embodied in the form of a ROM, and thus technically hardware, was irrelevant and the application was dismissed.

A slightly different approach is taken where the invention includes a computer program but is not the program itself. If the machine in question meets the criteria for patentability, without the program, it can be patented. The Technical Board of Appeal in the European Patent Office provided useful guidance on this point in *Vicom Systems Incorporated's Application* [1987] OJ EPO 14, when it stated that what would be decisive is the technical contribution that the invention makes to the known art. This decision influenced the Court of Appeal in *Merrill Lynch's Application* [1989] RPC 561. There, the application concerned a data processing system for making a trading market in securities. This invention used a known computer system controlled by a program coded in any known programming language. The Court of Appeal defined 'technical effect' as some technical advance on the prior art in the form of a new result. Although the subject of the application met that requirement, it was really a method of doing business, which is also excluded from patentability under s.1(2). The applicants failed to prove that what they had produced was more than a computer program or that, if it was, it was anything more than a method of doing business 'as such'.

In *Fujitsu Ltd's Application* [1997] RPC 608; CA [1997] EWCA Civ 1174 the application was for a method and apparatus for modelling a synthetic structure for designing inorganic materials. It involved a computer programmed so that an operator could select an atom, a lattice vector and a crystal face in each of two crystal structures displayed by the computer. The computer then converted data representing the physical layouts of the crystal structure that would have been obtained by combining the original two structures in such a way that the two selected atoms were superimposed, the two selected lattice vectors were superimposed and the two selected crystal faces were superimposed. The resulting data were then displayed to give an image of the resulting combined structure.

The applicant argued that this was not merely a thought process or a program for a computer 'as such' but that the images displayed were a technical contribution to the manufacture of new inorganic materials. Laddie J, whose decision was followed by the Court of Appeal, disagreed. On the issue of exclusion, the court was interested in substance over form. Even if the program made the computer perform in a novel way, it was still necessary to look at precisely what the computer was doing. If all that was being done, as a matter of substance, was the performance of one of the excluded activities (for example, a discovery, a method of doing business), it still could not be protected as a patent. In *IBM's Application* [1999] RPC 861, which concerned computer programs that were engaged in window management and provided a system whereby information displayed on a junior window was rearranged so that the entirety of the information in that window was visible notwithstanding that it was overlapped or obscured by a senior window, the Examining Division of the EPO found that the claims in question were directed to a computer program 'as such' and therefore not patentable.

On appeal to the Technical Board of Appeal, the following observations were made:

(a) There was no doubt that Article 52(2)(C) of the European Patent Convention 1973 provided that programs for computers should not be regarded as inventions and thus patents for them were not available. However, the exclusion was limited to claims for computer programs 'as such', which meant that not all programs for computers were to be excluded. Hence, where a claim was being made for something other than a computer program 'as such', then without other objections it would be patentable. Therefore the meaning of the words 'as such' were the key to determining the scope and limits of the patentability of computer programs.

(b) The exclusion of computer programs 'as such' should be construed as meaning that a computer program was considered to be a mere abstract creation which was lacking in technical character. Therefore, the main problem for the interpretation of the exclusion from patentability was to define the meaning of 'technical character'.

(c) Such a technical character could be said to be the effect of execution of the program where the software solved a technical problem. If such was the case, then the underlying computer program was patentable. A patent could therefore be granted not only in the case of an invention where a computer program was employed to control an industrial process or a piece of machinery or the working of a piece of machinery, but in cases where the computer program was the only means, or one of the necessary means, of obtaining a technical effect, including a technical effect which was achieved by the internal functioning of the computer itself.

Since 2000, the European Patent Office has taken what is referred to as the 'Pensions Benefit' approach (see *Pensions Benefit T931/95* [2001] OJ EPO 441). This is to ask two questions:

(1) Does the claimed invention have any technical features? If there are no technical features at all, then the application should be rejected as not being an invention.

(2) Is the claimed invention old or obvious? In deciding whether it is old or obvious, the Examiner must ignore anything that is not a 'technical feature'. What is the difference between the *Vicom* 'technical contribution test' and the 'Pensions Benefit' test? With the former, the subject matter of the application (for example a business method) would be excluded before such stages as the novelty and inventive step were considered, while the Pensions Benefit test would involve an examination at the same stage. This approach has been endorsed by English practitioners. *CFPH LLC's Patent Applications* (GB0226884.3) [2005] EWHC 1589 concerned whether an invention for reducing delays in online betting were unpatentable business methods within s.1(2) and *Halliburton Energy Services Inc.* v. *Smith International (North Sea) Ltd* [2005] EWHC 1623 concerned the computerised system for designing drill bits. In both cases the judges (Prescott QC in *CFPH* and Pumfrey J in *Halliburton*), were of the opinion that the Pensions Benefit test of considering novelty, obviousness and excluded matter should be adopted by courts in the United Kingdom. The Patent Office has since confirmed that the 'technical contribution test' is no longer the right approach and the newer EPO test will be adopted instead.

There had been a draft Directive (Proposal for a European Parliament and Council Directive on the patentability of computer-implemented inventions (COM 2002/0047)). The aim of the proposal was to clarify the law in Europe as distinct from the more liberal approach taken in the United States. The Directive was rejected by the European Parliament on 6 July 2005. However the European Commission has given an undertaking to work with the European Parliament in order to decide on a future course of action.

Biotechnology

There are further exclusions to patentability in s.1(3). This has been modified by the Patent Regulations 2000 (SI No. 2037), which implement Directive 98/44/EC (the biotechnology Directive). Patents are not to be granted whose commercial exploitation would be contrary to public policy or morality. Morality must be something more than 'illegality' (s.1(4)). Schedule 2A to the Patents Act 1977 deals with biotechnological inventions. These are defined as:

'(a) inventions concerning products consisting of or containing biological material or (b) processes by means of which biological material is produced processed or used.' (Schedule 2A, para. 1)

'Biological material' is defined as any material containing genetic information and which is capable of reproducing itself or being reproduced in a biological system (para. 2).

Paragraph 3 sets out the subject matter that is not allowed:

(a) the human body, at various stages of its formation and development and the simple discovery of one of its elements, including the sequence or partial sequence of a gene;
(b) processes for human cloning;
(c) processes for modifying the germ line genetic identity of human beings;
(d) uses of human embryos for industrial or commercial purposes;
(e) processes for modifying the genetic identity of animals which are likely to cause them suffering without any substantial medical benefit to humans or animals; and animals resulting from such processes;
(f) any variety of animal or plant or any essentially biological process for the reproduction of animals or plants, not being a micro-biological or other technical process or product of such a process.

For an interesting case concerning the issues see *Harvard/Onco-Mouse* [2005] EPOR 31 where the Technical Board of Appeal of the European Patent Office had to consider, among other things, the morality of creating a genetically altered mouse with susceptibility to cancer as against the potential benefit in the possible discovery of a cure for cancer.

Article 53 of the European Patent Convention has been amended to take account of the Directive.

3.3 Novelty and Publication

As the grant of a patent provides the patentee with a monopoly for up to 20 years, it would seem only fair that one of the conditions for such a grant is that the subject of the application is 'new', in other words, something that has never been done or made before.

Under s.2(1) of the Act, an invention is new if:

'it does not form part of the state of the art.'

This means that the subject matter should not have been available to the public before the date of the application. Section 2(2) goes further:

'The state of the art in the case of an invention shall be taken to comprise all matter (whether a product, a process, information about either, or anything else) which has at any time before the priority date of the invention been made available to the public (whether in the United Kingdom or elsewhere) by written or oral description, by use or in any other way.'

Cases decided under this section cover a number of issues. They concern, for example, information found in journals, information in previous (but, at the relevant time, unpublished) applications, prior use of the invention claimed and the inventor's own disclosure. Before considering these issues in turn, let us consider the question of 'availability to the public'.

Material is available to the public if it is available anywhere in the world. Published material is clearly available to the public. This is defined by s.130(1), which states:

> ' "published" means made available to the public (whether in the United Kingdom or elsewhere) and a document shall be taken to be published under any provision of this Act if it can be inspected as of right at any place in the United Kingdom by members of the public.'

So even if the relevant information is contained in a journal shelved at the University of Buea, it will be deemed available to the public if it is possible to gain access to it. In *Quantel Ltd* v. *Spaceward Microsystems Ltd* [1990] RPC 83, one of the issues was whether the subject matter of an infringement action had been anticipated by demonstrations at various institutions in the United States and elsewhere. Although Falconer J held that the invention satisfied the test of novelty, the case did make clear that prior use (including in a demonstration) would amount to anticipation. Returning to our example, Buea is not in the United States and few people may know that it is in the West African state of Cameroon. Common sense has to prevail and one must consider how readily available the information is. In *General Tire & Rubber Company* v. *Firestone Tyre & Rubber Co. Ltd* [1972] RPC 457, Sachs LJ suggested that the state of the art will not include matter that would not have been discovered during the course of a diligent search. This seems a reasonable test.

If a 'diligent search' results in a discovery of documentary information concerning the subject matter of the proposed patentee's application, then the product or process *prima facie* lacks novelty. In order for prior documentary information, or indeed any 'prior art', to invalidate a patent on the grounds that it lacks novelty, that information must amount to a clear disclosure of the invention. Traditionally the courts have approved the 'planting the flag' test set out in the Court of Appeal's judgment in *General Tire & Rubber Company* v. *Firestone Tyre & Rubber Co. Ltd* [1972] RPC 457 at page 485, namely that:

> 'To anticipate the patentee's claim the prior publication must contain clear and unmistakable directions to do what the patentee claims to have invented ... A signpost, however clear, upon the road to the patentee's invention will not suffice. The prior inventor must be clearly shown to have planted his flag at the precise destination before the patentee.'

Such disclosure must be what the courts refer to as 'enabling disclosure'. This was reinforced by the House of Lords in *Asahi Kasei Kogyo KK's Application* [1991] RPC 485 where Lord Oliver said:

'I do not see how an invention can be said to have been made available to the public merely by a published statement of its existence, unless the method of working is so self evident as to require no explanation.'

It is not possible to create a 'mosaic' of documents to challenge an application on novelty. If several documents are to be read together for the purposes of challenging a patent application on the grounds of novelty, the documents must be such that they would naturally be read together (for instance, because they cross-refer to one another). This principle is confirmed in the *European Patent Office Guidelines*.

In *Bristol-Myers Squibb Co.* v. *Baker Norton Pharmaceuticals* [2001] RPC 1, a lecture given by the patentee's Director of Research before the priority date on use of the taxol drug to treat ovarian cancer over a shorter infusion period amounted to 'enabling disclosure'. Aldous LJ (at page 46) said that using the information from the lecture, members of the public could carry out the procedure without the need for any further information from the patent. The lecture contained 'clear and unmistakable directions' to carry out what was being claimed in the patent.

3.4 Novelty and Earlier Application

The 'state of the art' referred to in s.2(2) includes information contained in other patent applications with earlier priority dates. This is confirmed in s.2(3), which states:

'The state of the art of an invention to which an application for a patent or a patent relates shall be taken also to comprise matter contained in an application for another patent which was published on or after the priority date of that invention, if the following conditions are satisfied, that is to say –
(a) that matter was contained in the application for that other patent both as filed and as published; and
(b) the priority date of that matter is earlier than that of the invention.'

To an extent, this puts the applicant at a disadvantage. He will have no means of knowing the contents of other applications until they are published. Yet those details may jeopardise his application. His claim would be invalidated by information that is not technically 'available to the public'.

This reinforces the importance of the priority date. As stated in Chapter 2, it is possible to file an application and then file a fuller application within the next 12 months claiming the priority date of the earlier application. So it is not unusual to have the following scenario: *A* puts in an earlier application with sufficient details to satisfy the requirements of the Patents Act. *B* then puts in his application. *A* then files a fuller application which contains information that would anticipate *B*'s claim and, because of the earlier priority date, it does anticipate and, therefore, invalidate *B*'s claim.

However, the possible inequity of this is mitigated by the practice of interpreting s.2(3) in the same way as s.2(2). Information contained in the earlier application must be 'enabling information'. In *Asahi Kasei Kogyo KK's Application* [1991] RPC 485, a major issue was whether the application in suit lacked novelty because of an earlier application. The application in suit described and claimed a physiologically active polypeptide (human tissue necrosis factor) produced by genetic engineering and useful in treating human tumours. A competitor's application was actually filed after the priority date of the application in suit, but it claimed priority from an earlier application. That earlier application disclosed the polypeptide but did not describe any method of preparing it. The House of Lords held that the earlier disclosure had not been an 'enabling disclosure' and there was, therefore, no anticipation. Passages from Lord Oliver's judgment indicate the unfairness of deciding otherwise. At page 542, he says:

> 'No doubt the claim is "matter contained" in an application but the claimant may in fact not even know whether the compound can be produced in practice. If nothing further is added . . . the application must fail and be refused. It would be a most unreasonable result that this failed application should nevertheless be capable of being cited as an anticipation of a subsequent application on the basis of the priority of an invention which it was never in a position successfully to claim.'

On the face of it *Asahi* appears to conflict with s.5(2) of the Patents Act.

Section 5(2) allows for the filing of applications from which a later, fuller application, filed within 12 months of the applicant's first application, can claim priority and not be anticipated by an intervening, otherwise anticipatory, application. Section 5(2) is useful for researchers who may have found a solution to a particular problem but need time to pursue it further. They can be rewarded for being the first to come up with the solution, even if they cannot immediately specify how the solution works, provided they can disclose the full story within the statutory 12 months. However, to avoid possible injustices where applications are filed merely to block out competitors, the first application must disclose the elements of the later application in suit. In *Asahi* Lord Jauncey felt that for the purposes of s.5(2), information in the earlier application should also be 'enabling'. At page 457, he states:

> 'an invention is only supported by prior matter for the purposes of paragraph [5(2)(a)] if the earlier relevant application not only describes the invention but also contains an enabling disclosure.'

See also *Evan's Medical Ltd's Application* [1998] RPC 517.

In *Synthon BV v. SmithKlineBeecham plc* [2005] UKHL 59, the House of Lords appears to have made adjustments to the principles laid down in *Asahi*. In giving the leading judgment, Lord Hoffman separated disclosure from enablement. In assessing whether a prior art document anticipates a claimed invention, he said first one had to look at what the prior art document disclosed (to the skilled man):

'. . . the matter relied upon as prior art must disclose subject matter which, if performed, would necessarily result in an infringement of the patent' (at para. 22)

Secondly one had to look at whether that disclosure enabled the claimed invention to be performed (by the skilled man):

'Enablement means that the ordinary skilled person would have been able to perform the invention which satisfies the requirement of disclosure . . .' (at para. 26)

3.5 Novelty and Use

Prior use of the invention in question is also considered part of the state of the art. This is based on the principle that a monopoly should not be granted to stop individuals from doing what they had been doing legitimately before the date of the application. This principle dates back to the Statute of Monopolies 1623 and is best summed up by Lord Denning's question in *Bristol/Meyers (Johnson)* [1973] RPC 157 at page 164:

'If this patent were granted, would it stop the prior user from doing what he was doing before?'

From a number of cases, it is also clear that for prior use to anticipate, it must be 'enabling use', in other words, the use must give information as to how the invention works.

In *Windsurfing International Inc.* v. *Tabur Marine (GB) Ltd* [1985] RPC 59, the plaintiffs were the owners of a patent on a sailboard that featured a Bermuda rig with a wishbone spar. In an infringement action brought by the plaintiffs, the defendants argued that there had been an anticipation ten years before the patent had been granted. This involved the use in public by a 12-year-old boy, who had built his own sailboard and used it for two summers off the coast of Hayling Island. The booms of that sailboard differed slightly in that they were straight (whereas those of the plaintiffs were curved) but, while in use, they were flexible enough to bend like those of the plaintiffs. The prior use was held to have anticipated the plaintiffs' patent and the patent was declared invalid. This can be contrasted with *Quantel Ltd* v. *Spaceward Microsystems Ltd* [1990] RPC 83 where it was held that the use during demonstrations did not anticipate, because in that case the use did not show how the invention worked.

In *PLG Research Ltd* v. *Ardon International* [1995] RPC 287 Aldous J said that prior use only forms part of the state of the art if it discloses the necessary information about the invention in question. The Technical Board of the European Patent Office appears to favour this principle, making it possible in some cases to obtain a patent for a new use of an existing patent. In *Mobil/Friction Reducing Additive* [1990] EPOR 73, the claimed invention was for the use of compounds as friction reducing additives in lubricant compositions. A prior document disclosed the use of the same compounds as additives in engine oil to inhibit rust. The question was whether the friction reducing properties of the claimed compounds had been made available to the public by the prior disclosure. The Technical Board of Appeal did not think so. In its view, 'available' meant more than just knowledge of the patent. All the technical features of the claimed invention must be communicated to the public, or laid open for inspection. In other words, the prior document or use must communicate its technical features to the public.

It seems that *Mobil* confirms that it is possible to claim a new use for an old patent, as long as the new use has a new technical effect, and the prior use did not disclose or enable the public to understand that new technical effect. How does this reconcile with the traditional principle that a person should not be granted a monopoly to stop others from doing what they were doing before and with the statement quoted earlier from *General Tire*? As already suggested, *General Tire* makes room for the assumption that two people can arrive at a solution from two different directions which inevitably lead to the invention. As we will see in Chapter 6 on defences, *Mobil* and other decisions should not stop others from doing what they were doing before, because of s.64, which allows a person acting *bona fide* to carry on any activities in which they were engaged before the patent was granted. So, if *A* was using the invention before *B*'s application but *C* was not, this defence will only be available to *A* and not to *C*.

What effect has *Mobil* had on English courts? In *Merrill Dow* v. *Norton* [1996] RPC 76, the House of Lords said that courts in the United Kingdom must have regard to the decisions of the European Patent Office on the construction of the European Patent Convention on which the Patents Act 1977 is based. In *Merrill Dow* the plaintiffs were a pharmaceutical company that had patented an anti-histamine drug called terfenadine. Unlike other anti-histamines, this did not cause drowsiness. The patent was obtained in 1972 and expired in 1992. Other companies were then allowed to make and market terfenadine. The plaintiffs had researched terfenadine and discovered that it worked by forming an acid metabolite in the liver. They analysed its chemical composition, then produced and patented their own acid metabolite in 1980 for anti-histamine drugs. They claimed that the sale of terfenadine by other companies infringed their patent for the acid metabolite because acid metabolite is automatically produced in the liver when terfenadine is swallowed. The sale of terfenadine, it was claimed, was an infringement because it involved knowingly supplying consumers with the means of producing the patented acid metabolite.

To deal with the issue of infringement the House of Lords had to consider the issue of novelty. It was claimed as a defence that there had been anticipation of the acid metabolite patent by use and disclosure. The anticipation by use had taken place when the terfenadine was made available to, and used by, volunteers in clinical trials between 1977 and 1978. Acid metabolite had been produced in their livers and they had experienced its anti-histamine effects. Anticipation by disclosure was claimed in the specification of the terfenadine patent. According to Lord Hoffman at page 86:

> 'An invention is a piece of information. Making matter available to the public within the meaning of s.2(2) therefore requires the communication of information. The use of a product makes the invention part of the state of the art only so far as that use makes available the necessary information.'

This confirms that prior use will only anticipate if that use illustrates how the invention works. So each case will depend on the workings of the invention in question. If the mechanics are simple, as in *Windsurfing*, then use anticipates, but if they are very technical or, indeed, cannot be seen, even on close inspection, then use is less likely to anticipate. In *Merrill Dow*, Lord Hoffman made the following observation about the 'infringement test' from *General Tire*:

> 'Acts done secretly or without the knowledge of the relevant facts, which would amount to infringements after the grant of the patent, will not count as anticipations before.'

Such use as there was, did not amount to 'enabling use', so there was no anticipation by use. There was, however, anticipation by disclosure. After *Merrill Dow*, on anticipation and use, see *Evan's Medical Ltd's Application* [1998] RPC 517. This concerned a patent for pertactin, a surface antigen of the whooping cough bacterium *Bordatella pertussis*. At the priority date, Takeda's vaccine was already on the market. This must have contained pertactin, although at the time no one appreciated this. Relying on comments made in *Merrill Dow*, the proprietor therefore argued that the prior use in Takeda's vaccine did not invalidate the patent because no one knew that the pertactin was present. Laddie J, however, made a distinction. In *Merrill Dow*, the patients in question were never in possession of a product containing the acid metabolite, whereas in *Evan's*, the Takeda vaccine was a product within the claims. *Mobil* was endorsed but distinguished on the facts of the *Merrill* case. It is felt by some academics and practitioners that the House of Lords should have used *Merrill Dow* to put *Mobil* right. See *Bristol-Myers Squibb* v. *Baker Norton* [1999] RPC 253, where

Mobil has been questioned but it was felt that national courts should not depart from a decision of the enlarged Board of Appeal lightly. In fact it was a matter of the utmost seriousness and only to be done by a higher court.

The implications of these decisions on the abuse of patent rights can, at this stage, only be imagined. If the plaintiffs in *Merrill Dow* had succeeded, they would, in effect, have been able to add more than ten years to their original monopoly. As indicated above, these decisions will need to be considered in the light of Lord Hoffman's statements in *Synthon*.

In his article, 'Disclosure and enablement: The House of Lords clarifies the law on novelty' (*Journal of Intellectual Property Law & Practice*, 2006, Vol. 1, No. 3 at page 163), Rowan Freeland states that by separating 'enablement' and 'disclosure', the decision provides a 'new and elegant' test for disclosure. On the test for 'disclosure', he states that it can readily be seen whether an express disclosure, if performed would fall within the scope of the later patent. On the 'enablement' test, the author states that this addresses whether the requirement 'if performed' in the disclosure test is satisfied in fact. With respect, it is not really clear why the distinction is required, or indeed whether it adds anything new to the requirement for 'enabling disclosure'. According to Freeland:

> 'The decision provides a new and elegant test for disclosure in the context of novelty to which the courts may well refer for decades to come.'

We look forward to seeing how the decision is applied in subsequent cases.

One interesting type of anticipation is by the inventor himself. This is illustrated by *Fomento* v. *Mentmore* [1956] RPC 87, where the plaintiffs had a patent for making a particular type of improved ballpoint pen. It was claimed that the patentees themselves had anticipated their application by providing the public with pens, which were the subject of the invention, before the priority date. The Court of Appeal held that, as the pens came into the hands of those who were free at law and equity to do whatever they liked with them, they anticipated the invention claimed in the application. However, as with other types of anticipation, providing goods to the public in this way will only anticipate if it is easy to understand how the patent works by using it. Further, if the inventor has made it clear that the invention is being shown for purely experimental purposes, or is disclosed on a confidential basis, the invention will not be anticipated by their prior use or the disclosure. In *Pall Corp.* v. *Commercial Hydraulic* [1990] RPC 329, the patentee's delivery of membrane samples, in confidence, to those who were aware that the samples were being supplied for experimental purposes and on a secret basis did not constitute making the invention 'available to the public'. This underlines the importance for inventors of only disclosing inventions to those who are under an obligation of confidentiality; this obligation may be implied in certain fiduciary relationships (such as between a solicitor and client or patent agent and client) or imposed by a contractual agreement (see Chapter 7).

Sections 2(4)–(6) define specific types of disclosure that will not anticipate a patent application. These include information obtained unlawfully, information disclosed through a breach of confidence, and disclosure at a recognised international exhibition. Prior use to treat humans and animals will not invalidate for lack of novelty.

In particular, s.2(6) makes clear that just because a substance or composition is part of the state of the art, that does not stop its being patentable as an invention if the particular use which is applied for is a method of treatment of a human or animal body which was not part of the state of the art. This section of the Act has been interpreted as allowing patents for the first discovered medical use of a known substance, but not second and subsequent discovered medical uses of the same substance. However, the EPO has been willing to entertain applications for second (and further) medical uses when they are presented in the form approved by the Swiss Patent Office, namely, 'an application' for use of the substance for the manufacture of a medicament for the treatment of a particular condition. This has become known as the 'Swiss form'.

Hot Topic . . .

BIOTECHNOLOGY AND MORALITY

The developments in biotechnology are exciting yet raise great concern. The possibilities for treating serious illness to ending world poverty signal the desire by governments and business to invest in this area of science. Yet the use of biological material for research leading to possible commercial gain raises a number of ethical issues. In their article, 'The importance of the Morality Exception under the European Patent Convention' Thomas and Richards commenting on the *Onco-Mouse* litigation outline two possible objections; these are concerns for animal welfare and objections on religious or other grounds to the patenting of life-forms. Both are essentially matters of morality and as such are difficult to quantify. How is morality to be assessed? In *Plant Genetic Systems/Plant Cells (Opponent: Greenpeace)* [1995] EPOR 357, the Technical Board of Appeal stated:

'the concept of morality is one which is related to the belief that some behaviour is right whereas other behaviour is wrong, this belief being founded on the totality of the accepted norms which are deeply rooted in a particular culture which, in the case of the European Patent Convention, is the culture inherent in European Society and civilization.'

It is respectfully suggested that this in itself does not reveal much. Clearly public opinion will be a factor but there is also the issue of how to solicit and assess that opinion. The Boards of Appeal have had to consider issues of morality in a number of cases. Perhaps the most well known is the *Onco-Mouse*. Laboratory mice that had been genetically altered to increase their suspectibility to developing cancer were then used for research into anti-cancer drugs. Here the conflict is clearly between animal welfare and the possible alleviation of human suffering.

The Technical Board of Appeal adopted a two stage test in *Onco-Mouse*.

(1) If there is likely to be suffering to animals from the application of the invention and no likelihood of substantial medical benefit to people or other animals, the patent must be refused.

(2) Even if there is substantial medical benefit as well as animal suffering, consider whether a patent should nevertheless be refused under the traditional Article 53(a). In other words, a balance must be made between animal suffering against usefulness to mankind.

We suggest that the issues are complex and more so when the issue concerns the use of human biological materials – see *Hormone Relaxin Opposition* [1995] OJ EPO 338. Linked to this has been the debate concerning research into human stem cells. According to Graeme Laurie:

'Research using the human embryo is ethically problematic for a number of reasons, all of which centre around the moral status of this organism. While some consider it to be a human being from conception and deserving of full respect, most people do not see it that way, and most legal systems accord the embryo a special status which falls short of conferring the protection of full legal human rights and privileges. But whatever view we might take of its status, most agree that the human embryo is somehow unique . . .'

Yet such research can provide scientists with the means to repair or replace diseased or damaged cells in conditions such as Parkinson's disease, heart failure and injuries to the spinal cord. Even if such research is to be supported should it lead to the grant of patents? Laurie suggests that a way forward is to separate the ethical objections to the scientific developments themselves from the ethical concerns about the scope of patent monopoly and the consequences of granting that

monopoly. Consider the use of biological material to obtain a patent without the donor's consent. In *Moore* v. *Regents of the University of California* [1990] (793P. 2d.479), Moore suffered from hairy-cell leukemia and was treated at the defendant's hospital. He authorised the surgical removal of his spleen as part of his treatment. The defendants conducted research on cells derived from Moore's spleen and established a cell-line from the *T. lymphocytes*. They applied to patent the cell-line and negotiated commercial exploitation agreements with third parties. When he found out, Moore took legal action claiming the tort of conversion for the use of his body cells without permission. The case centred on the ownership of body cells. As other common law jurisdictions, the Supreme Court in the United States does not recognise the ownership of body cells. The patented cell-line was said to be factually and legally distinct from the cells taken from Moore's body. The defendants therefore had the right to the patent.

·Summary

3.1 To obtain a patent, the product or process must be new, involve an inventive step, be capable of industrial application and not be excluded under s.1(2) or s.1(3).

3.2 Whereas computer programs 'as such' are excluded from patentability, a product containing a program may be patented if it makes a technical contribution to the science.

3.3 The European Patent Office and the European Union recognise that some forms of software will be patentable.

Summary cont'd

3.4 Information about material parts of the invention that is available on or before the priority date can defeat a patent application for want of novelty, if it can be discovered following a diligent search.

3.5 Information in earlier, but unpublished, applications can affect the application but only if it is 'enabling information'.

3.6 Prior use will also defeat a patent application, but only if it is 'enabling use' in the sense that it allows the user to determine how the patent works.

Exercises

3.1 What are the basic requirements for obtaining a patent?

3.2 What is the significance of the words 'as such' in relation to the patentability of computer progams? Outline the arguments for allowing software to be patented.

3.3 In 1997, *A* invented a formula for use in drugs to control weight gain. It works by breaking up fat tissue in the body. In 1993, a research student at the University of Benin had written about the need for a fat busting drug to fight obesity. How will this affect *A*'s patent application?

3.4 What exactly is 'enabling disclosure'?

3.5 *A*'s formula and compound for reducing weight is patented as obsetabolite. *A* discovers that, when mixed with stomach juices, it produces a substance called X-it that breaks up fat tissue. *A* has found a method of producing X-it in the laboratory. Advise her of the likelihood of obtaining a patent for X-it.

Further reading

Laurie, *Patenting Stem Cells of Human Origin* [2004] EIPR 26(2), 59–66.

Schertenleib, *The Patentability and Protection of DNA Based Inventions in the European Patent Office and the European Union* [2003] EIPR 25(3), 125–38.

Thomas and Richards, *The Importance of the Morality Exception under the EPC* [2004] EIPR 26(3), 97–104.

Chapter 4

Patentability (2)

Key word

▶ **Inventive step** – the subject matter of the application should not merely be the next logical step in the science.

4.1 Inventive Step

Even after satisfying the test of novelty, the application must involve an inventive step. This means that it must move the science on and not be merely something that would be 'obvious' to anyone skilled in the art if they had put their mind to it (see *Pfizer Ltd's Patent* [2002] EWCA Civ 1). Section 3 states:

'An invention shall involve an inventive step if it is not obvious to a person skilled in the art, having regard to any matter which forms part of the state of the art.'

This is based on the philosophy, similar to that in novelty, that the public should not be prevented from doing anything that is merely an obvious extension or workshop variation of what was already known. Unlike novelty, it is possible to make a 'mosaic' of documents or information, in other words, put together documents or pockets of separately available information and claim that the invention is obvious. However, the documents must be in the same field, and the 'mosaic' will only establish *prima facie* obviousness. It is still possible to argue that the combination of the documents has resulted in an unexpected technical advantage and that there has, therefore, been an inventive step.

The question to ask is: 'to whom must the invention be obvious?' In *Technograph Printed Circuits Ltd* v. *Mills & Rockley (Electronics) Ltd* [1972] RPC 346 at page 355, Lord Reid suggested the 'skilled but unimaginative worker' test. If the product or process would have been obvious to someone with some knowledge of the technology or science within which the invention lies, then it is obvious. In *Rockwater Ltd* v. *Technip France SA* [2004] EWCA Civ 381, the skilled but unimaginative worker is described as 'a nerd but not an android' (see paragraphs 7, 10 and 11). If the invention is not obvious to even skilled and inventive technicians it must involve an inventive step. The definition of the skilled technician will depend on the type of science or industry. If the work involves high levels of research, it may be that a researcher with a PhD is the skilled technician; in which case even though the invention may not be 'obvious' to the average technician, it will still fail the inventive step test if obvious to others in the industry having that type of qualification (*Genentech Incorporation's Application* [1989] RPC 147). In *Minnesota Mining & Manufacturing Co.* v. *ATI Atlas Ltd* [2001] FSR 514, Pumfrey J said that it could also be a person with a practical interest in the development of the invention. For further guidance on the skilled addressee, see *Mayne Pharma (2), Mayne Pharma Plc* v. *(1) Debiopharm SA* [2006] EWHC 1123.

A product may be satisfactory and useful, but that will not make it inventive. See *Rocky Mountain Traders Ltd* v. *Hewlett Packard GmbH & Others* [2002] FSR 1.

For 1949 Act patents, the steps to be taken to establish whether an invention is obvious were suggested by Oliver LJ in *Windsurfing International Inc.* v. *Tabur Marine (GB) Ltd* [1985] RPC 59. At pages 73–4, he stated that to answer the question of obviousness, one had to follow four steps:

(1) identify the inventive concept embodied in the patent;
(2) import to a normally skilled, but unimaginative, addressee what was common general knowledge in the art at the priority date;
(3) identify the differences, if any, between the matter cited and the alleged invention; and
(4) decide whether those differences, viewed without any knowledge of the alleged invention, constituted steps that would have been obvious to the skilled man or whether they required any degree of invention.

This was confirmed as a useful test for 1977 Act patents by the Court of Appeal in *Mölnlycke AB* v. *Procter & Gamble Ltd (No. 5)* [1994] RPC 49. See also *Union Carbide Corp.* v. *BP Chemicals* [1999] RPC 409 where the patent in question related to a continuous heating process for the production of polymers. According to the invention, the recycled gases were cooled to below the dew point of the gas stream to produce a two-phase gas–liquid mixture before reintroduction to the reactor. It had been thought necessary to keep the temperature of the reactor gas above the dew point of the recycled gases in order to prevent the introduction of liquid. This invention provided the advantages of a cooler recycled gas stream and cooling from the latent heat of evaporation of the liquid.

In an action for infringement, the defendants claimed the invention was obvious in view of a disclosure referred to as 'Mitsui'. This described a similar polymerisation process in which the recycled gases were cooled to condense and separate the liquid, but did not say how the separated liquid was introduced into the reactor.

The Court of Appeal held on the issue of obviousness:

To decide whether the claim in question was obvious, the first step was to identify the inventive concept embedded in the patent. In this case, this was the introduction into the reactor of the two-phase mixture of gas and entrained liquid, not limited to a place where the reintroduction took place or to a requirement that the gas consisted of recycled gases rather than make-up monomer. 'Mitsui' nowhere suggested entrainment of liquid with gas to provide a two-phase gas–liquid mixture, and there was nothing in 'Mitsui' that would make that obvious.

Does the *Windsurfing* test always apply?

Davina Wheatley v. *Drillsafe Ltd* [2001] RPC 133 concerned a patent that claimed an improved method for drilling a new threaded hole in the lid of underground tanks. In reversing the decision of Ferris J, the Court of Appeal maintained that *Windsurfing* sets out the structured approach to be followed in deciding whether a patent is obvious. The second limb of the test requires the court to adopt the mantle of the notional unimaginative skilled addressee and impute to him what, at the priority date, was the common general knowledge in the art in question. Aldous LJ went on to point out that Ferris J did not follow the *Windsurfing* test in his judgment and this failure led him 'into the trap of hindsight reasoning'.

In *Sabaf SpA* v. *MFI* [2005] RPC 10, the court considered the relevance of *Windsurfing*. It concerned a patent for a burner for gas cookers and hobs. In particular the issue was whether one or two inventions were being claimed. The stated features were:

(1) the drawing of primary air in from above the hob unit; and
(2) use of a flow path under the flame spreader in which a Venturi effect would be present.

At first instance, Laddie J, applying the law of collocation, stated that both inventive features were obvious in the light of the prior art. In doing so, he referred to *Windsurfing* but considered that the law of collocation did not fit easily into its structural approach and given the obviousness of the subject matter did not see the need to apply it.

The Court of Appeal held that where a case involved a 'mere collocation' of two known concepts, the question was whether it would be obvious to the skilled person to combine the concepts. Peter Gibson LJ considered that Laddie J had taken a 'dangerous short cut' in not directly applying the *Windsurfing* structural approach.

The House of Lords reversed the Court of Appeal's finding that although there was no exception to s.3, it was necessary to decide whether there was one or more inventions before applying s.3. The judge had been correct to find that there were two alleged inventions and correct in finding that there was virtually no difference between the relevant prior art and the invention.

The main problem for inventors in this area is one of hindsight. Once something has been done, it may appear to have been obvious. It is quite easy to think 'I could have thought of that'. This will be the case, particularly, if there have been pockets of information in the field and the inventor appears to have simply put them together. The courts have never really favoured this argument, particularly when it is advanced by competitors. In *British Westinghouse Electric & Manufacturing Co. Ltd* v. *Braulik* (1910) 27 RPC 209, Fletcher-Moulton LJ made the following statement:

> 'I confess that I view with suspicion arguments to the effect that a new combination bringing with it new and important consequences in the shape of practical machines, is not an invention because, when it has once been established, it is easy to show how it might be arrived at by starting from something known, and taking a series of apparently easy steps. This *ex post facto* analysis of invention is unfair to the inventors and, in my opinion, it is not to be countenanced by English patent law.'

In *Technograph Printed Circuits Ltd* v. *Mills & Rockley (Electronics) Ltd* [1972] RPC 346, Lord Reid said that, rather than considering what is obvious to the court in hearing a dispute, one has to look at what was obvious at the date of the application.

One way of dealing with the issue of hindsight is to ask: if the product or process was obvious, why had it not been done before, particularly if it satisfies a 'long-felt' need? In *Lux Traffic Controls Ltd* v. *Pike Signals Ltd* [1993] RPC 107, it was claimed that some of the plaintiff's patents in traffic control signals were invalid because they were obvious. One of the patents in question was for a means of varying the 'inter-green' period (that is, the safety period between the lights in one direction changing to red before the lights in the other direction change to green). The court held that, although simple, the invention represented an advance and technical contribution to the art. If the process had been obvious, it would have been proposed before.

Likewise, in *Parkes Cramer Co.* v. *G.W. Thornton & Sons Ltd* [1966] RPC 407, where the invention was a method of cleaning floors between rows of textile machines, made up of an overhead vacuum cleaner which moved back and forth between the textile machines, with a long vertical tube attached to it. It was argued that this was obvious because every competent housewife knows that dust can be removed from a floor using a vacuum cleaner. This argument was rejected. There had been many unsuccessful attempts to find a satisfactory solution, but none of them had actually worked. The fact that the invention was also a commercial success once it entered the market, demonstrated that it satisfied a long-awaited need that would have been met long before had the plaintiff's invention been so 'obvious'. Of course, if an invention is not a commercial success, this does not mean that it was obvious.

The problem solution approach was also considered in *Haberman & Another* v. *Jackel International Ltd* [1999] FSR 683. Mrs Haberman had the patent for the ANYWAYUP Cup, a trainer cup for toddlers. The plaintiff's cup had a valve fitted to the lid, which would open when the baby sucked and close when it stopped, thereby solving the problem of leakage. The cup was an immediate commercial success. The defendants produced and launched a rival product, 'Super-Seal'. In an action for infringement, the defendants claimed that the plaintiff's patent was invalid on the grounds of 'obviousness'. Laddie J found that, even though the invention in question only involved a 'very small and simple step', it was sufficiently inventive to deserve the grant of a patent. The invention itself was quite simple but it had solved a problem to which many had sought a solution, that is, leakage in infant trainer cups. While its commercial success could have something to do with other factors such as marketing, it also demonstrated that this was a problem to which a solution had been sought. It satisfied a need. The success of the product was found to be attributable to the solution it gave to the long-felt need for a spill-proof cup.

The decision in *Dyson Appliances Ltd* v. *Hoover* [2001] EWCA Civ 440 suggests that the response, or lack of it, to the patent holder's solution, at the priority date, is also important. The dispute between the parties has been well documented in the press. Dyson invented a bagless vacuum cleaner, whose use of cyclones rids the air of dirt. Before the priority date no vacuum cleaner manufacturer had commercially sold or proposed a bagless vacuum cleaner. According to Sedley LJ (at para. 89):

'The vacuum-cleaner industry was functionally deaf and blind to any technology which did not involve a replaceable bag.'

In *Biogen Inc.* v. *Medeva plc* [1997] RPC 1, the plaintiffs had obtained a patent for recombinantly produced DNA molecule coding for the Hepatitis B virus (HBV). At the priority date, HBV DNA had not been sequenced nor had the viral proteins been expressed. It was claimed that the step taken was one that was 'obvious to try', in the light of a paper published by an expert in the field. Aldous J held that Biogen had taken the initiative and attempted something uncontemplated by others. This demonstrated that their approach was not obvious and demonstrated an inventive step. Sadly this decision was overturned by the Court of Appeal (and the Court of Appeal decision was upheld in the House of Lords). In the view of the Court of Appeal, the step taken was based on a commercial decision to pursue an identified goal by known means. To spend time and money on a project, where others would have regarded the odds against success as too long to justify the investment, was a business judgment rather than an inventive step. In the House of Lords, Lord Hoffman (at page 44) felt that reference to a commercial decision was less than helpful. In his view there was no reason why a chosen experimental strategy should not involve an inventive step simply because it had been adopted for commercial reasons. His Lordship went on to state that the inventiveness in this particular case was of a very unusual kind. It was said to consist of attempting something, which a man less skilled in the art might have regarded as obvious, but which the expert would have thought so beset by obstacles as to be not worth trying. The House of Lords found the invention to be inventive but invalid for want of sufficiency.

The Court of Appeal's decision may be justified on the grounds that the plaintiffs merely took a gamble, which paid off when others were not prepared to take the risk. However, there are surely many inventions that are the result of a lucky discovery.

The Court of Appeal has stated that 'obviousness' is a jury-type question for a judge at first instance who has heard all the technical evidence. The Court of Appeal should therefore be slow to come to a different conclusion from that of the judge when the conclusion was one to which he was entitled to come. See *Raychem Corp.'s Patents* [1999] RPC 497 at page 516.

In *David J. Instance Ltd* v. *Denny Bros Printing Ltd* [2001] EWCA Civ 939; [2002] RPC 114, it was stated that the Court of Appeal should only interfere with a judge's conclusion on obviousness if he had erred in principle (see para. 16).

4.2 Industrial Application

Even if the invention satisfies ss.2 and 3, under s.4 it will only be patentable if it can be manufactured and is marketable in any industry, including agriculture. For this reason, methods of treatment for people or animals are not covered under s.4A(1), which states that an invention which consists of a method of treatment (by surgery or therapy) or a method of diagnosis cannot be patented. But any drugs produced for treatment are capable of industrial application and are, therefore, patentable if the other conditions are satisfied (see s.4A(2)). This links with s.2(6) on novelty, which states that prior use to treat humans and animals will not invalidate a patent for want of novelty. See *Bristol-Myers Squibb Co.* v. *Baker Norton Pharmaceuticals* [2001] RPC 1.

It is generally accepted by academics (see, for example, Bainbridge, and Holyoak and Torremans) that it makes sense for policy reasons that professionals like doctors should not be able to obtain a monopoly to restrain the use of improved methods of treatment. To be excluded, a method of treatment must be by way of surgery, therapy or diagnosis, and must be carried out on the living human or animal. This means that treatments such as methods of contraception and cosmetic treatment of nails or hair can be patentable (although in some countries, methods of contraception have fallen foul of the national equivalent of s.1(3)(a) – this shows how the political and religious climate of a country can influence patent law).

Summary

4.1 To be patentable the invention should not be obvious to the skilled but unimaginative technician.

4.2 It must be possible to manufacture and sell the product in any industry including agriculture.

Exercises

4.1 What is the 'skilled but unimaginative worker test'? Is it a realistic test?

4.2 Many things may seem 'obvious' once invented. How can inventors overcome the problem of hindsight when their patents are challenged?

4.3 A doctor develops a revolutionary method of treating cancer of the colon. Is it fair that she cannot obtain a patent for that method?

Chapter 5

Ownership

> ▶ **Employee-inventor** – an individual who is employed to invent.
> ▶ **Inventor** – the person who devised the inventive product or process.

5.1 Introduction

Section 7 of the Patents Act 1977 provides that 'any person can apply for a patent'. This would imply that there are no conditions as to nationality of the applicant or the country where the invention was made, unlike the position in copyright law. Section 7(2) states that patents can be granted to (a) the inventor and joint inventor, (b) other persons entitled to property in the invention or (c) successors in title. Sections 8 and 9 deal with disputes regarding the ownership of patents and s.10 provides guidance on how disputes between joint applicants are to be handled.

The person to whom the patent is granted (the proprietor) is the only person entitled to manufacture, use, sell or import the product or process. If the proprietor does not wish to work the patent the licence can be assigned to another. An assignment gives the assignee full rights in the patent whereas the terms of a licence might only allow the licensee to do certain things.

5.2 Who Can Apply?

Whereas s.7(2)(a) states that a patent may be granted primarily to the inventor or joint inventors, s.7(2)(b) recognises that others may have a legal claim to the patent. A patent can be granted to:

> 'any person or persons who by virtue of any enactment or rule of law, or any foreign law or treaty or international convention, or by virtue of an enforceable term of any agreement entered into with the inventor before the making of the invention was or were at the time of the making of the invention entitled to the whole of the property in it other than equitable interests in the United Kingdom.'

The inventor may have been engaged as a consultant to solve a problem for a firm and under the terms of the consultant's contract it may have been expressly provided that any resulting invention would belong to the firm. Alternatively, the 'inventor' may be an employee and any inventions made will belong to the employer by virtue of s.39 of the 1977 Act. Without this section, the inventor would have to apply for and then assign or license the patent to the employer. While assigning and licensing of patents takes place, the inventor is often not able to afford the cost of making an application. Further, if the invention is made under a consultancy agreement or in the course of employment, the rightful owners should be able to apply and register their property interest from the outset.

5.3 The Inventor

The inventor is defined under s.7(3), as the 'deviser of the invention'. As there is no further explanation of what is meant by the 'deviser' and no definition of the word 'invention' within the Act, we have to rely on common sense; the inventor will be the person who has worked out the subject matter of the patent application through his own efforts. In *Markem Corporation* v. *Zipher Ltd (No. 1)* [2004] RPC 10, Fysch J stated that the word 'devise' had a slightly broader signification than 'make' or 'implement', that of planning a particular course of action before even that course of action is actually implemented.

As already indicated, the inventor will not always be the person applying for the patent. Even so, the inventor has the right to be named as the inventor under s.13(1). Inventors are also, to some extent, protected by s.13(2). Section 13(2) states that any person, other than the inventor, who is making an application must identify the inventor and state the grounds on which the applicant is entitled to the patent. Failure to comply with this section could result in the application being refused.

As s.7(1) states, an application can be made either by an individual alone or jointly with another. Any disputes between inventors as to the prosecution of the application are handled by the Comptroller-General under s.10.

Each individual inventor is entitled to be named on the patent by virtue of s.13(1). However, there may be cases where an individual inventor feels that the other's contribution was so insignificant that he is the only one entitled to be mentioned. When this happens, he can make an application under s.13(3) to have the other inventor's name removed. However, as shown by *Staeng Ltd's Patents* [1996] RPC 183, the onus is on the applicant to prove his right to sole ownership.

5.4 Employee Patents

Most ownership disputes are between employee-inventors and their employers. The law on ownership of patents for inventions devised by employee-inventors is set out in ss.39–43 of the Patents Act 1977.

In settling disputes about employee-inventions, the starting point is to confirm that the inventor is actually an 'employee'. Traditionally, a number of factors determined whether there was an employer/employee relationship between the inventor and alleged owner of the invention. These could include: responsibility for the deduction of income tax and national insurance contributions, provision of any equipment used, and the supervision and control of the inventor's activities. Section 130 of the Patents Act 1977 defines an employee as someone 'who works or has worked under a contract of employment or in employment within a Government department, or serves or has served in the navy, military or air forces of the Crown'.

Once it is settled that the inventor can be classified as an employee, the next step is to determine whether the invention belongs to the inventor or the employer. Before the 1977 Act, the court would analyse the inventor's contract of employment for an indication of whether it was the employee's responsibility to invent. In *Electrolux* v. *Hudson* [1977] FSR 312 (decided under the 1949 Act, which did not have equivalent provisions to ss.39–43), Hudson was employed as a senior storekeeper for the electrical manufacturers, Electrolux. In his spare time, Hudson and his wife invented an adaptor for a vacuum cleaner taking disposable bags.

Electrolux, whose products included vacuum cleaners, claimed to be the owners of the resulting patent. The claim was based on a term in Hudson's contract of employment that stated that anything invented, or any process ascertained or discovered, in relation to any of Electrolux's products in the United Kingdom or elsewhere, had to be disclosed to Electrolux and any such invention or process would belong to Electrolux. Dismissing the claim, Whitford J was of the opinion that the clause was too wide even to cover a person employed to research and invent and, on common law rules of restraint of trade, was more than was necessary to protect the employer's legitimate business interests. In his view, the validity of any clause concerning patent ownership would depend on the type of work done by the employee. Hudson was employed as a storekeeper. It was not his responsibility to invent.

Section 39(1) of the Patents Act 1977 is quite specific about the ownership of an employee patent. A patent resulting from an invention devised by an employee belongs to the employer if:

'(a) it was made in the course of the normal duties of the employee or in the course of duties falling outside his normal duties, but specifically assigned to him, and the circumstances in either case were such that an invention might reasonably be expected to result from the carrying out of his duties; or

(b) the invention was made in the course of the duties of the employee and, at the time of making the invention, because of the nature of his duties he had a special obligation to further the interests of the employer's undertaking.'

An interpretation of s.39(1) was attempted in *Re Harris Patent* [1985] RPC 19. Harris was employed as a manager in the wey valve department for company *R*, which operated under licence from a Swiss company, *S*. *R* had no research facilities and never undertook any creative design activity. Major problems were referred to company *S*. Harris's primary duties were to sell valves made by *R* under the licence from *S* and to use his specialist knowledge to assist his employer's customers. During the period of his redundancy notice, Harris invented a slide valve. His employer claimed ownership of the patent.

In the Patents Court, Falconer J held that an employee's duties in s.39(1)(a) were the normal duties which he was employed to perform. The 'circumstances' referred to were the circumstances under which the particular invention in suit was made, rather than the circumstances in which any invention whatsoever might be made. Harris's employer never took it upon itself to solve the design problems in the valves, so it could never have been part of any of its employees' normal duties to invent. And the invention had not been made under circumstances such that an invention might reasonably be expected to have resulted from the carrying out of Harris's normal duties. On s.39(1)(b), Falconer J was of the opinion that the nature and extent of an employee's obligation to further the interests of the employer's undertaking depended on the employee's status, with its attendant duties and responsibilities. Harris's only real obligations were to sell valves and provide after-sales services to customers.

In *Staeng Ltd's Patent* [1996] RPC 183, the court stated that in applying s.39(1), one should first decide what constituted the employee's normal duties, then decide whether the circumstances were such that an invention might reasonably be expected to result from the execution of those duties.

Section 39(1) was also applied in *Greater Glasgow Health Board's Application* [1996] RPC 207. A junior doctor was employed as a Registrar by the Health Board in the Department of Ophthalmology. His job description stated that his responsibilities were mainly clinical but indicated that he was also expected to participate in undergraduate and postgraduate teaching, although the latter were not described as duties. He was also expected to avail himself of the research facilities provided. While revising for Fellowship examinations at home, he invented a device for examining the retina. The Health Board claimed ownership. In the Patents Court, Jacob J followed the approach taken by the Court of Appeal in earlier copyright cases concerning ownership of copyright in employees' work. He held that, whereas the device was a useful accessory to the doctor's contracted work, it was not an integral part of it. A factor that might have persuaded the court was the fact that, in evidence, the inventor's manager stated that the junior doctor would not have been failing in his duties if he had not invented anything. This is a useful guide in interpreting s.39(1)(a). Would the employee in question have been failing in his duties had he not sought to invent? That test is equally relevant to s.39(1)(b), which is concerned more with the status of the employee, which indicates a general duty to further the interest of the employer, and which does not necessarily require a duty to invent.

5.5 Employee Compensation

If it is agreed or determined that the patent belongs to the employer under s.39, s.40 allows an employee to claim compensation if he can show that *either the invention*, patent *or both* is of 'outstanding benefit' to the employer, taking into account the employer's size and type of business.

Benefit means 'benefit in money or money's worth' (s.43(7)) and Patent Office practice is to consider the actual rather than the potential benefit to the employer; potential benefit is only relevant to decide the level of compensation if it is to be awarded.

In practice, it proved difficult to succeed in a claim for a s.40 award. There appears to be no recorded case where an employee has successfully claimed the award. The words in italics were added by the Patents Act 2004, to try to redress the balance. A selection of cases below indicates the difficulties encountered by employees.

In *GEC Avionics Ltd's Patent* [1992] RPC 107, the Patent Office read s.40 in the context of s.39 and reached the view that, if it is agreed that the employee is employed to invent, then he already receives a reward for inventive activity in the form of salary. Hence the need for the 'benefit' to the employer to be 'outstanding' if an additional award is to be made. In *Elliot Brothers' Patent* SRIS 0/47/89 it was held that 'outstanding' means something out of the ordinary and not such as would be expected to arise from the duties the employee is paid for.

Another factor is the level of investment by the employer in the project. As s.40 refers to the size and nature of the employer's undertaking, an inventor working for a business with high turnover and profits will find it difficult to prove 'outstanding benefit'. This is illustrated by *British Steel plc's Patent* [1992] RPC 117, where the patent concerned an outlet valve for vessels containing molten material. It was regarded as a great technological advance in its field and the annual benefits to British Steel were up to

£500,000. However, because this represented no more than 0.01 per cent of the company's annual turnover and 0.08 per cent of its profits, the employee's claim for compensation under s.40 failed.

In *GEC Avionics Ltd's Patent* [1992] RPC 107, the patent in question related to an optical system for providing a 'head-up display' (HUD) in an aircraft cockpit. Whereas the inventor's employers had secured a contract worth $72 million involving the patent, they had previously secured contracts worth $75 million for HUDs not involving the patented system. Again, the Patent Office refused the employee's claim. The Patent Office's approach appears to be that if the employer is habitually involved in contracts worth many millions, an employee's contribution is not 'outstanding' or 'out of the ordinary' even if it also attracts contracts worth many millions.

If there was evidence of previous dealings with a particular customer, irrespective of the patent in question, the inventor's task in making a s.40 claim is even more onerous. In *Memco-Med Ltd's Patents* [1992] RPC 403, the patent in question concerned units to detect a person near lift doors, the idea being to prevent the doors from closing on people. The employers had previous contracts to build lift door detector units for O Elevator Co. Ltd. Sales of their products had gone to O Elevator in the past. The history of the business relationship between Memco and O Elevator supported the view that it would have continued whether or not a patent had been granted for the invention. Accordingly, the employee's invention had not been of outstanding benefit. *Memco* also suggests that, even where an employee-inventor can show a substantial increase in sales of his employer's product, the onus is on him to demonstrate that the increase was due to the patent and not other factors such as the price, marketing or quality of the employer's general product range.

Although the employee-inventor's task may seem onerous in claiming s.40 compensation, the employer has quite a heavy burden in surpassing s.39. Additionally, an employee who is contracted to invent will no doubt draw a salary whether he invents or not. The employer bears the cost and effort of trying to realise the initial concept. For every successful patent, there will have been many discarded attempts and the project can take years to develop. Meanwhile the employee draws a salary without the risks. The modification introduced by the Patents Act 2004 is not exactly radical. The onus will still be on the employee to prove that the invention or patent is of outstanding benefit. But it may be prudent for employers in research industries to introduce employee-inventor incentive schemes.

5.6　Dealings in Patents

Patents and patent applications are personal property and accordingly may be assigned, mortgaged and transferred as part of a person's estate. These transactions must be in writing and signed by both parties (except in the case of transfers on death, where only the personal representatives need to sign). Where there are joint owners, all must sign for a transaction to be valid. Different provisions apply to Scotland (s.31).

When a patent has been transferred, the new owner should register his interest on the Patents Register. Failure to register the interest could result in the new owner losing his rights to a third party who subsequently acquires rights in the same patent without knowledge of the earlier transaction.

Where the patent is owned by two or more persons, each of them is entitled on his own behalf to do any of the acts in respect of the patent which would otherwise be an infringement.

The owner or owners of the patent may also license others to work the patent. Licensees in these circumstances will be limited to activities covered within the licence agreement. Under s.46, the owner may also apply for an entry to be made in the register that licences as of right are available. This is useful to a proprietor who discovers, after the patent has been granted, that she is not in a position to exploit the patent effectively.

After a patent has been granted for three years, any person may apply for a compulsory licence to work the patent, or apply for an entry on the Register that licences are available as of right. Generally such applications are made if it is felt that the patentee is either not making full use of the patent or refusing to grant licences on reasonable terms. The exact grounds are listed in s.48(3). These are:

(a) The patent is capable of being commercially worked but is not being worked to its fullest potential as far as is reasonably practicable.
(b) The demand in the United Kingdom for the patented product is not being met on reasonable terms, or is being met to a substantial extent by importation.
(c) The patent is capable of being commercially worked in the United Kingdom and such work is being prevented or hindered.
(d) The proprietor's refusal to grant a licence on reasonable terms has resulted in:
　(i)　a market in the export of the patented product made in the United Kingdom not being supplied, or
　(ii)　the working or efficient working in the United Kingdom of any other patented product which makes a substantial contribution to the art is prevented from or hindered, or

  (iii) the establishment or development of commercial activities in the
        United Kingdom is unfairly prejudiced.
(e) The terms imposed by the proprietor in licence agreements are unfairly
    prejudicial to commercial or industrial activities in the United Kingdom.

As stated in Chapter 2, these provisions redress the balance against allowing
a patentee to abuse the monopoly granted.

Summary

5.1 The Patents Act 1977 allows an individual inventor, joint inventor, other
persons entitled to the invention and successors in title to apply for a patent.

5.2 If the applicant is not the actual inventor she must justify ownership, and the
inventor is entitled to be named.

5.3 The inventor is the person who devised the subject matter of the application.

5.4 An employee-invention will only belong to the employer if it was part of the
employee's duty to invent or the employee has special responsibilities to
further the interests of the employer's business.

5.5 Although it is possible for an employee to obtain compensation for a
patentable invention of 'outstanding benefit', in practice this is difficult if the
employers habitually secure profitable contracts irrespective of the invention.

Exercises

5.1 How is the actual inventor protected against others making a false claim on
his invention?

5.2 *A* is a senior member of the research team at *B* Pharmaceutical. *B* have been
developing a non-habit-forming drug to aid restful sleep. It contains the
compound dormalite. *A*, who is a keen gardener, makes up the formula at *B*'s
laboratory and takes it home to try on her weak plants. The formula works as
a very effective fertiliser and *A* decides to apply to patent this use on plants.
Advise *B* Pharmaceutical.

Key words

▶ **Claims** – the monopoly claimed by the patent holder.
▶ **Pith and marrow** – a consideration of whether the adjustments made to a patented product or process by an alleged infringer are fundamental or merely cosmetic.

6.1 Introduction

The whole point in obtaining a patent is to gain a monopoly in the invented product or process. Thus once a patent has been granted, the proprietor (the patentee) has the right to stop others from manufacturing, using, selling or importing the subject of the patent for 20 years from the priority date. The patentee may protect his interest by suing for infringement. An exclusive licensee also has rights against infringers (s.67), as long as his interest has been registered (s.33). Where there are joint owners of a patent, any of the owners may commence infringement proceedings but must notify the other owners.

The general right to take action and obtain remedies for infringement is covered by ss.60 and 61. There are risks in commencing infringement actions. Section 70 creates a right to claim damages and other remedies for groundless threats, and many claims for infringement are defended by a challenge to the validity of the patent (s.72).

6.2 Acts of Infringement

A patented product is infringed under s.60(1) by the following activities in the United Kingdom: making the product, disposing of it, offering to dispose of it, using or importing it or keeping it (whether for disposal or otherwise), all without the patentee's consent. A patented process is infringed by its use, or offer for use, in the United Kingdom, in circumstances where the infringer knows, or it is obvious to the reasonable person, that such use without the patentee's consent is an infringement. It is also infringement of a patented process to do any of the acts that would be an infringement of a patented product in respect of any product 'obtained directly by means of that process'. What is meant by a product 'obtained directly by means of that process' was considered in the case of

Pioneer Electronics Capital Inc. v. *Warner Music Manufacturing Europe GmbH* [1997] RPC 757. The case involved a patent for a process to manufacture masters for optical discs. The defendants had manufactured and sold optical discs, but three further stages were introduced between the manufacture of the master disc and the manufacture of the discs which were made by the defendants. The Court of Appeal approved the decision of the High Court that the defendants' products were not obtained directly from the patented process.

For a brief discussion of how the English court's approach to the protection of a product from a process differs from that of the rest of the EPO members see *Kirin-Amgen Incorporated and Others* v. *Hoechst Marion Roussel Ltd & Others* [2004] UKHL 46, at paras 89–91.

Section 60(2) states that it is an infringement for anyone, other than the patentee, to provide others with the means to make a patented product or use a patented process. This amounts to 'indirect infringement', so the wrongdoer in this case must know, or the circumstances must be such that it is obvious to the reasonable person, that sufficient means are being provided to put the invention into effect in the United Kingdom. Section 60(3) allows the supply of a 'staple commercial product', even if covered by a patent, provided that product is not being supplied for the purpose of inducing the person supplied to commit one of the infringing acts under s.60(1).

It is possible to infringe even if part of the infringing apparatus is located overseas. See *Menashe Business Mercantile Ltd* v. *William Hill Organisation Ltd* [2003] 1 All ER 279 (CA).

6.3 The Significance of the Claims

The extent of an invention is set out in the claims (see s.125 Patents Act 1977: Article 69 EPC). In any action for infringement, the court will therefore start by considering the claims within the specification. The claims map out the extent of the patentee's monopoly. According to Lord Russell in *Electric & Musical Industries Ltd* v. *Lissen Ltd* (1939) 56 RPC 23:

> 'The function of the claims is to define clearly and with precision the monopoly claimed, so that others may know the exact boundaries of the area within which they will be trespassers. Their primary object is to limit and not extend the monopoly. What is not claimed is disclaimed.'

According to Laddie J, in *Merck & Co.* v. *Generics (UK) Ltd* [2003] EWHC 2842; [2004] RPC 31:

> 'The purpose of a patent is to convey to the public what the patentee considers to be his invention and what monopoly he has chosen to obtain. These are not necessarily the same. The former is primarily to be found in the specification and

the latter is primarily to be found in the claims . . . It is his duty to communicate his invention and his assertion of monopoly to the public in language it will understand . . .' (para. 38).

For this reason, claims need to be drafted very carefully. A specification containing broad claims covering every possible variation may be rejected, but one drafted too narrowly allows competitors to add insignificant modifications and escape infringement actions.

6.4   Interpretation of the Claims

There appears to be a difference in the approach to the interpretation of claims across Europe. In Germany, for example, the claims were said to be treated simply as a guide to determine the scope of the protection. By contrast, English case law suggests that, in examining the claims, English judges have found it difficult to move away from the traditional approach adopted in interpreting statutes and other legal documents. Judges will either take a strict literal approach or, where there is some ambiguity, a purposive approach. The former approach is said to be justified for statutes because it is up to Parliament to correct any discrepancies. In patent law, this approach is justified on the grounds that the patentee was given the opportunity to map out his monopoly when he drafted the specification. In *C van der Lely NV* v. *Bamfords* [1963] RPC 61, Viscount Radcliffe said:

'After all, it is [the patentee] who has committed himself to the unequivocal description of what he claims to have invented, and he must submit in the first place to be judged by his own action and words.'

Although English judges are more at home with a literal approach, it has been argued that such an approach is inappropriate for patent specifications. In *Rodi & Wienenberger AG* v. *Henry Showell Ltd* [1969] RPC 367, in a dissenting judgment at page 378, Lord Reid said:

'Claims are not addressed to conveyancers: they are addressed to practical men skilled in the prior art, and I do not think that they ought to be construed with that meticulousness which was once thought appropriate for conveyancing documents.'

Instead it is recommended that judges study the specification and what the alleged infringer has done. If the defendant's activities fall within the claims, then there is infringement. If there are variations, the court should determine whether they are fundamental differences between the patentee's invention and what the alleged infringer has produced. This is referred to as the 'pith and marrow' approach to the interpretation of patent claims. It involves looking at each element or section of the claim (the 'integers') and considering how many integers have been taken by the defendant, and the extent to which those integers are vital to the working of the invention.

Even with the pith and marrow approach, competitors have been able to avoid infringement by making cosmetic modifications. In *C van der Lely NV* v. *Bamfords*, the plaintiff had a patent for a mechanical hay-rake with movable wheels at the back ('hindmost'). The defendant's machine had movable wheels at the front ('foremost'). The court decided that it could not regard 'hindmost' in the plaintiff's claims as the same as 'foremost', and the plaintiff's action for infringement, therefore, failed. *Rodi & Wienenberger AG* v. *Henry Showell Ltd* concerned a patent for expanding metal bracelets for wrist watches. The House of Lords held that the defendant's replacement of two U-shaped bows with a single C-shaped bow meant that its product did not infringe the plaintiff's patent. The court decided that the U-shaped bow was an essential integer. Lord Pearce (who dissented) felt that it was not enough to say that the U-shaped bow was an essential integer and that the defendant's bracelet did not infringe by having a C-shaped bow. As far as he was concerned, both connected to adjacent sleeves by a bridge between two parallel limbs that lay in the sleeves and pivoted in the spring. The differences were not essential.

6.5 Has There Been Infringement?

The leading case on patent infringement is *Catnic Components Ltd* v. *Hill & Smith Ltd* [1982] FSR 60. The plaintiffs had a patent for load-bearing steel lintels, which had a rear support member, described in the claims as 'vertical'. The defendants made a similar lintel but the rear support member was inclined between six and eight degrees from the vertical. This meant that its load-bearing capacity was slightly less than that of the plaintiffs but not enough to make a significant difference in its practical use. The plaintiffs had described another part of their lintel as 'substantially horizontal', and the defendants claimed that, as the reference to the 'vertical' support had not been qualified in the same way, the defendants' lintel would have to be exactly vertical to infringe. The House of Lords rejected this argument and held that the patent had been infringed.

According to Lord Diplock, the real question was whether persons skilled in the art would understand that strict compliance with a particular descriptive word or phrase was intended by the patentee to be an essential requirement of the invention, so that any variant would fall outside the monopoly, whether or not it had any material effect on the way the invention worked. This introduced a purposive approach to the interpretation of claims.

Catnic concerned a 1949 Act patent. There has been a debate about whether this is appropriate for patents granted under the 1977 Act and, indeed, whether this is compatible with the Protocol adopted at the Munich

Conference (which established the European Patent Convention), on the Interpretation of Article 69 EPC. The Protocol was a compromise between the perceived differences of approach across the Member States, the UK and German approaches being at the two extremes. It states that the interpretation of a claim should combine fair protection for the patentee with a reasonable degree of certainty for third parties. *Catnic* appears to be compatible with that objective and the actual wording of the Protocol.

The approach suggested by *Catnic* is to follow a process involving three main questions:

(1) Does the variant have a material effect upon the way the invention works? If 'yes', a variation will not infringe; if 'no', the second question is considered.

(2) When the specification was published, would it have been obvious to the skilled reader that the variant had no material effect? If 'no', the variant does not infringe; if 'yes', consider the final question.

(3) Would the skilled reader understand that the patentee intended that strict compliance with the claim was essential? If 'yes', the variant does not infringe; if 'no', there is infringement.

This process was apparently followed by Hoffman J in *Improver Corp.* v. *Remington Consumer Products Ltd* [1990] FSR 181. The plaintiffs had a European patent for a hair-removing device called 'Epilady'. This removed hair by a helical spring, which rotated to pluck out the hairs. The defendants brought onto the market a similar device called 'Smooth and Silky', which removed hair by an elastomeric rod with slits to pluck out hair. In what has become known as the '*Improver* Questions', Hoffman J stated:

(1) Does the variant have a material effect on the way the invention works? If 'yes', the variant is outside the claim. If 'no':

(2) Would this (i.e. that the variant had no material effect) have been obvious at the date of the publication of the patent to a reader skilled in the art? If 'no', the variant is outside the claim. If 'yes':

(3) Would the reader skilled in the art nevertheless have understood from the language of the claim that strict compliance with the primary meaning was an essential requirement of the invention? If 'yes', the variant is outside the claim.

His Lordship went on to decide that there was no infringement. In his view, the variant had no material effect on how the invention worked, but on the third question, he felt that because the claim referred to a helical spring, it could not be interpreted broadly to include a rubber rod.

It is our view that to reach this decision, Hoffman J applied the literal interpretation approach, criticised by Lord Reid in *Rodi & Wienenberger* and by Lord Diplock in *Catnic*. As a point of interest, the same parties appeared before a German court, concerning the same patent. In the German courts, applying a more purposive approach, the defendants' device was held to infringe the 'Epilady' patent.

In *PLG Research Ltd* v. *Ardon International* [1995] RPC 287, Millett LJ in the Court of Appeal was of the opinion that, if the *Catnic* test was the same as the Protocol, it was no longer necessary and if it differed, its continued use would be dangerous. (But Lord Hoffan in *Kirin-Amgen Incorporated & Others* v. *Hoechst Marion Roussel Ltd & Others* [2004] UKHL 46; [2005] RPC 9 specifically disagreed, see below.) In *Assidoman Multipack Ltd* v. *The Mead Corp.* [1995] FSR 225, Aldous J decided to continue to follow *Catnic*. The purposive approach recommended by Lord Diplock in *Catnic* was also followed in *Kastner* v. *Rizla & Another (No. 1)* [1995] RPC 585, which concerned a patented method and machine for interleaving and severing paper used, in particular, in relation to cigarette papers. In deciding whether the defendant's machine infringed the plaintiff's patent, Aldous LJ (as he became) in the Court of Appeal adopted a purposive approach to the whole of the patent specification. In *Catnic*, Lord Diplock had merely stated that the purposive approach should be used to interpret 'a particular descriptive word or phrase appearing in a claim'. The purposive approach was given far broader application by the Court of Appeal in *Kastner*.

In *Consafe Engineering (UK) Ltd* v. *Emitunga UK Ltd* [1999] RPC 154, Pumfrey J held the question to be decided was whether, on a true construction of the claim in its context in the specification, the patentee had intended that strict compliance with any particular descriptive word or phrase was an essential requirement of the invention, so that any variant would fall outside his monopoly even if the variant would have had no effect upon the way that the invention worked and a skilled man would have appreciated that to be so. This question was conveniently approached by way of Hoffman J's questions in *Improver*, designed to result in a fair protection for the patentee with a reasonable degree of certainty for third parties.

See also *Auchinloss* v. *Agricultural & Veterinary Supplies Ltd* [1999] RPC 397 where the Court of Appeal held *inter alia* that the patent with its claims must be construed as a whole according to the guidelines given in the Protocol on the Interpretation of Article 69 of the European Patent Convention. The purposive construction was therefore the correct approach.

In *Union Carbide Corp.* v. *BP Chemicals* [1999] RPC 409, the Court of Appeal held that the ambit of the monopoly lay between the extremes of literal construction and the use of the claims only as a guideline, and was to be interpreted as defining a position which combined fair protection for the patentee with a reasonable amount of certainty for third parties. To find that position the court should apply purposive construction in accordance with the guidance given in *Catnic* and explained in *Improver*.

See also *Davina Wheatley* v. *Drillsafe Ltd* [2001] RPC 133 and *Amersham Pharmacia Biotech AB* v. *Amicon Ltd* [2001] EWCA Civ 1042.

In *Kirin-Amgen Incorporated & Others* v. *Hoechst Marion Roussel Ltd & Others* [2004] UKHL 46; [2005] RPC 9, Lord Hoffman was able to confirm the *Catnic* Test as compatiable with the Protocol. The case concerned the alleged infringement of Amgen's European patent relating to the production of erythropoietin (EPO) by recombinant DNA technology:

Claim 1 related to a DNA sequence for use in securing the expression of EPO in a host cell.

Claim 19 concerned a product by process claim to EPO having particular physical and biological properties made from any exogenous DNA, i.e. by means of a process of expressing an exogenous DNA sequence.

Claim 26 covered a product by process claim to EPO made in a eukargotic host cell by the process of expressing the specific DNA sequence that was set out in claim 1.

TKT had made EPO by activating a naturally present endogenous gene in a human cell and the dispute centred on whether this infringed claims 19 and 26, and whether the claims themselves were valid.

6.6 Defences

When faced with an action for infringement, the alleged infringer has a number of options available.

First, he can challenge the validity of the plaintiff's patent, using ss.72 and 74. The grounds upon which a patent can be challenged are:

(a) the invention was not patentable in the first place (*Windsurfing*);
(b) the patent was granted to someone who was not entitled to it (although this is only available during the two years after the grant of the patent, unless the patentee knew at the time of the application that he was not entitled);
(c) the specification does not disclose the invention with sufficient clarity and fullness for it to be performed by a person skilled in the art;
(d) what is disclosed in the specification extends beyond what was disclosed in the application for the patent as filed; or
(e) the protection conferred by the patent has been extended by an amendment which should not have been allowed.

A successful challenge will result in the patent being revoked or amended.

It is also possible to argue that there has been no infringement, because the defendant's activities vary sufficiently from what is contained in the claims. Cases like *Improver Corp.* v. *Remington Consumer Products Ltd* [1990] FSR 181 demonstrate this. A defendant can accordingly also apply to the courts under s.71 for a declaration of non-infringement.

Section 60(5) lists the general statutory defences which are:

(a) the infringing activity took place privately and was not for commercial purposes;
(b) the infringing activity took place for experimental purposes;
(c) the activity involved the extemporaneous preparation in a pharmacy of medicine for an individual in accordance with a registered medical or dental practitioner's prescription;
(d) use of the invention was in relation to certain ships, aircraft or vehicles temporarily or accidentally in or crossing the United Kingdom.

Further, s.60(4) provides a defence to certain acts of infringement if it can be shown that the patentee's rights have been exhausted under the competition law of the European Community. Exhaustion of rights is discussed in more detail in Chapter 24. Broadly, this section provides that once the patented product, or products resulting from the patented process, have been put into circulation in any part of the European Economic Area by or with the consent of the patentee, the patentee cannot use an action of infringement to prevent subsequent sale, importation or use of the same products anywhere in the European Economic Area.

Apart from the above, there is protection for the *bona fide* prior user in s.64. This states that acts done in good faith before the priority date are allowed to continue. This maintains the principle that a monopoly should not be granted to stop individuals from doing what they were legitimately doing before the grant.

Anti-competitive practices are discouraged by the statutory defence in s.44. This refers to certain restrictive practices, such as requiring licensees of patents to take non-patented products as a condition of the licence. Such agreements are void and s.44(3) provides a defence against infringement of a patent if, at the time of the alleged infringement, such an agreement was in force in respect of the patent with the consent of the plaintiff. The effects of this provision were felt by Chiron Corporation in the case of *Chiron Corp.* v. *Murex Diagnostics Ltd (No. 12)* [1996] FSR 153.

Government departments are exempt from infringement action under s.55, if the use of the patent is for the use of the Crown, subject to payment of a royalty.

At common law, there is an implied licence to use or resell a patented product acquired through ordinary purchase of that product (as illustrated by *Betts* v. *Willmott* [1871] LR 6 Ch App 239) and an implied licence to repair patented goods even if that involves an activity that would otherwise infringe the patent (as illustrated by *Solar Thomson Engineering Co. Ltd* v. *Barton* [1977] RPC 537). In *Solar Thomson* the defendants had to repair part of a patented product supplied to them by the plaintiffs. They replaced a part of the patented product with one they had manufactured, which had an identical design to the plaintiffs' product. The Court of Appeal held that it was permissible to carry out repairs without infringing the patent covering the repaired product, provided the work of repair did not amount to the manufacture of a new article. But note *United Wire Ltd* v. *Screen Repairs Services & Others* [2001] RPC 439.

As with all equitable remedies, a failure on the part of the patent holder to take immediate action against infringers might prevent him from obtaining certain remedies.

6.7 Remedies

If successful in an infringement action, the patentee is entitled to the following remedies under s.61:

(a) an injunction restraining the defendant from any apprehended act of infringement;
(b) an order for the defendant to deliver up or destroy any patented product which relates to the infringement;
(c) damages in respect of the infringement;
(d) an order for an account of the profits made from the infringement; and
(e) a declaration that the patent is valid and has been infringed.

Remedies (c) and (d) are alternatives and will not both be awarded.

In the case of *Gerber Garment Technology Inc* v. *Lectra Systems Ltd* [1997] RPC 443 the court agreed with the plaintiff that damages for patent infringement could be based not only on lost sales of products covered by the patent, but also on other related sales and supplies which the patent owner might have made if it had not been for the infringer's activities. In that case, the plaintiff successfully claimed damages in respect of loss of sales on spare parts for the patented product, loss of income for servicing the patented product and the so-called springboard damages in respect of sales that could have been made after expiry of the patent.

For further guidance on assessing accounts of profits see Laddie J in *Celanese International Corp.* v. *BP Chemicals Ltd* [1999] RPC 203.

6.8 Criminal Offences

The Patents Act creates some criminal offences attracting criminal penalties, but these are not related to acts of infringement. The specific offences are: falsification of the Patents Register; misrepresenting a connection with the Patent Office; falsely representing oneself as a patent agent or patent attorney; falsely claiming that a product is patented; and falsely claiming that a patent has been applied for. Obviously, there may be situations where an applicant has prepared goods having the word 'patented' applied to them in expectation of obtaining the patent or without expectation that the patent will be revoked. In such a case, a reasonable period is allowed to prevent the commission of further offences by having the articles in question amended. It is also a defence to prove that due diligence had been exercised by the person charged to prevent continuance of the offence.

As with other criminal offences under intellectual property statutes, where the offender is a corporate body and the act was done with the consent, knowledge or connivance of an officer, the officer may also be found personally guilty of the offence.

6.9 Groundless Threats of Infringement

Section 70 of the 1977 Act introduced protection against groundless threats made against alleged defendants that did not exist in the 1949 Patents Act. The provision is there to prevent patentees from threatening unwarranted legal action. Infringement actions are quite complex and expensive to defend. Patentees are aware of this and some may be tempted to threaten legal action on the weakest of cases, knowing that the other party will cease the alleged infringing activity without a fight. The section, which has been significantly amended by the Patents Act 2004, provides that where anyone, by whatever means, threatens another with infringement proceedings, anyone aggrieved by the threats may claim relief against the person making the threats. The courts will consider threats that are both express and implied. The test is an objective one, assessing whether the language used would convey to the reasonable man an intention to bring infringement proceedings (see *Jaybeam Ltd* v. *Abru Aluminium* [1976] RPC 308). The 'person aggrieved' is defined in broad terms to include anyone whose 'commercial interests are likely to be adversely affected in a real, as opposed to a fanciful or minimal way' (see *C&P Developments Co. (London)* v. *Sisabro Novelty Co.* (1953) 70 RPC 277). A good explanation of s.70 both prior to and following the 2004 amendment can be found in Nettleton & Cordery, 'Walking the groundless threats minefield', *Journal of Intellectual Property Law & Practice* (2005) Vol. 1(1), 51. There, the authors point out that prior to 2005 (when the amendment took affect), the section did not apply to alleged primary infringements that involve making or importing products or using a process. The provision is intended to protect the potentially innocent middleman who is merely selling or using a product covered by the patent and who might, on receipt of such a threat, cease selling the product regardless of the validity of the action. However, the patentee's position is strengthened slightly in that permitted threats now cover all threats made to primary infringers. This will affect the decision in *Cavity Trays Ltd* v. *RMC Panel Products Ltd* [1996] RPC 361 concerning the meaning of s.70(4), which is the provision that removes the right to bring a threats action where the threat of proceedings was in respect of making or importing a product for disposal or in respect of using a process. In *Cavity Trays*, the threat of proceedings made against the plaintiffs, who were the manufacturers of the allegedly infringing products, was in respect of the acts of manufacture, promotion, marketing, advertisement and sale. The defendant argued that s.70(4) was aimed at removing the right to bring a threats action from primary infringers (that is, manufacturers) and was intended to protect secondary infringers further along the chain of supply. The court did not agree. Section 70(4) clearly provided an exception in respect of threats made about certain acts, and not in respect of threats made against types of person. Accordingly, since the defendant had threatened proceedings for infringements in respect of activities other than manufacture and importation of a product or use of a process, the plaintiff was entitled to its remedies under s.70. This is now not good law.

It is still a defence to a claim for unjustified threats that the threats were justified – this involves proving that the acts complained of were indeed infringements of a valid patent. Where the patent was found to be invalid, the defence was not available. The case of *Patrick John Brian* v. *Ingledew Brown Bennison & Garrett and Riso National Laboratory* [1996] FSR 341 underlines the risk of making threats of patent infringement on the basis of a patent application (as opposed to a granted patent). In that case, the threats were made at a time when the patent in question was an application being considered by the EPO. The EPO refused the application and sent it to the Examining Division for consideration. However, the court agreed with the plaintiff that it was entitled to an early decision on the threats action and that it should not have to wait for final determination on the validity of the patent. The defence of justification has now been widened to the extent that the patentee can avoid liability if he can show that he did not know and had no reason to suspect that the patent would be held invalid.

Summary

6.1 Once a patent is granted, the owner of the patent has the right to stop others dealing in the invention without his consent.

6.2 Making the invention, using it, or otherwise dealing with the invention all amount to acts of infringement.

6.3 To determine whether there has been infringement, the court will consider whether the defendant's activities fall within the claimant's claims.

6.4 English judges are being encouraged to adopt a more purposive approach to interpreting patent claims.

6.5 Slight modifications to the patent will still amount to infringement if there is no material difference in the working of the invention.

6.6 The general statutory defences are listed in s.60(5). A defendant can also claim that because of modifications made to the patent, there is no infringement. There is also the risk that a defendant will challenge the validity of the patent.

6.7 The general intellectual property remedies apply in respect of patent infringement and are listed in s.61.

6.8 The criminal offences under the Patents Act 1977 relate to false claims about whether a patent has been applied for and granted. It is also a criminal offence to misrepresent a connection with the Patent Office. Infringement of a patent is not a criminal offence.

Exercises

6.1 If the applicant has had the opportunity to prepare a patent specification, why should it not be interpreted literally for infringement purposes?

6.2 What exactly is the *Catnic* approach? Assess its validity for 1977 patents.

6.3 In 1980, *A* Toys obtained a patent for 'Josie the storytelling elephant', a cuddly toy whose voice is activated when her tummy is squeezed. *B* Toys have begun making 'Marty lullaby bear'. He is activated to play soothing music when a baby starts crying. Advise *A* Toys.

6.4 *C* acquired a licence to make and sell 'Josie the storytelling elephant'. Under the terms of the licence they agreed the following:

    (a) not to produce a similar toy for five years after the expiry of *A*'s patent;

    (b) to purchase the materials to make Josie from sources recommended by *A* Toys; and

    (c) not to challenge the validity of the patent for the term of the licence agreement.

C have produced 'Charlie the chatty chipmunk'. His voice is activated by a cuddle from a child or adult. He automatically switches off after five minutes to save the batteries. The idea for their design came from a member of staff who remembered having a soft cuddly doll in the 1970s that sang when her tummy was squeezed.

Advise *A* Toys, the owners of Josie.

Chapter 7
Breach of Confidence

Key words

▶ **Obligation of confidence** – those who are party to certain relationships have a responsibility not to disclose confidential information.
▶ **Trade secret** – sensitive information in relation to a manufacturing or productive process.

7.1 Introduction

This area of law has developed through the common law and equity. It is aimed at protecting secrets, and should not be confused with laws available in other countries providing a right to privacy (see *Kaye* v. *Robertson* [1991] 2 All ER 599); although it has been argued that in '*Campbell* v. *Mirror Group Newspapers* [2004] UKHL 22, English Law took a significant step closer to the protection of privacy as such' (Brazell, *EIPR* [2005], 27(11), 405–11). Invasions of privacy can be dealt with under the Human Rights Act 1998 and their Lordships in *Campbell* unanimously acknowleged that the values of privacy and free speech set out in the European Convention on Human Rights now form part of the cause of action for breach of confidence.

Breach of confidence complements other aspects of intellectual property, as an obligation of confidence can arise even before the work in question is tangible. So, for example, whereas the idea for a television programme cannot attract copyright protection until it is recorded in some way, the person to whom the idea is disclosed can be prevented from publicising that idea to others or exploiting the idea by the use of an action for breach of confidence. In *Fraser* v. *Thames Television Ltd* [1984] 1 QB 44, three actresses and a composer devised an idea for a television series based on the story of three female rock singers who formed a band. They discussed the idea with Thames Television and offered Thames first option on the idea, subject to the three actresses being given the parts of the three rock singers.

A dispute arose, and Thames made the programme without engaging the actresses. The plaintiffs claimed for breach of confidence. The defendant argued that the idea disclosed was not entitled to protection unless it was a developed idea that had been recorded in some permanent form. The court did not agree – those requirements were more relevant to the issue of copyright protection – and accepted the plaintiffs' argument of breach of confidence. Hirst J did, however, state that to be capable of protection by the law of confidence an idea must be 'sufficiently developed, so that it would be seen to be a concept ... which is capable of being realised as an actuality'.

The law of breach of confidence also protects the applicant for a patent by allowing him to impose an obligation of confidence on those who are in a position to know, or who need to know, the details of the invention before a patent application is filed. This is important because if the details of an invention are made public before the patent application is made, as we have seen it could fail for lack of novelty. Section 2(4)(b) of the Patents Act 1977 states that publication made in breach of confidence will not invalidate the patent application.

The law here is not limited to commercial or industrial situations. The obligation of confidence has been enforced to protect secrets between husband and wife (*Argyll* v. *Argyll* [1967] Ch 303), secrets between friends (*Stephens* v. *Avery* [1988] 1 Ch 457), drawings by members of the Royal family (*Prince Albert* v. *Strange* [1849] 1 Mac & G 25) and state secrets (*Attorney-General* v. *The Observer Ltd* [1989] AC 109).

7.2 Historical Background

Since the mid-nineteenth century, the law has recognised that an obligation of confidence can exist, although the action was not necessarily referred to as breach of confidence. In *Prince Albert* v. *Strange* [1849] 1 Mac & G 25, the Prince Consort was able to prevent the exhibition of prints taken from etchings he had produced of Queen Victoria. The House of Lords recognised a proprietary interest in the prints but stated that the plaintiff would have been equally protected if the etchings had been disclosed by actions for breach of trust, confidence or contract.

Another case from this period is that of *Morison* v. *Moat* (1851) 9 Hare 492. Morison invented 'Morison's Universal Medicine' and entered a partnership with Moat senior to market and sell it. The recipe was given in confidence to Moat senior. Before his death, Moat senior appointed his son as his successor in the partnership. Morison and his family believed that Moat senior had not passed the recipe on to Moat junior but, in fact, he had. On termination of the partnership agreement, Moat junior went into business on his own account, using Morison's recipe. The plaintiff was successful in restraining Moat junior from using the recipe. Turner VC felt that the disclosure by Moat senior to his son amounted to a breach of faith, as well as a breach of contract. This case also illustrates that it is possible to obtain protection for a longer period by relying on the obligation of confidence rather than the patent system. 'Morison's Universal Medicine' had not been patented. We know from the previous chapters that the details of patents are published and can be inspected by members of the public and it is possible for a competitor to work the patent after the patent has expired. However, where there has been no patent application, provided the details of the invention are kept secret by the owner, and by anyone to whom it is disclosed, it cannot be inspected in the same way, thus maintaining the invention's secrecy.

7.3 The Basic Requirements

The conditions for imposing an obligation of confidence were stated in Megarry J's decision in *Coco* v. *A.N. Clark (Eng.) Ltd* [1969] RPC 41. The plaintiff, who had designed an engine for a moped, entered into negotiations with the defendant company to discuss manufacture of the engine. All the details of the design were disclosed during these discussions. The parties subsequently fell out and the defendant decided to make its own engine, which closely resembled the plaintiff's. The plaintiff failed in his attempt to get an injunction to stop the defendant manufacturing his engine. Instead, the court required the defendant to deposit royalties on sales of the engines into a joint account until the full hearing. According to Megarry J, to be able to claim breach of confidence, a plaintiff needed to satisfy three conditions. First, the information must have the necessary quality of confidence. Second, the information must have been imparted in circumstances importing an obligation of confidence. Third, there must be unauthorised use of the information. In *Coco* v. *Clark* the court felt that the plaintiff could only satisfy the second condition.

Let us consider each requirement in detail.

7.4 The Necessary Quality of Confidence

The first condition is that the information must have the necessary quality of confidence. In other words, it should not be in the public domain. In a commercial or industrial context, this might be a trade secret. But what is a trade secret? Obviously it will cover technical information, like the mechanics of an invention that is yet to be the subject of a patent application. Price lists, customers' names and addresses and delivery routes might also be covered. A useful (but not conclusive) test is provided by Lord Parker in *Herbert Morris Ltd* v. *Saxelby* [1916] 1 AC 688. If the information is so detailed that it cannot be carried in the head, then it is a trade secret, but if it is simply a general method or scheme that is easily remembered, it is not.

Even where the information is not a trade secret, it can be classified as information of a confidential nature if it has 'the necessary quality of confidence about it, namely it must not be something which is public property and public knowledge' per Lord Greene MR in *Saltman Engineering*

Co. v. *Campbell Engineering Co.* [1963] 3 All ER 413 at page 415. The question is how do we tell whether the information has the 'necessary quality of confidence about it'? According to Megarry vc in *Thomas Marshall (Exports) Ltd* v. *Guinle* [1979] 1 Ch 227 there are four elements that should be taken into account. First, the owner must believe that the release of the information would be injurious to him or of advantage to his rivals. Second, the owner must believe that the information is confidential or secret. Third, the two first beliefs must be reasonable. Finally, the information must be considered taking into account trade practice. This would appear, initially, to be a subjective test in that it considers what the owner of the information believes. However, such belief must be reasonable suggesting an objective element (see Holyoak and Torremans).

The important point is that the owner of the information has not placed it in the public domain. Confidential information can come into the public domain in a number of ways, including by applying for a patent. When a patent is applied for, details of the patent application are published on the Patents Register and, as a result, come into the public domain. In *Mustad (O.) & Son* v. *S. Allcock & Co. Ltd and Dosen* [1963] 3 All ER 416, Mustad took over a business that had formerly employed Dosen. Dosen had acquired knowledge of the business's trade secrets but had been advised that he was no longer under an obligation of secrecy. He passed his knowledge on to his new employers. Mustad, who had acquired the trade secrets with the business, applied for a patent to protect one of the business's inventions and sued to restrain Dosen from passing on the trade secrets connected with it. The House of Lords held that, as the essential parts of the invention had been disclosed through publication of the patent application, the information was no longer confidential. The defendant must know that information is confidential (see *PCR Ltd* v. *Dow Jones Telerate* [1998] FSR 170) and it must be possible to isolate the information that is claimed to be confidential (see *Inline Logistics Ltd* v. *UCI Logistics Ltd* [2001] EWCA Civ 1613).

Disclosure and the 'springboard' doctrine

Although general disclosure or publication of the information in question generally removes the obligation of confidence, a person under an obligation of confidence may nevertheless be held to that obligation for a certain period of time after the general disclosure or publication. This is referred to as the 'springboard' doctrine. The following two cases are examples of this doctrine in practice.

In *Terrapin Ltd* v. *Builder's Supply Co. (Hayes) Ltd* [1967] RPC 375, the defendants made prefabricated portable buildings designed by the plaintiffs. During the period of their agreement, the plaintiffs disclosed details of their designs to the defendants in confidence. After the agreement ended, the defendants produced their own buildings, which were similar to those designed by the plaintiffs. At this stage the information was not confidential because the buildings could be inspected by any member of the public, but Roxburgh J granted an injunction on the basis that the defendants should not be in the position where they could make use of information gained in confidence from the plaintiffs to compete with the plaintiffs. As Roxburgh J said in that case:

> 'A person who has obtained information in confidence is not allowed to use it as a springboard for activities detrimental to the person who made the confidential communication, and springboard it remains even when all the features have been published or can be ascertained by actual inspection by any member of the public.'

In *Cranleigh Precision Engineering Ltd* v. *Bryant* [1964] 3 All ER 289, the defendant was the managing director and inventor for the plaintiff company, which made above-ground swimming pools. Before leaving the plaintiff company, the defendant was informed of another type of pool for which there was a patent (the Bischoff patent). This information was not disclosed to his employers. The defendant left the plaintiff company and set up business in competition, having acquired the Bischoff patent. He used the Bischoff patent, incorporating features from the plaintiff's pools. The plaintiff company applied for an injunction to prevent the defendant from making use of information about the plaintiff's pools. Although details of the Bischoff patent were available for inspection, the injunction was granted. The defendant's position had placed him at an unfair advantage. The information acquired as an employee meant that he could 'springboard' when setting up his own business.

These cases illustrate the principle that, even if the information becomes available to the public, those previously under an obligation of confidence in respect of the information should not have an unfair advantage as a result of having previously obtained that information.

What is confidential?

Apart from the 'springboard' doctrine, once the information is available to the public, it ceases to be confidential. Tom Jones and other celebrities were unable to stop the publication of details of their extramarital activities in *Woodward* v. *Hutchins* [1977] 2 All ER 751, because a number of those activities took place in public places and were well known. Further, the Court of Appeal felt that the plaintiffs had been quite happy to pursue publicity that portrayed them in a positive light, while attempting to suppress information that displayed their true characters. According to

Lord Denning MR it was in the interests of the public to know the truth. In *Attorney-General* v. *The Observer Ltd* [1989] AC 109 the House of Lords refused an injunction against the serialisation of *Spycatcher*, a book written by Peter Wright, an ex-member of MI5, because the book's publication abroad meant that its contents were no longer secret.

However, just because a secret is disclosed to another person, that does not necessarily place it in the public domain. This is illustrated by *Stephens* v. *Avery* [1988] 1 Ch 457. In that case, the plaintiff confided to a friend that she had been involved in a lesbian relationship with the deceased wife of a known criminal. The 'friend' disclosed the information to a Sunday newspaper, claiming that the disclosure to her meant that the information ceased to be confidential. Sir Nicholas Browne-Wilkinson did not agree:

> 'The mere fact that two people know a secret does not mean that it is not confidential. If, in fact, information is secret, then in my judgment it is capable of being kept secret by the imposition of a duty of confidence on any person to whom it is communicated. Information only ceases to be capable of protection as confidential when it is in fact known to a substantial number of people.'

It is clear then that if a person is told something as a secret they will be under an obligation of confidence. *Stephens* v. *Avery* involved a secret told to one person. The question is how many people can be told the secret before a 'substantial number' know of it and it ceases to be confidential? We suggest that a court will take the objective view and consider what is reasonable in each case. In *A* v. *B* [2003] QB 195, a so-called 'kiss and tell' case, Lord Woolf CJ stated that a duty of confidence will arise whenever a person is in a situation where he knows or ought to know that the other person can reasonably expect his privacy to be protected. As previously stated, the enactment of the Human Rights Act 1998 has perhaps reinforced the protection. In *Douglas* v. *Hello* [2005] EWCA Civ 595, the Court of Appeal held that when considering what information should be protected as confidential, the courts are required as a result of the Human Rights Act 1998 to adopt and develop the law of breach of confidence in such a way as to give effect to the competing rights of privacy and freedom of expression. Private information includes personal information not intended to be made public (see also *Campbell* v. *Mirror Group Newspapers* [2004] UKHL 22.

Even if a large number of people have been told the information, if they have all been bound to an obligation of confidence, the information is clearly not in the public domain. For instance, a software company may allow its licensees to have access to the computer source code (the human-readable coding, rather than the machine-readable code known as object code) for the purposes of error correction and development, subject to obligations of confidentiality. Even if the software is licensed to a large number of people, provided the obligations of confidentiality are imposed on and enforced against all the licensees, the source code will remain confidential information.

7.5   The Obligation of Confidence

The second condition from *Coco* v. *Clark* is that the information must have been 'imparted in circumstances importing an obligation of confidence'. Here we are looking at the relationship between the person imparting the information and the person who receives it. This relationship may be based on contract, trust, friendship or, even, marriage.

Contractual relationships

This is the most straightforward. The parties to a contractual agreement may have express terms of confidence in their agreement. Even if there are no express terms, an obligation of confidence might be implied. See *Saltman Engineering Co.* v. *Campbell Engineering Co.* [1963] 3 All ER 413. *Coco* v. *Clark* confirms that the obligation extends to precontractual disclosures, even if no contract materialises.

The law has imposed an obligation of confidence on a variety of contractual relationships. In *Tournier* v. *National Provincial & Union Bank of England* [1924] 1 KB 461, it was held that a bank was under an obligation of confidence to its customers, unless required to disclose information by law. Partnership agreements also impose duties of confidentiality on all the partners concerned (as illustrated by *Morison* v. *Moat*), as do agreements between directors and the companies they represent (cases such as *Cranleigh* and *Thomas Marshall* illustrate this). The above contracts also give rise to fiduciary relationships where the law will also impose a duty of confidence.

What would be the position if the owner of the information wrongfully repudiates the contractual relationship? In *Naomi Campbell* v. *Frisbee (Vanessa)* [2002] EWCA Civ 1374, the defendant had been employed by the claimant, a well-known cat-walk model. The latter sued when the defendant disclosed details of her personal life to a national newspaper. In deciding the effect that the claimant's wrongful repudiation of contract would have on any obligation of confidence, the Court of Appeal held that the principles were not clearly defined.

Contracts of employment

The obligation of confidence is also part of the contract of employment (although there is no duty to keep a secret about the employer's wrongful or unlawful act) (see *Initial Services* v. *Putterill* [1968] 1 QB 396). The duty imposed on employees is illustrated by *Hivac* v. *Park Royal Science*

Instruments Ltd [1946] 1 All ER 350. Park Royal, the plaintiff's competitor, was restrained from employing Hivac's employees. The employees had been working for the defendant in their spare time and, although there was no proof that confidential information had been disclosed, the Court of Appeal accepted that there was a risk that this could happen. For an employee's obligation of confidence, see also *Polymasc Pharmaceutical plc* v. *Stephen Alexander Charles* [1999] FSR 711 and *SBJ Stephenson Ltd* v. *Mandy* [2000] FSR 286.

In *FSS Travel & Leisure Systems Ltd* v. *Johnson* [1999] FSR 505, it was stated that it is critical to distinguish the trade secrets that the employer could claim as his property from the skill, experience, know-how and general knowledge that the employee could regard as his property, as only the former could be subject to an obligation.

The obligation of confidence can continue even after the contract of employment has been brought to an end. However, this is subject to quite a stringent test. In *Faccenda Chicken Ltd* v. *Fowler* [1987] 1 Ch 117, the plaintiff, who sold fresh chickens from refrigerated vans, applied for an injunction to restrain two former employees from using their knowledge of sales, prices and customers' details, when they set up a competing business. Neill LJ said, at pages 137–8, that in deciding whether the former employees owed a duty of confidence in respect of this information a number of factors should be considered:

(1) The nature of the employment. Was confidential information habitually, normally or only occasionally handled by the employee?
(2) The nature of the information itself: only trade secrets or information of a highly confidential nature would be protected.
(3) Whether the employer impressed upon the employee the confidential nature of the information.
(4) Whether the relevant information could be isolated easily from other information that the employee was free to use or disclose.

While Fowler (one of the former employees) was still employed, there was information that could be regarded as confidential and could not be disclosed by him or used for any other purpose, as he would be in breach of contract. However, when the contract of employment ended, such information that had become part of his own skill and knowledge ceased to be confidential and the employee was entitled to make use of that information and those skills.

Independent contractors, while not under a contract of employment, are usually under a duty of confidence by virtue of terms expressed or implied by law in a contract for services.

Non-contractual relationships

The obligation of confidence is not restricted to contractual relationships. *W. v. Edgell* [1990] 1 Ch 359 shows that it does apply to fiduciary relationships such as that between doctor and patient, subject to the public interest defence. *Stephens* v. *Avery* confirms that even a secret disclosed to a friend gives rise to an obligation based on the relationship of trust. What ties the different types of relationship together is that, as stated by Megarry J in *Coco* v. *Clark* at page 48:

> 'the circumstances are such that any reasonable man standing in the shoes of the recipient of the information would have realised that upon reasonable grounds the information was given to him in confidence.'

However, in *Carflow Products (UK) Ltd* v. *Linwood Securities (Birmingham) Ltd* [1996] FSR 424 the judge applied a different test to decide whether, in the absence of a contractual agreement, any confidentiality obligation could be implied. The judge applied a 'subjective test' – what obligations did the parties intend to impose and accept? In that case, because both parties wanted to invalidate a third party's registered design right by showing that it had previously been available in the public domain, both parties agreed that they did not intend the information to be treated as confidential. The judge also described an objective test (which could have been used if the subjective test had not answered the question). This test was the same test used in *Coco* v. *Clark*. The interesting point about the *Carflow* case is that the judge felt that, in the circumstances of the case, the reasonable bystander would have realised that the design in question would be protected by intellectual property rights and would, therefore, not assume that the information was disclosed in confidence. We think this attributes a degree of knowledge about intellectual property rights that most bystanders would not possess. In any event, even if other intellectual property rights were available to protect the information, as we have already said, obligations of confidentiality can provide additional and potentially unlimited protection, whereas most intellectual property rights expire after a period of time.

The position of third parties

The obligation will extend to a third party if it is obvious (to that party) that the information is of a confidential nature. So, as with cases such as *Stephens* v. *Avery*, the media are also under an obligation not to publish information of a confidential nature passed on by the recipient. Similarly, where an ex-employee is under an obligation of confidence, his new employer will also be held to an obligation of confidence in respect of the matters covered by the employee's obligation. In *Morison* v. *Moat* (1851) 9 Hare 492, Turner VC suggested that a third party would only escape the obligation of confidence if he were a purchaser for value of the secret without notice of the obligation. In other words, if the information is acquired by a third party who has paid for that information and who has no reasonable grounds to suspect that it is confidential, there is no obligation of secrecy. In *Susan Thomas* v. *Pearce* [2000] FSR 718, the first defendant kept a list of the clients of her former employer, which she gave to the second defendant, who used it. The Court of Appeal stated that the correct test was whether the third party had acted honestly. Behaviour that is considered careless, naive or stupid is not enough. The third party must have acted dishonestly, with conscious knowledge of the breach or at least deliberately closed their mind to it. The test would appear to be very similar to that used for holding a third party liable for assisting in a breach of trust.

This would appear to cover another interesting possibility. The third party may be unknown to both the person confiding the information and the person to whom he is disclosing it. For example, the information may be disclosed in a telephone conversation to which another party is listening in. Is that party also under an obligation of confidence? Technically, that third party owes no such obligation. Is it possible to owe an obligation to a person who does not know you exist? Turner VC's guidance is helpful here because a third party obtaining information from listening in on a telephone conversation is not, in our view, a 'purchaser for value'. This view is not, however, supported by the decision in *Malone* v. *Metropolitan Police Commissioner (No. 2)* [1979] 1 Ch 344. In that case, the plaintiff was charged with handling stolen goods. The prosecution case was based on information obtained by the tapping of the plaintiff's telephone conversations with the authority of the Home Secretary. The plaintiff sought an injunction to prevent use of the information. Megarry J refused to grant the injunction. In his view, anyone using a telephone to disclose confidential information had to accept the risk of being overheard. We think it would have been better if his Lordship had decided the issue on the question of public interest alone. Clearly, in this case, permission had been given by the Home Secretary, the objective being the detection and prevention of crime. To decide that, because of faults on the line, we take a risk when we disclose information on the telephone is less than satisfactory.

Malone was distinguished in *Francome* v. *Mirror Group Newspapers* [1984] 2 All ER 408. Here the information concerned had also been obtained by telephone tapping. The plaintiff was a well-known jockey, the defendants the proprietor and journalists of a tabloid newspaper. The defendants obtained information that suggested that the plaintiff had taken part in illegal activities. This information had come from an unknown source who had illegally tapped conversations from the plaintiff's telephone. Here the

Court of Appeal held that the plaintiff had the right to protect the confidentiality of his telephone conversations. The distinguishing factor between the two cases appears to be that in *Malone* the tapping took place legally whereas in *Francome* it did not. Megarry J's view in *Malone* was not followed here.

7.6 Unauthorised Use of the Information

Megarry J's third condition in *Coco* v. *Clark* was that the information has been used without the owner's authority. Within an agreement involving obligations of confidence, there will be implied as well as express terms. It will be clear that certain information is confidential. However, it may be necessary to disclose the information to others not directly party to the agreement. Where one party is engaged to manufacture the subject of the agreement, employees on the shop floor will need to have access to the information covered by the agreement in order to produce the end product, as will subcontractors. The authority to disclose in this instance will be implied into the agreement, even if not expressly contained.

Disclosure of the information includes using it to produce goods in order to compete with the person owning the information, as well as disclosing it to others. In *Seager* v. *Copydex* (*No. 1*) [1967] 2 All ER 415 the plaintiff and defendant had discussed the plaintiff's design for a stair carpet grip. Some time later the defendant designed its own carpet grip, which inadvertently incorporated some of the plaintiff's ideas. The Court of Appeal held this to be a case of unconscious copying and use of the plaintiff's idea and found in favour of the plaintiff. As shown by this case, the state of the defendant's mind is irrelevant, but it will be relevant when the court determines the plaintiff's remedy.

There is some doubt as to whether the disclosure or use of the information has to be detrimental to the plaintiff for the claim of breach of confidence to succeed. In *Coco* v. *Clark*, Megarry J suggests that it is part of the definition. If this is so, detriment must be proved in order for the plaintiff to succeed. We suggest that in most cases the detriment can be implied or assumed, even if it is not obvious or proven. Where the information is of a commercial nature, then disclosure to the plaintiff's competitors is bound to have an effect on his trade. The competitor will, for example, be able to use the information to produce competing goods without the investment costs incurred by the plaintiff and, therefore, sell those goods at a lower price. Even disclosure of personal information can lead to detriment. For example, the plaintiff in *Stephens* v. *Avery* would have suffered emotionally from unwanted media attention.

In *Drummond Murray* v. *Yorkshire Fund Managers Ltd and Michael Hartley*

[1998] FSR 372, the concern was whether a co-owner of information can prevent its use by the other co-owners.

The plaintiff was a marketing expert involved in the purchase of companies. He joined a team of five for the purpose of a management buy-in/buy-out of a company. The team created a business plan to attract venture capitalists. The business plan and the price to be paid for the assets were highly confidential information. Each member of the team was a co-author of the business plan with equal rights in it. But there was no agreement between the team members as to how this confidential information would be used.

The team approached the defendants as potential investors. The business plan and the price to be paid for the assets were discussed. The first defendant was interested in investing in the company but questioned the plaintiff's involvement as managing director and the team, other than the plaintiff, agreed to the latter being replaced by the second defendant. The plaintiff sued for breach of confidential information, contending that the confidential information was given to the defendants for the purpose of deciding whether to invest. The second defendant was therefore not entitled to use that information for any other purpose and had breached this obligation by using the information for the purpose of replacing him as managing director. The Court of Appeal held that the confidential information was incidental to the relationship between the team members. The confidential information ceased to be the plaintiff's property once this relationship was dissolved. He could not, therefore, prevent the other team members from using it as they pleased. As there had been no agreement concerning the relationship between the team members, the plaintiff could not prolong that relationship once he ceased to be a team member.

7.7 Defences

Confidential information and the public interest

The only real defence to this form of action is that disclosure of the information is in the public interest. For example, in *Lion Laboratories Ltd* v. *Evans & Others* [1984] 2 All ER 417, the plaintiff company made and supplied the police with intoximeters that were used to test the breath of drivers for the presence of alcohol under s.12 of the Road Traffic Act 1972. The defendants had been employed as technicians in developing the device and were aware of information that questioned its reliability. Concerned that the police were making use of an inaccurate and unreliable device, the defendants decided to pass the information on to a newspaper. The plaintiff sought an injunction to stop them. In the Court of Appeal, the defendants argued that it was in the public interest to disclose the possible unreliability of a device from which results were used as evidence against an individual charged with a criminal offence. The court agreed. The defence of public interest was available if it was in the public interest to publish the information. The Court of Appeal stated that it had to weigh up the public interest in maintaining secrecy in the plaintiff's documents against the public interest in the accuracy and reliability of an approved device that was used to determine whether a defendant facing a drink-driving charge should be convicted and suffer a penalty, possibly as serious as imprisonment.

In the earlier decision of *Hubbard* v. *Vosper* [1972] 2 QB 84, the Court of Appeal refused to grant an injunction to the leader of the Church of Scientology, L. Ron Hubbard. Vosper had agreed, on joining the Church, to keep certain aspects of the Church's activities secret. When he left, he wrote a book about its activities using material from Hubbard's book and certain other confidential information. The Church applied for an injunction to prevent publication of the book. The Court of Appeal considered that it was in the public interest that details of the activities of the Church be published.

Public interest as a defence also succeeded in *W.* v. *Edgell* [1990] 1 Ch 359. The fact that there is a duty of confidence between a doctor and patient is very clear. The plaintiff, a mental patient, had been convicted of manslaughter. In preparation for release into the community, he sought a transfer to a regional secure unit. To support an application to a mental health review tribunal, the plaintiff was examined by the defendant, an independent consultant psychiatrist. The defendant was concerned that the plaintiff was still a danger to the public and consequently his report was not favourable and the application was withdrawn. This meant that the consultant's report was not seen by the tribunal or by the medical officer at the secure unit. The defendant, concerned that his report should be shown to those treating the plaintiff, disclosed the report to the medical officer and the Secretary of State. The plaintiff sued claiming breach of the doctor–patient confidential relationship. The Court of Appeal held that there was certainly a duty of confidence between a doctor and patient, but this duty had to be balanced against the public interest in protecting others from possible violence.

In limited circumstances, confidence may be breached in the prevention of crime. In *Hellewell* v. *Chief Constable of Derbyshire* [1995] 1 WLR 804, the police circulated photographs of the plaintiff, who had previous convictions for theft. The photographs were circulated to local shopkeepers as part of a neighbourhood watch scheme. The plaintiff sued, claiming that a duty of confidence arose whenever the police took a photograph of a suspect. Laws J accepted this argument but held that where the photograph was being used for the prevention and detection of crime, the police had a public interest defence to any action for breach of confidence. However, not all information collected by the police can be disclosed on the basis of this defence. In *Marcel* v. *Commissioner of Police* [1991] 1 All ER 845, it was held that information seized by the police under the Police and Criminal Evidence Act 1984 could not be disclosed to a third party for use in civil proceedings.

7.8 Remedies

Damages for breach of confidence will generally be calculated on the basis of compensating the claimant for the conversion of property, although Holyoak and Torremans make a distinction between whether the breach is contractual or non-contractual. They suggest that for a contractual breach, damages should be assessed on the basis of contractual principles. That would appear to be logical. Where the breach is non-contractual, several commentaries appear to agree with Lord Denning in *Seager* v. *Copydex (No. 2)* [1969] RPC 250. His Lordship suggested considering the value of the information in question. If there is nothing particularly special about the information, such that it could have been obtained by employing a competent consultant, then damages should be assessed on the basis of the cost of hiring such a consultant. If, on the other hand, the information is special, perhaps involving an inventive step, then damages should reflect the price a willing buyer would pay for the information on the open market. In *Indata Equipment Supplies Ltd* v. *ACL Ltd* [1998] FSR 248, the Court of Appeal stated that damages should be assessed on a tortious basis, that is, such sum as would have put the claimant into the position he would have been in had it not been for the tort, or breach of confidence.

As with infringement of other intellectual property rights, the claimant may request an account of profits where the information has been used commercially. This is an equitable remedy that is at the court's discretion, as is an order for the delivery up and destruction of goods made using the confidential information.

As this area of law is concerned with secrets, the most usual remedy that the claimant seeks is an injunction preventing disclosure of the information. To restrain publication by an interloctory injunction the claimant has to satisfy a particularly high threshold test, since the enactment of the Human Rights Act 1998 (see *Creamm Holdings Ltd* v. *Bannerjee* [2005] 1 AC 253. If the information is already in the public domain, this is impractical and an injunction will not be granted, as illustrated by *Attorney-General* v. *The Observer Ltd* [1989] AC 109, where publication abroad of Peter Wright's book, *Spycatcher*, made it impractical for the House of Lords to restrain British newspapers publishing extracts. The 'springboard' doctrine is, however, an exception to this. As already stated, an individual under an obligation of confidence can be held to it even after general disclosure of the information, if it is felt that previous knowledge of the information places him at an unfair advantage over the plaintiff's other competitors.

Hot Topic . . .

PUBLIC INTEREST, MORALITY AND CELEBRITIES

Public interest and morality

If an individual puts herself forward to stand as a leadership contender for her political party, should details of her private life be made available to the public?

If the lead defender of a premiership football team spends the night in a brothel the night before a decisive match, do supporters have the right to know? What about season ticket holders?

The answers to these questions are perhaps not relevant in a textbook on intellectual property, but these are issues that are becoming relevant in the area of confidential information.

Like copyright, the law of confidence is not available to protect confidential information that is considered immoral. The defendants in *Stephens* v. *Avery* [1988] 1 Ch 457 claimed that the law should not enforce an obligation of confidence in relation to matters that have a grossly immoral tendency. However, Sir Nicholas Browne-Wilkinson pointed out that in 1988, details of a lesbian relationship were not necessarily regarded as grossly immoral. His Lordship, therefore, rejected the defendants'

submission. His Lordship pointed out, there was no common view that sexual conduct of any kind between consenting adults was grossly immoral. Following that approach, it is difficult to see when information of a sexual character can be disclosed using the public interest defence. *Woodward* v. *Hutchins* [1977] 2 All ER 751 may be cited as an example, but here the Court of Appeal were not making a judgment about the morality of the plaintiff's sexual activities, rather their Lordships felt that the plaintiffs had misrepresented their image to the public and were seeking to suppress information that would undermine such a representation.

Likewise, if the claimant confides to a 'friend' that he is a homosexual, there is an obligation of confidence. However, we would argue that if that claimant is a public figure who portrays a homophobic image, the practice of 'outing', although unpleasant, may be excused on this sort of argument. Here we see a link with the defences available in an action in defamation. In cases like *Lion Laboratories* and *Woodward* the defendant was able to argue that he would be in a position to plead the defence of justification to an

action in libel if he could disclose certain information. Where a defendant can make such a claim, the public interest defence is available against an action for breach of confidence. In *Naomi Campbell* v. *Mirror Group Newspapers Ltd* [2002] EWCA Civ 1373, the well-known cat-walk model sued a national newspaper for disclosing details of her visits to a narcotics support group. The Court of Appeal had held that where a public figure chooses to make untrue pronouncements about his or her public life, the press would normally be entitled to set the record straight (but now see Case note at the end of the chapter on *Campbell* v. *Mirror Group Newspapers* [2004] UKHL 22).

Public interest and the Human Rights Act 1998

Since the Human Rights Act 1998 came into force, the law of confidence must be considered in the light of the principles of the European Convention on Human Rights. Article 8 provides for a right to privacy, an apparent contrast to Article 10 which provides for freedom of expression. Where claimants are public figures, the courts will have to weigh up the merits of protecting the conflicting rights identified. The Court of Appeal did this in *Flitcroft* v. *Mirror Group Newspapers Ltd* [2002] EWCA Civ 337. A sporting personality sought to restrain details of his extramarital affairs. Jack J's discussion of the issues is in our opinion of great assistance. In his view, the court had to consider whether publication is in the public interest. If the public interest is great then any justification for suppressing that publication had to be strong in order for it to prevail. Conversely where the public interest in publication was very slight, or non-existent, a lesser justification would be sufficient. On appeal, the Court of Appeal, perhaps influenced by the fact that the individuals wanting to disclose were party to the extramarital relationship, allowed freedom of the press to prevail.

Public interest, the Human Rights Act 1998 and the celebrities' right in their own images
Another aspect of incorporating principles of Human Rights into the law of confidence is the control it may provide to celebrities in the use of their image. Celebrities and owners of fictional characters have found it difficult to use the law to curtail unauthorised use of their characters (see Chapter 11). In *Douglas* v. *Hello* [2005] EWCA Civ 595, the first and second claimants were well-known actors who signed an agreement with the third claimant giving the latter exclusive coverage of their celebrity wedding. The defendants managed to get photographs of the event which they subsequently

published. In an action for breach of confidence, the Court of Appeal held (*inter alia*) that the claimants had a reasonable expectation that the information would remain private. The contract with the third party was not a defence and the court recognised the rights of the claimants to commercially exploit their private wedding by authorising the publication of their photographs by the third claimants. It is suggested that although not a form of intellectual property in itself, this recognition of the right to commercially exploit a family occasion or indeed in any case where a celebrity has an exclusive agreement concerning media access, provides the celebrity with further armour.

Summary

7.1 The law of confidence can be used to impose secrecy in a variety of relationships.

7.2 The basic requirements for a successful action are to be found in Megarry J's judgment in *Coco* v. *Clark*.

7.3 To be protected, the information must be of a confidential nature. In other words it must not have reached the public domain unless the 'springboard' doctrine applies. The court will also consider whether it is in the public interest that the information is disclosed.

7.4 The obligation of confidence may arise from a number of relationships from contractual to relationships of trust and confidence.

7.5 Use of the information must be unauthorised but it is questionable whether use must be detrimental to the plaintiff.

7.6 The normal intellectual property remedies apply to breach of confidence actions.

7.7 The law of confidence has been reinforced to some extent by the Human Rights Act 1998.

Case note

▶ *Campbell* v. *Mirror Group Newspapers* [2004] UKHL 22

The claimant was a well-known cat-walk model undergoing treatment for drug addiction. The defendants published photographs of her leaving her Nacotics Anonymous sessions. In her action for breach of confidence, the House of Lords held that the threshold test was to ask whether a reasonable person of ordinary sensibilities if placed in the same situation as the subject of disclosure (i.e. the claimant), rather than its recipient (readers), would find the disclosure offensive. The details of the claimant's therapy for her addiction related to her physical and mental health. They were akin to private and confidential information contained in medical records.

Further reading

Brazell, *Confidence, Privacy and Human Rights, English Law in the 21st Century* [2005] EIPR 27(11), 405–11.

Singer and Scott, *The 21st Century Journalist* [2006] Ent LR 17(2), 55–7.

Part II

Trade Marks and Passing Off

Chapter 8

Trade Marks

Key word

> ▶ **Trade mark** – a word, sign or symbol on goods and services which allows consumers to make a distinction between similar goods and services.

8.1 Introduction

The following chapters are concerned with trade names and devices that have been registered under the Trade Marks Act 1938 or the Trade Marks Act 1994. Unregistered trade names and devices might be protected by means of a common law action for the tort of passing off (see Chapter 11) and, in some cases, by copyright.

The enactment of the Trade Marks Act 1994 radically changed the law on registered trade marks. The legislation harmonises the trade mark law of the United Kingdom with that of the rest of the European Community and implements the First Council Directive (89/104/EEC) to approximate the laws of the Member States relating to trade marks. The Government used the new Act as an opportunity to bring the law in this area up to date with current business practices. It was felt that the needs of commerce were not catered for by the Trade Marks Act 1938 despite a number of piecemeal amendments over the years to that Act. The 1994 Act has also made the process of registering trade marks and the administration of the Trade Marks Register more efficient.

8.2 What is a Trade Mark?

A trade mark can be described as a sign or symbol placed on, or used in relation to, one trader's goods or services to distinguish them from similar goods or services supplied by other traders. Section 1 of the Trade Marks Act 1994 defines a trade mark as any sign capable of being represented graphically which distinguishes the goods or services of one business from those of another. This is a much broader definition than that provided by s.68 of the 1938 Act, which required that the mark was used or proposed to be used in relation to goods to indicate a connection between the goods and the person entitled to use the mark.

The 1938 definition of a trade mark did not provide adequately for the registration of shapes of goods or their packaging, even though shape is as good an identifier of one trader's goods as any other type of trade mark. This was illustrated in *Coca-Cola Trade Mark Applications* [1986] 2 All ER 274 in which Coca-Cola filed an application to register the shape of the distinctive Coca-Cola bottle as a trade mark. Coca-Cola's application failed because, the Registrar said, it was trying to register 'the thing itself' as a trade mark. The Registrar and the court took the view that the definition of a trade mark in the 1938 Act required the mark to be 'something distinct from the thing marked'. The House of Lords was also concerned that by granting a trade mark in respect of the bottle itself, it would be allowing an undesirable monopoly in containers to develop.

The 1994 Act allows for the registration of words, designs, letters, numerals and the shape of goods or their packaging. In theory it is even possible for sounds and smells to be registered, although in practice this has proved difficult for applicants.

8.3　Possible Functions of Trade Marks

A trade mark may satisfy a number of functions. Its main function is indicated in the definition given above, namely, to differentiate one trader's goods or services from those of another. As mass production and self-service in the wholesale and retail markets have replaced limited product ranges and personal service, the trade mark allows the consumer to distinguish between similar products.

A good trade mark can be an essential tool for selling goods. As such, it is invaluable to the producer. In a market swamped by competing goods, the trade mark is a shorthand description for the product. Without a trade mark it would be necessary, each time a purchase is contemplated, to compare products by reference to ingredients, function and consumer experiences, which would be very long-winded. The trade mark is useful to the consumer as she will choose goods based on personal or vicarious experiences of a product and the trade mark allows easy identification of the product which previously gave satisfaction, thus leading to repeat purchases. This leads to another possible function of the trade mark: its guarantee function. Once a customer has tried a product with a particular name and found it satisfactory, repeat purchases of goods bearing that name will guarantee repetition of that satisfaction.

Equally, where a consumer has had a bad experience with a product, the trade mark can act as a warning against further purchases. Traders thus have an interest in protecting the good name of their mark by only attaching it to quality goods. Provided that the mark is imbued with this good reputation, the trader can use it to increase and generate sales by investing in promotions and advertising, and by using the mark.

The European Court of Justice, in *SA CNL-Sucal* v. *Hag GF AG* [1990] 3 CMLR 571, 608 at paras 13 and 14, described the essential function of a trade mark as giving the consumer or the ultimate user 'a guarantee of the identity of the origin of the marked product by enabling him to distinguish, without any possible confusion, that product from others of a different provenance'.

In *Philips Electronics NV* v. *Remington Consumer Products* [1999] RPC 809, at page 815, the Court of Appeal stated:

'The function of a trade mark is to identify the trade origin of goods and services. That function is important to protect both traders and consumers. It is a requirement of a trade mark under European law just as much as it has been under UK law.'

Thus in legal terms the main function of a trade mark is to identify the source of the goods and services to which it is attached; according to Lord Nicholls, in *Scandecor Developments AB* v. *Scandecor Marketing AV & Others* [2001] UKHL 21 at para. 16, it is a 'badge of origin'. His Lordship elaborated further in paras 18 and 19. Use of the trade mark would encourage producers of the goods or services to which they are attached to set and maintain quality standards. Consumers would then rely on the quality of goods not because there is a legal guarantee of quality but rather because 'the proprietor has an economic interest in maintaining the value of his mark'. The guarantee of origin function has been confirmed by the European Court of Justice in Case C-206/01, *Arsenal Football Club* v. *Reed* [2002] ECR I-10273. Implementation of the Directive has therefore led to a shift in focus with regard to the trade mark's function. One reason why it was so difficult to gain registration under the 1938 Act was the underlying 'public interest' or 'consumer protection' function. It could be argued that was one of the reasons s.68 required that the mark should be used or proposed to be used in relation to goods to indicate a connection between the goods and the person entitled to use the mark. 'Trafficking' in trade marks was also prohibited.

8.4 Historical Background

From the earliest times, traders have distinguished their goods by marking them. According to the Mathys Committee Report 1974, goods have been marked in various ways since Greek and Roman times. By the nineteenth century it was clear that marks applied to goods that had become distinctive had an intrinsic value and were worthy of some form of legal protection. Such protection was available through the use of Royal Charters and court action.

Protection from the courts came through two forms of action. First, a manufacturer could seek an injunction and damages against another person who was passing off his goods as those of the manufacturer. The basis for such an action was the plaintiff's reputation acquired by use of the mark. The second form of action was for infringement of a trade mark, an action developed by the courts of Chancery, which viewed the trade mark as a form of property. The main difficulties with this second form of action were that each time the plaintiff had to prove title to the mark and the court had to resolve the problem of what exactly constituted a trade mark.

The Trade Marks Registration Act 1875 was passed to overcome the difficulties encountered in such infringement actions. The Act established a statutory Register of trade marks that is still in use today. The Register provides the trade mark owner with evidence of legal title to, and exclusive rights of use of, the trade mark for the goods in respect of which it is registered. Entry of a mark on the Register is *prima facie* evidence that the proprietor has property in the mark and is entitled to prevent its unauthorised use by third parties. The Act of 1875 also laid down the essentials of a trade mark, giving practitioners and the courts the criteria for determining what could legally amount to a trade mark and, therefore, benefit from registration.

There then followed a number of repealing and amending Acts including the Patents, Designs and Trade Marks Act 1883, the Trade Marks Act 1905 and the Trade Marks Act 1919. Each Act moved the law relating to the registration of trade marks forward in line with changes in commercial practice, culminating in the 1938 Trade Marks Act. Apart from amendments made by the Trade Marks (Amendment) Act 1984 (which introduced the registration of service marks – trade marks used in relation to services rather than goods) and the Copyright, Designs and Patents Act 1988 (which made forgery of a trade mark a criminal offence), the 1938 Act governed trade mark law in the United Kingdom for nearly 60 years – until the 1994 Trade Marks Act came into force.

8.5 Background to the Trade Marks Act 1994

The need to reform trade mark law had been perceived in the United Kingdom for some time. In 1972, the Mathys Committee met to examine the state of British trade mark law and practice. Its report of 1974 made a number of recommendations for amending the law, but apart from the introduction of registration for service marks as a result of the Trade Marks (Amendment) Act 1984, none of these recommendations was implemented.

Certain aspects of the Trade Marks Act 1938 led to a great deal of judicial frustration. The Act lacked clarity for interpretation purposes and it failed to cater for modern commercial activities, such as character merchandising (as displayed by the Holly Hobbie case, discussed below). The impetus for change to trade mark law in the United Kingdom finally came from the European Community and the international stage.

In December 1988, the Council of the European Community adopted EC Directive 89/104/EEC, which aimed to harmonise, as far as possible, trade mark law throughout the European Community. While leaving individual Member States to determine certain procedural details of application, revocation and infringement proceedings, the Directive sought to harmonise the criteria for registrability and to minimise any differences in law between Member States that might affect the free movement of goods. The Directive prescribes what can and cannot be registered as a trade mark, the extent of the trade mark right, certain mandatory grounds for revocation and the means of licensing trade marks. It also confirms the obligation to use a trade mark to avoid cancellation of the mark.

In December 1993, the Council also adopted Commission Regulation 40/94/EEC, which was aimed at the creation of a Community Trade Mark, a single trade mark that would apply throughout the European Community (see Chapter 12).

Meanwhile, there was also pressure on the international stage for the United Kingdom to ratify the Protocol to the Madrid Agreement and various provisions of the Paris Convention (which are discussed in Chapter 12). While legislating to enable the United Kingdom to fulfil its obligations under European Community law (that is, to implement Council Directive 89/104/EEC) and various international conventions, the Government identified other areas in need of reform. It recognised, for example, that statutory amendments to the 1938 Act, and case law on that Act, had made the legislation complicated to interpret and administer. A particular culprit was s.4 of the 1938 Act on infringement (discussed further in Chapter 10).

Another specific problem with the 1938 Act, which had resulted in many commercially contradictory decisions, was the definition of a trade mark (under s.68), which limited the scope of what could amount to a trade mark. Distinctive shapes, smells and sounds could not be registered, while in other cases trade marks comprising distinctive colour combinations were allowed. The 1994 Act neither specifically allows nor excludes the registration of marks consisting of shapes, smells or sounds, but allows for a trade mark to be any sign that is capable of being represented graphically, and that distinguishes the goods or services of one undertaking from those of another. It goes on to state that a trade mark may consist of words (including personal names), designs, letters, numerals or (subject to a few limitations) the shape of goods or their packaging. This places the onus on a trader to convince the Registrar that the subject of the application can function as a trade mark, without placing any technical barriers in the way once that has been proved.

The Trade Marks Act 1938 also failed to cater for a number of common business practices. For example, under s.3, registration of a mark had to be for particular goods within one of the 42 internationally standard classes of goods. This meant that a trader wanting to register a mark in respect of goods falling within several classes had to file a separate application for each class, which was inconvenient and expensive. It is now possible to make a single application to cover goods and services in several classes at a reduced cost. So a mark can be registered to cover, say, drinks (Class 32) and sweets (Class 30) without the need for two separate applications. There is a small additional cost for each additional class.

Additionally, s.28(6) of the 1938 Act was a particular irritant for those engaged in the practice of licensing fictional characters and celebrities, as it stated that:

> 'The Registrar shall refuse an application . . . if it appears to him that the grant thereof would tend to facilitate trafficking in a trade mark.'

The full effect of this provision was felt in *American Greetings Corp.'s Application* [1984] RPC 329 (known as the Holly Hobbie case). The applicants were an American greetings card company, wanting to register 'Holly Hobbie', a mark comprising a drawing of a little girl called Holly Hobbie in a distinctive dress. The applicants' intention was to license others to use the mark on various items, including stationery and bedding, and with that intention they filed applications in numerous classes. Registration was refused on a number of grounds, but in particular because of s.28(6). The House of Lords upheld the Registrar's refusal to register, holding that the applicants were attempting to deal in the trade mark as a commodity in its own right and not for the purpose of identifying or promoting merchandise in which they were interested. The feelings of the business community and practitioners at that time were best summed up by Lord Bridge, who said:

> 'though I can find no escape from s.28(6) of the Act of 1938, I do not hesitate to express my opinion that it has become a complete anachronism and that the sooner it is repealed the better.'

Section 28(6) has been repealed by the 1994 Trade Marks Act.

A further change introduced by the 1994 Act relates to the Register itself. Since 1919, the Trade Marks Register has been divided into two parts, Part A and Part B. To be registered in Part A a mark had to be 'adapted to distinguish' the applicant's goods or services, while for Part B it was sufficient that it be, or had become, 'capable of distinguishing' the goods or services, for instance, as a result of long use. The criteria for registration in

Part B were less onerous but offered less protection against infringement. A great deal of time was spent in considering whether a mark should be registered in Part A or Part B of the Register. The 1994 Act has resulted in the two parts being combined into a single Register with the same requirements of distinctiveness and the same level of protection.

8.6 Conclusion

International obligations and the desire to administer trade mark law more efficiently, taking account of current trade practice and the decisions in numerous trade mark cases, finally led to the enactment of the Trade Marks Act 1994. The Act was brought into force by statutory instrument on 31 October 1994 and applies to all trade marks registered under the 1938 and 1984 Acts. In the following chapters we look at the registration, protection and enforcement of trade marks under the 1994 Act.

Summary

8.1 A trade mark is a sign distinguishing the goods and services of one trader from those of another.

8.2 If consumers are able to identify goods by reference to a trade mark, this will allow for repeat purchases and, equally, avoidance of low quality products. In this way, trade marks can be seen to add value to the goods and services to which they are applied.

8.3 The 1994 Trade Marks Act has resulted from the EC Directive on harmonisation of trade mark laws and the needs of modern commerce, and has also enabled the United Kingdom to ratify the Madrid Protocol and to implement the Community Trade Mark registration system.

Chapter 9

Registration of Trade Marks

Key words

- **Capable of distinguishing** – the mark should make it possible for consumers to make a distinction between the trade mark owners' goods and services and the goods and services provided by others.
- **Graphic representation** – it should be possible to visualise the mark.
- **Olfactory marks** – scented trade marks.

9.1 Introduction

The 1994 Trade Marks Act would appear to be more flexible than earlier trade mark legislation. On the face of it, the scope of what can be registered has been broadened. It also allows for more parties to register an interest in trade marks. The definition of a trade mark is not now limited to being in any particular form, as long as it can be graphically represented and as long as it functions as a trade mark (that is, as an identifier of one person's goods or services).

The producer of the goods or services to which the mark will be applied, or the person who designed the mark, can apply to register by virtue of s.32. Section 23 recognises joint ownership and s.30 recognises the interests of licensees. Licensees can also sue for infringement if their interests have been registered under s.25. For the first time, the interests of a mortgagee in a trade mark are recognised, with the possibility under s.25 of registering security interests on the Register.

9.2 The Application Process

Section 32 requires the following documents for registration of a trade mark:

(a) request for registration;
(b) information about the identity and address of the applicant;
(c) a statement about the goods and/or services in respect of which the mark is being registered;
(d) a graphic representation of the mark;
(e) payment of the appropriate fees (although payment can be delayed);
(f) a statement from the applicant that she is using the trade mark, or that it is being used with her permission, in relation to goods or services, or that she has a *bona fide* intention to do so.

Once the application is received at the Trade Marks Registry, it will be examined as required by s.37 to make sure that the rules and requirements of the legislation have been satisfied. If it is accepted, it will be published in the *Trade Marks Journal* (s.38), so that interested parties have the opportunity to oppose the trade mark within a specified period (three months from the date of publication).

If no opposition is filed, or an opposition is unsuccessful, the mark will be registered under s.40.

Each separate trade mark must be the subject of a separate application. Applications can be filed for a series of marks if they are sufficiently similar so as not to be considered as different marks by the Registrar.

Under the 1938 Act it used to be possible to associate marks that were similar or identical and that were registered for similar goods and/or services. Associated marks were useful, as use of one associated mark counted as use of all other associated marks (for the purposes of non-use challenges). The disadvantage was that once associated, such marks had to be held by the same owner, unless special procedures were followed. The 1994 Act does not provide for association of marks.

9.3 What is a Registrable Trade Mark?

Section 1(1) defines a trade mark as:

'any sign capable of being represented graphically which is capable of distinguishing goods or services of one undertaking from those of another.'

Under the 1938 Act, before a trade mark could be registered in Part A, it had to consist of or contain one of the 'essential particulars' listed in s.9. These particulars were names, signatures, invented words, words having no direct reference to the goods or services in question and any other distinctive mark. This more restrictive definition was seen not to admit trade marks which consisted purely of shape, sound or smell.

Section 9 of the 1938 Act also expressly prohibited the registration of geographical names and surnames. Names that were words in ordinary usage as well as being, coincidentally, geographical names could be registered (if they passed all other registrability tests). Surnames were held unregistrable in Part A of the Register if they appeared more than twice in the English telephone directory and unregistrable in Part B if they appeared more than five times in the English telephone directory. This Registry practice for determining whether a surname was common or not was strictly adhered to by the Registry. It is obvious that this test had its limitations – a truly 'common' surname could be registered if people with that name did not possess telephones or were ex-directory. This practice, which has survived the Act of 1994, has been criticised by the European Court of Justice in *Nichols Plc* v. *Registrar of Trade Marks* (Case C-404/02) [2005] RPC 12.

The position has changed under the 1994 Act because the absolute bar on geographical names and other names indicating type, origin and so on (s.3(1)(c)) is subject to a proviso if the name has acquired a secondary meaning.

So what is included?

Colours

There is a continuing debate about whether colours qualify as trade marks. It is clear that the law wishes to balance the needs of all traders by allowing the legitimate use of particular colours, while making it possible for proprietors to benefit from the use of colours in a distinctive manner. In *Redaway & Co.'s Application* (1914) 31 RPC 147, three lines of coloured thread interwoven in, and running the length of, canvas hose was held acceptable as a trade mark. *Smith, Kline & French Laboratories Ltd* v. *Sterling-Winthorp Group Ltd* [1975] 2 All ER 578 was decided under the stricter 1938 Trade Marks Act. This concerned an application to register ten colour combinations used on various drug capsules to distinguish the sustained release drugs in them. Most of the drugs were only available on prescription. There was sufficient evidence to show that widespread marketing and sales had made these colours distinctive of the appellant's product. The House of Lords held that distinctiveness was the important factor, and the coloured capsules had become distinctive through use. Registration was allowed.

In its White Paper, *Reform of Trade Mark Law* (Cm 1203), the Government made it clear that applications for trade marks consisting of colours would have to be accompanied by evidence of a secondary meaning; in other words, evidence that the colour has or colours have been used so extensively by the applicant that they are perceived by the public as distinguishing the applicant's goods or services from those of others. The courts have always appeared willing to allow registration of colours where drugs are concerned. In addition to the *Smith, Kline & French* decision, see *Parke Davis & Co.'s Application* [1976] FSR 195 where the High Court in Ireland was prepared to accept that the applicant's mark, consisting of a blue band encircling a capsule, was distinctive to chemists as representing the applicant's goods. But in *Wyeth (John) Coloured Tablet Trade Mark* [1988] RPC 233 the Registry was not prepared to register the colours blue and yellow as applied to tranquilliser drugs. A single colour (either blue or yellow) was being applied to the whole surface of the drug to indicate its strength. Whereas it was possible for a single colour to be a trade mark, in this case the Registry felt that the colours in question were being used to denote dosage rather than as a trade mark. The colours, blue and yellow, were common in the pharmaceutical industry and could not, therefore, acquire a secondary meaning.

In *Unilever's Trade Mark* [1984] RPC 155, the registration of red and white stripes for toothpaste was not allowed. The red stripes were functional in that they carried the mouthwash in the product and red was one of a limited number of colours available to toothpaste manufacturers to use for this purpose.

The question is whether these decisions are applicable under the 1994 legislation. The answer is 'yes'. Section 1(1) outlines the need for a trade mark to be capable of distinguishing goods or services of one undertaking from another. The colours in *Smith, Kline & French* and *Parke Davis* did just that. The colours in *Wyeth* and *Unilever* did not.

Colours as trade marks

As well as the ability to distinguish, there is the question of whether a colour can be represented graphically as required by s.1(1). This has been the subject of debate for both national and Community Trade Mark officials. According to Charlotte Schulze (see *Registering Colour Trade Marks in the European Union* [2003] 25(2) EIPR 55–67):

> 'Unless a colour mark is clearly defined it is impossible to assess the exact scope of protection, i.e the degree of monopoly use of a colour or colours.'

In Case R7 / 97–3, *Orange Personal Communications Ltd's Application* [1998] ETMR 460, the mark was simply described by the applicant as 'orange'. This was judged as not sufficiently precise to be a representation of a colour. The Third Board of Appeal of the Community Trade Mark Office observed that:

> 'An uncountable number of different colour shades, ranging in the specific case from dark to light and from the yellowish to the reddish tones, are conceivable which would fall under the wide generic term "orange".'

On its own, the mark as represented was vague and did not provide enough information to tell others what the mark to be protected actually was.

There is also a need for interested parties to be able to determine what is actually being protected, without having to engage in a complicated exercise to find out what the trade mark is.

In *Ty Nant Spring Water Ltd's Application* [2000] RPC 55, the applicant applied to register a trade mark for a selection of bottled waters. The application defined the trade mark in terms of characteristic optical properties represented in the following terms:

> 'A blue bottle of optical characteristics, such that if the wall thickness is 3 mm the bottle has, in air, a dominant wavelength of 472 to 474 nanometres, a purity of 44 to 48%, an optical brightness of 28 to 32%.'

The sign in question consisted of a blue bottle of any shape or size made from any material which would, if the wall thickness of the bottle was adjusted to 3 mm, be found to produce readings within the ranges specified when its ability to absorb and reflect white light was measured with the aid of a spectrophotometer. The colour presented to the eye by light radiating within the ranges specified is known as cobalt blue.

The application was refused, on the basis that it lacked the ability to be represented graphically, and because it was devoid of any distinctive character under s.3(1)(b). On appeal, Geoffrey Hobbs QC (12 July 1999) identified a number of problems with the application. First, he pointed out that those reading the application would need to take certain steps, that is, use a spectrophotometer to obtain the necessary readings in order to determine whether a bottle was of a particular hue. The representation had not mentioned the colour cobalt blue, nor had it included a graphic example of the relevant colour. Second, it was unclear whether the application necessarily implied a need to carry out a test to measure for compliance with the filed representation, and, if so, whether there was a standard test using standard equipment under standard conditions. Third, the words 'if the wall thickness is 3 mm' added to the uncertainty by providing that bottles made from materials which might appear to be radiating differing shades of blue at the wall thicknesses they actually possessed, should nonetheless be regarded as manifestations of the sign put forward for registration if it could be established that readings within the ranges specified would be obtained if they possessed a wall thickness of 3 mm.

Slogans

Applications to register slogans do not encounter the same difficulties as other non-traditional marks, since the graphic representation requirement can easily be satisfied. There is however still the issue of whether slogans can function as trade marks in the sense that consumers can distinguish the goods or services to which they are applied. There is also the need to ensure that a monopoly is not gained in phrases that other legitimate traders would want to use. So in *Fieldturf* v. *Office for Harmonisation in the Internal Market*, T.216/02, the Court of First Instance upheld the refusal to register the phrase 'looks like grass . . . feels like grass . . . plays like grass' for synthetic lawns and related services. (See also T.281/02, Mehr für Ihr Geld, 'more for your money'.) However lack of imagination in the slogan selected does not necessarily amount to lack of distinctiveness (see Case C-64/02P, *Office for Harmonisation in the Internal Market* v. *Erpo Möbelwerk GmbH*). In Case C-353/03, *Société Des Produits Nestlé SA* v. *Mars (UK) Ltd*, the main issue was whether Nestlé could register the words 'Have a break' as a trade mark without the rest of the well-known phrase used in its advertising. The European Court of Justice had to consider whether that part of the phrase had acquired distinctive character. In Advocate General Kokott's opinion, the reflex reaction from relevant consumers ('. . . have a KitKat') would not be sufficient (see para. 34). The Court agreed with this but went on to hold, taking into account the factors it had identified in *Windsurfing Cheimsee* on acquired distinctiveness, that such a mark may acquire distinctiveness through the use made of it (see section 9.5 below).

Shapes

Before 1994, the registration of shapes was hampered by a statement of Lindley LJ in *James* v. *Soulby* [1886] 33 Ch D 392:

> 'A mark must be something distinct from the thing marked. A mark itself cannot be a mark of itself.'

Coca-Cola Trade Mark Applications [1986] 2 All ER 274 concerned an application to register the famous Coca-Cola bottle as a trade mark. The House of Lords held that the legislation was there to protect marks, and not the article marked. The mark should distinguish the goods rather than be the goods themselves. Lord Templeman was concerned about granting a monopoly in respect of containers. He felt that rival manufacturers should be free to use any container of a similar shape provided it was labelled and packaged differently. This was an interesting conclusion, given that Coca-Cola would undoubtedly have had good grounds for an action in passing off if anyone else had used a bottle with the same shape. This is confirmed by the House of Lords' decision in *Reckitt & Colman Products Ltd* v. *Borden Inc. (No. 3)* [1990] 1 All ER 873, which we shall discuss in Chapter 11.

The decision in Coca-Cola has effectively been overruled by the second part of s.1(1), which states:

> 'A trade mark may, in particular, consist of words . . . designs, letters, numerals or the shape of goods or their packaging.'

The Trade Marks Registry has now accepted the shape of the Coca-Cola bottle as a trade mark. It has also accepted many other containers as trade marks, and even the shape of a peppermill. It is questionable whether all of these shapes do, in fact, function as trade marks – but, for now, they are getting on to the Register. However, not all shapes will be registrable. Section 3(2) states that a sign will not be registered if it consists exclusively of the shape that gives substantial value to the goods or is necessary to obtain a technical result. It also prohibits the registration of shapes that result from the nature of the goods themselves. In *Procter & Gamble Co's TM Application* [1998] RPC 710 to register a three-dimensional mark for soap, the

Registry gave some helpful statements in relation to the registrability of shape marks. The Hearing Officer in that case said that a shape was only likely to be held as functioning as a trade mark if 'the shape in question immediately strikes the eye as different and therefore memorable' and that if a shape was held by the public to be serving a functional purpose, operating as a convenience feature or having a purely decorative or aesthetic purpose, then it would be 'unlikely to be regarded as performing a trade mark function'.

Sounds and smells

These are potentially registrable, but the question is how will they satisfy the condition that they should be represented graphically? It has been suggested that an application could include musical notation for sounds and a chemical equation for smells. However, will this allow interested parties to know what the trade mark is? A suggested method of representing an olfactory mark is to describe it. However, the description should provide information that is so clear and precise that anyone reading it has 'an immediate and unambiguous idea of what the mark is' when used in connection with the goods or services to which it is applied. This certainly appears to be the approach taken by the Office for the Harmonisation of the Internal Market (formerly the Community Trade Marks Office).

The case of *Venootsschap onder Firma Senta Aromatic Marketing's Application* [1999] ETMR 429 concerned an application to register 'the smell of fresh cut grass' to tennis balls. In considering whether the application complied with Article 4 of the Community Trade Mark Regulation (equivalent to s.1(1) of the 1994 Act), the Second Board of Appeal of the Community Trade Marks Office made the following observations:

'The question then arises whether or not this description gives clear enough information to those reading it to walk away with an immediate and unambiguous idea of what the mark is when used in connection with tennis balls.

'The smell of freshly cut grass is a distinct smell, which everyone immediately recognises from experience. For many, the scent or fragrance of freshly cut grass reminds them of spring, or summer, manicured lawns or playing fields, or other such pleasant experiences.

'The Board is satisfied that the description provided for the olfactory mark sought to be registered for tennis balls is appropriate and complies with the graphical representation requirement of Article 4 of the CTMR.'

This now has to be considered in the light of the European Court of Justice decision in Case C-273/00, *Ralf Sieckmann* v. *Deutsches Patent- und Markenamt* [2002] ECR I-11737, which was that although a trade mark can consist of a sign which is not of itself capable of being perceived visually, a smell could not be registered as a trade mark by means of a chemical formula, a description in words or the deposit of an odour sample (para. 73). The applicant had applied to register an olfactory mark at the German patent and trade mark office. The application contained a chemical formula and was accompanied by an odour sample of the scent. It was also described as 'balsamically fruity with a slight hint of cinnamon'. The Court accepted the submission from the UK and the EC Commission that a chemical formula does not represent the odour of a substance, but the substance as such, and nor is it 'sufficiently precise' (at para. 69). While the description was 'graphic', it was not sufficiently 'clear, precise and objective' (para. 70). The deposit of a sample did not constitute a graphic representation. In what is now referred to as the '*Sieckmann* criteria', non-visual marks will have to be: 'clear, precise, self-contained, easily accessible, intelligible, durable and objective.'

It will be difficult to register olfactory marks on the basis of the above decision. Clearly samples and chemical formulae are unacceptable. Owners of such marks will have to find a way to describe the scent in a way that satisfies the above criteria.

The Registry has also issued a practice notice on sound marks in the *Trade Marks Journal*, giving examples of musical notations which have been accepted (*prima facie*) and also specifying the following examples as not acceptable without further evidence of factual distinctiveness (for example, children's nursery rhymes for children's goods or services, national anthems, songs commonly used as chimes for ice-cream vans such as 'Greensleeves'). In Case C-283/01, *Shield Mark BV* v. *Joost Kist (Trading as Memex)* (Case C-283/01) [2004] RPC 315, the ECJ stated that sounds could be registered if the *Sieckmann* criteria are met.

9.4 Conditions for Registration

These are the matters which the Examiner will consider under s.37. Section 1(1) establishes two basic conditions for registrability. The mark must be:

(1) capable of being represented graphically; and
(2) capable of distinguishing one trader's products from those of others.

Graphic representation

The objective here is to make it possible for interested parties to judge the monopoly given. In *Intellectual Property Law*, 2nd edn, at page 770, Bentley and Sherman identify three main functions of the graphic representation requirement. These are: the property function, to determine exactly what sign is protected; the administrative function, to assist the trade mark authorities in dealing with the sign; and the information or publicity function, where third parties can search the *Trade Marks Journal* not only to be aware of the trade mark owners' rights but also to determine whether a fresh application conflicts with earlier marks. As stated above, the *Sieckmann* criteria will also apply. Words and symbols will pose no problems and a two-dimensional drawing can represent a three-dimensional shape. However, as highlighted earlier, there are some interesting cases for sounds and smells.

Capable of distinguishing

Under previous law, to obtain superior trade mark protection under Part A of the Register, the mark had to be inherently distinctive. That is to say, it had to convey no meaning to the consumer except in the context of the applicant's goods or services, for example, an invented word like KODAK.

Lesser protection through registration in Part B of the Register was granted to trade marks that were 'factually distinctive'. These could be common words or symbols that had been used so extensively by the applicant that consumers recognised the sign as identifying the applicant's goods or services. However, strict judicial interpretation led to situations where even proof of factual distinctiveness failed to provide applicants with even the basic protection provided by Part B registrations. In *York Trailer Holdings* v. *Registrar of Trade Marks* [1982] 1 All ER 257, the applicants tried to register a mark that consisted of the word 'YORK' in white block capital letters on a black rectangular background with a maple leaf drawn inside the letter 'O'. There was evidence to show that the applicants' use in this way was distinctive of their products. There would have been a strong case in passing off, if others had used the mark. Nevertheless, the House of Lords refused the application. 'Capable of distinguishing', in their view, meant 'capable in law'. In other words, the House of Lords were looking for inherent distinctiveness.

Contrast this with the attitude of the Irish judges in *Waterford Trade Mark* [1984] FSR 390, who were satisfied that the extensive use of 'Waterford' on crystal had made it 'capable of distinguishing' and allowed the registration.

Section 3(1)(c) of the 1994 Act states that a trade mark designating a geographical origin is not capable of registration, unless the mark has acquired a distinctive character through use. The proviso has the effect of overruling *York Trailer*. The wording of s.1(1), and the qualification at the end of s.3(1) on absolute grounds of refusal, suggest that factual distinctiveness will be sufficient under the Trade Marks Act 1994.

Even if a mark appears to satisfy s.1, it could fail to achieve registration because of s.3 and/or s.5. Section 3 covers absolute grounds of refusal and s.5 covers relative grounds.

9.5 Absolute Grounds for Refusal

These are to be found in s.3(1), which states:

'The following shall not be registered:
(a) signs which do not satisfy the requirements of s.1(1),
(b) trade marks which are devoid of distinctive character,
(c) trade marks which consist of signs or indications which may serve, in trade to designate the kind, quality, quantity, intended purpose, value, geographical origin, the time of production of goods or of rendering of services, or other characteristics of goods or services,
(d) trade marks which consist exclusively of signs or indications which have become customary in the current language or in the bona fide and established practices of the trade:

Provided that, a trade mark shall not be refused registration by virtue of paragraph (b), (c) or (d) above, if before the date of registration, it has in fact acquired a distinctive character as a result of the use made of it.' [our italics]

Signs which do not satisfy s.1(1)

These will be signs that cannot be represented graphically or are not able to distinguish the goods of one trader from those of another. In *Healing Herbs Ltd* v. *Bach Flower Remedies Ltd* [2000] RPC 513, BACH and BACH FLOWER REMEDIES were among marks registered by Bach Flower Remedies (BFR), for homeopathic products made according to the teachings of Dr Edward Bach. Healing Herbs (HHL), who also made products following the Bach method, applied under s.47 for declarations that each of the marks had been registered in breach of each of the paragraphs of s.3(1). On s.3(1)(a), the Court of Appeal held that as the words BACH and BACH FLOWER REMEDIES were commonly used to describe such products, the marks failed to satisfy s.1(1) of the Trade Marks Act 1994, in the sense that they did not distinguish goods produced by BFR from similar goods produced by other undertakings. As such they failed under s.3(1)(a). See also *1-800 Flowers Inc.* v. *Phonenames Ltd* [2001] EWCA Civ 721.

Trade marks devoid of any distinctive character

In *AD2000 Trade Mark* [1997] RPC 168, Geoffrey Hobbs sitting as the Appointed Person stated that to avoid refusal under this heading a trade mark had to be 'distinctive by nature or have become distinctive by nurture', in other words inherently distinctive as discussed earlier or made distinctive through use. See also *Procter & Gamble's TM Application* [1999]

RPC 673. The shape of the bottle in *Yakult's TM Application* [2001] RPC 753 for yogurt drinks had been described as 'pretty ordinary' by the Registrar. Laddie J agreed. In his view it lacked inherent distinctiveness and had failed to acquire any distinctiveness through use.

Traditionally it was felt that trade marks which are descriptive of the goods or services to which they are applied cannot be distinctive and therefore cannot be registered. In *H. Quennel Ltd's Application* [1954] 72 RPC 36, the mark 'Pussikin' for cat food was considered directly descriptive of cat food. As such it was inherently incapable of distinguishing it. A useful test was put forward by Lloyd-Jacob J – would other traders in good faith legitimately want to use the word in the course of business? If the answer is 'yes', the applicant should not get a monopoly of the word. This would suggest that the requirement for distinctiveness has also a public policy function. Some would also state that this requirement is the first line of protection for legitimate traders (see for example Pfeiffer, *The Impact of the Baby Dry Case* [2002] EIPR 373). However, statements from the European Court of Justice and the Court of First Instance, concerning similar provisions in EEC Commission Regulation No. 40/94 to register Community Trade Marks, would suggest that other legitimate traders have sufficient protection from the defences in the respective pieces of legislation. For example see *Procter & Gamble* v. *Office for Harmonisation in the Internal Market (Trade Marks and Designs)* (Case C-383/99P). This concerned an application to register the words 'Baby Dry' as a Community Trade Mark for disposable nappies. The Examiner refused registration, as did the First Board of Appeal. On appeal to the Court of First Instance, that court stated that since the purpose of nappies was to be absorbent, in order to keep babies dry, the term 'Baby Dry' merely conveyed to consumers the intended purpose of the goods without exhibiting any additional feature to render the sign distinctive (para. 7). However the European Court of Justice took a different view. First of all, to determine whether the word combination 'Baby Dry' is capable of distinctiveness, the Court stated that one had to place oneself in the position of an 'English-speaking consumer'. From that point of view, it was necessary to determine whether the word combination is the normal way of referring to the goods in question. The ECJ held that while the word combination alluded to the function the goods in question were meant to fulfil, it should not be disqualified. While each of the two words did form part of expressions of everyday speech to designate the function of babies' nappies, 'their syntactically unusual juxtaposition is not a familiar expression in the English language, either for designating babies' nappies or for describing their essential features' (para. 43). This tended to suggest that even descriptive words might be registered, provided they have acquired a secondary meaning. In other words, to the average consumer they serve to identify the applicant's goods and services.

The Court of First Instance appeared to follow this approach in *Zapf Creation AG* v. *Office for Harmonisation in the Internal Market* (Case T-140/00): *Office for Harmonisation in the Internal Market* v. *Zapf Creation AG* (Case C-498/01P), which concerned an application to register 'New Born Baby' for dolls and their accessories. The CFI annulled the Examiner's refusal to register. On appeal from the Office for Harmonisation in the Internal Market (OHIM), Advocate General Jacobs advised the European Court that although 'New Born Baby' was not descriptive of the goods in question, the word combination was a reference to the characteristics of the goods (the doll represented a new born baby). Following the Advocate General's opinion, the application to register was withdrawn. The position has been clarified by Case C-191/01P , *Wrigley Jr. Company* v. *Office for Harmonisation in the Internal Market* [2004] ETMR 9. Wrigley applied to register 'Doublemint' as a Community Trade Mark for chewing gum. This was refused as lacking distinctiveness. The OHIM was of the opinion that the word was descriptive of the product and that other legitimate traders may want to use the words. The Court of First Instance allowed Wrigley's appeal, stating that the ambiguity over whether the sign meant that the gum was flavoured by two types of mint, or that it was twice as minty, was enough to make the sign not exclusively descriptive. The CFI's judgment was anulled by the European Court. A sign is unregistrable if at least one of its possible meanings designates a characteristic of the relevant goods or services.

For the position on the registration of surnames see *Nichols Plc* v. *Registrar of Trade Marks* (Case C-404/02) [2005] RPC 12, where Nichols Plc applied to register the company name 'Nichols' for vending machines and the food and drink they contained. Trade Mark Office practice in the United Kingdom was to test for distinctiveness of surnames by consulting the London Telephone Directory. As the name appeared 483 times, it was classed as a common surname and devoid of distinctive character for use on the products but not for the vending machines. In response to a reference from the High Court, the ECJ stated that there was nothing to justify adopting different tests for different types of mark. Consulting the London Telephone Directory was applying a further test which was radically different from the rest of the European Union. All marks were to be given the opportunity to demonstrate distinctiveness through use following the test from *Windsurfing Chiemsee Produktions* v. *Huber* [1999] ETMR 585 (*Windsurfing Chiemsee*) – see below.

What is the relationship between s.3(1)(a) and s.3(1)(b) with regard to distinctiveness? We suggest, like others (for example Bainbridge, *Intellectual*

Property, 5th edn, at page 557), that the intention must have been to add a further requirement for applicants. In *AD2000 Trade Mark*, the applicants appealed against the Registrar's refusal to register the mark AD2000 as devoid of distinctive character. They argued that having accepted that the mark was a sign 'capable of distinguishing goods' for the purpose of s.1(1), the Registrar was precluded from finding that it was devoid of distinctive character under s.3(1)(b). Dismissing the appeal, Geoffrey Hobbs QC held that 'capable' in s.1(1) meant that the mark was not 'incapable' of distinguishing goods or services from one undertaking from those of others. Even if s.1(1) was satisfied, a sign had to be 'distinctive by nature or become distinctive by nurture'. Since the year 2000 was significant for trading purposes, the onus was on the applicants to show that their sign was incapable of fair and honest application to the goods and services of anyone else. See also Jacob J in *British Sugar plc* v. *James Robertson & Sons Ltd* [1996] RPC 281. In *Philips Electronics NV* v. *Remington Consumer Products* (Case C-299/99) 18 June 2002 [2003] RPC 2, the European Court of Justice considered Articles 2 and 3, the equivalent to ss.1(1) and 3. On the relationship between the provisions, the ECJ stated that if a sign is distinctive through either nature or use, then it would be treated by definition as 'capable of distinguishing' the goods as required in s.3(1)(a). Section 3(1)(a) and the other paragraphs should be read together (see paras 37 and 38):

The proviso to ss.3(1)(b)–(d)

> '*Provided that, a trade mark shall not be refused registration by virtue of paragraph (b), (c) or (d) above, if before the date of registration, it has in fact acquired a distinctive character as a result of the use made of it.*' [our italics]

What will be required to bring an applicant or trade mark owner within the proviso? Important guidance was given by the European Court of Justice in *Windsurfing Chiemsee Produktions* v. *Huber* [1999] ETMR 585 (*Windsurfing Chiemsee*). This concerned registration of a geographical place name for use on sportswear. The ECJ stated that for such words to become distinctive through use, such use must serve to identify the product as originating from a particular undertaking, thus distinguishing its products from those of other undertakings. The geographical designation must have gained a new significance and its connotation no longer descriptive to justify its registration as a trade mark. What is particularly useful about the ECJ's decision is that it indicated other matters that could be taken into account, such as:

> 'the market share held by the mark; how intensive, geographically widespread and long-standing use of the mark has been; the amount invested by the

undertaking in promoting the mark; the proportion of the relevant class of persons who, because of the mark, identify goods as originating from a particular undertaking; and statements from chambers of commerce and industry or other trade and professional associations.'

However it has been suggested that ECJ's case law after *Windsurfing Chiemsee* is in a state of confusion (see Bentley and Sherman, *Intellectual Property Law*, 2nd edn, at page 803).

To demonstrate that the mark in question has acquired a secondary meaning, in the words of Jacob J in *British Sugar plc* v. *James Robertson & Sons Ltd* [1996] RPC 281, it must be shown that its original meaning has been 'displaced' (at page 302). The claimants in *Premier Luggage & Bags Ltd* v. *The Premier Company (UK) Ltd* [2002] EWCA Civ 387; [2001] FSR 461, were able to do this. Although the word 'Premier' could be described as an ordinary word, or descriptive and laudatory, the claimants were able to demonstrate that customers recognised that luggage bearing that mark was of a certain quality. The claimant had achieved a reputation for reliability, quality and value for money.

Shapes that cannot be trade marks

Section 3(2) is based on Article 3(1)(e) of Directive 89/104/EEC. Section 3(2)(a) does not allow registration of a shape:

'which results from the nature of the goods themselves.'

This excludes shapes dictated by the actual function of the goods in question. This would make sense for to allow registration would result in prohibiting other legitimate traders from using shapes that are inherent in the goods in question. Examples include the shape of footballs, shoe horns and keys. For similar reasons, the shapes of goods necessary to obtain a technical result are also not permitted under s.3(2)(b).

In *Philips Electronics NV* v. *Remington Consumer Products* (Case C-299/99) 18 June 2002 [2003] RPC 2, the European Court of Justice explained that the rationale behind the provision was to:

'prevent trade mark protection from granting its proprietor a monopoly on technical solutions or functional characteristics of a product, which a user is likely to seek in the products of competitors.'

The ECJ went on to add that trade mark protection should not be used as an obstacle to prevent competitors from freely dealing in products incorporating such technical solutions or functional characteristics in competition with the owner of the trade mark. The reference from the Court of Appeal to the ECJ concerned the registration of a three-headed rotary electric shaver by Philips. When Philips sued Remington for infringing its mark by selling and offering to sell three-headed rotary razors, Remington claimed that the mark should not have been registered as it breached each of the paragraphs in s.3(1), as well as s.3(2). Confirming the decision of both the High Court and Court of Appeal, the mark was declared invalid.

We believe s.3(2)(c) will be the cause of much litigation, because it is not clear what the section is seeking to prohibit. It states that a sign will not be registrable if it consists exclusively of a:

'shape which gives substantial value to the goods.'

At this stage we can only speculate that, in interpreting this paragraph, courts will look to the consumer's motive for buying the product. Potentially it will cover products as diverse as luxury designer goods and biscuits shaped in the likeness of one of The Hundred and One Dalmatians.

Trade marks offending public morality and good taste

Section 3(3) states that:

'A trade mark shall not be registered if it is:
(a) contrary to public policy or to accepted principles of morality, or
(b) of such a nature as to deceive the public (for instance as to the nature, quality or geographical origin of the goods or service).'

In *Re H.N. Brock* [1910] Ch 130, one of the reasons why the Court of Appeal refused registration of the word 'orlwoola' was that, phonetically, it sounded like 'all wool' and would be deceptive if the goods to which it was applied were not made entirely of wool. In *Re Hallelujah Trade Mark* [1976] RPC 605, it was held that the religious connotation of the word 'Hallelujah' made it inappropriate as a trade mark for clothing.

Likewise in *Ghazilian's Trade Mark Application* (2232411) 28 November 2001, Simon Thorley QC upheld the Registrar's decision to refuse an application to register 'TINY PENIS' for clothing. The correct anatomical term for parts of the human body should be 'reserved for serious use and not be debased by use as a smutty trade mark for clothing'.

Trade marks prohibited by enactments and emblems

Section 3(4) is intended to stop the registration of marks whose use is prohibited in the United Kingdom by any enactment or rule of law or by any provision of European Community Law. This would include use of the Red Cross symbol, for example, which is protected in another part of the Act or the inappropriate use of the word 'champagne', which would contravene EC Regulation 823/87. See *Taittinger SA* v. *Allbev Ltd* [1993] FSR 641.

Specially protected emblems are covered in s.3(5) which complements s.4.

Section 4 protects certain national and international emblems including Royal Arms, national flags and emblems of Paris Convention countries, as well as those of certain other international organisations. None of these is registrable without the consent of the relevant authorities.

Bad faith applications

An application made in bad faith is prohibited by s.3(6). An example of a bad faith application is where the applicant has no intention of using the mark himself, but registers it to stop competitors using it. *Imperial Group Ltd v. Philip Morris & Co. Ltd* [1982] FSR 72 is an example of such a practice. The plaintiffs introduced king-sized cigarettes that they wanted to call 'Merit'. This would have been unregistrable as a mark for being descriptive and laudatory. To stop others using the name, they registered the mark 'Nerit'. In 1976, the plaintiffs heard that the defendants were to launch cigarettes called 'Merit' in the United Kingdom and organised further distribution of their brand 'Nerit' through 2,600 outlets, but without an extensive advertising campaign. They then sued the defendants for trade mark infringement. In response, the defendants argued that 'Nerit' should be taken off the Register as there was never any real intention to use the mark. The Court of Appeal agreed. The mark had been registered without any *bona fide* intention to use it. Such use as there was, was not substantial. In coming to this decision, the court considered the meaning of '*bona fide*' in the context of *bona fide* intention to use and *bona fide* use. The court felt that to be *bona fide*, the use or intention to use had to be 'ordinary and genuine', 'perfectly genuine', 'substantial in amount', 'a real commercial use on a substantial scale' and 'a real genuine use'.

Although decided under the 1938 Trade Marks Act, this decision is still valid as an example of a bad faith application. It also illustrates that, like patents, a proprietor suing for infringement has to be prepared for the possibility that his intellectual property right underlying his claim will be challenged on the grounds that it should not have been granted in the first place.

In *Peter Byford v. Graham Oliver & Another* [2003] EWHC 295 Ch, registration of SAXON, the name of a 1970s heavy metal band, was declared invalid. Former band members had obtained registration even though they had no title and had done so for the purpose of interfering with the rights of the others who did. Section 5(4), which we discuss later, also applied because passing off proceedings could prevent use of the word SAXON alone. See also *Harrison's Trade Mark Application* [2004] EWCA Civ 1028; [2005] FSR 10.

9.6 Relative Grounds for Refusal

Even if the applicant gets past the absolute grounds for refusal in s.3, she still has to jump the hurdle of s.5. The aim of s.5 is to protect prior rights of third parties. Generally speaking, under s.5 the Registrar should not allow registration of a mark that is the same as, or similar to, an earlier mark. An earlier mark is defined in s.6(1) as:

'(a) a registered trade mark, international trade mark (UK) or Community trade mark which has a date of application for registration earlier than that of the trade mark in question, taking account (where appropriate) of the priorities claimed in respect of the trade marks,

(b) a Community trade mark which has a valid claim to seniority from an earlier registered trade mark or international trade mark (UK), or

(c) a trade mark which, at the date of application for registration of the trade mark in question or (where appropriate) of the priority claimed in respect of the application, was entitled to protection under the Paris Convention as a well-known trade mark.'

Section 5(1) states that a trade mark that is the same as an earlier mark and is for the same goods or services will not be registered. Under s.5(2), a mark is not registrable if it is likely to cause the public confusion, where the mark is identical to an earlier mark and is for similar goods or services, or if it is similar to an earlier mark and is for identical or similar goods or services. An old authority provides us with an example. In *Aristoc* v. *Rysta* [1945] AC 68, the defendants repaired stockings manufactured by the plaintiffs. The defendants decided to apply the mark 'RYSTA' to repaired stockings and the stockings they manufactured. They were not allowed to do this as 'RYSTA' was phonetically too similar to 'ARISTOC'. If an applicant can show that the goods to which its mark will be applied are sold in different markets from the markets in which the goods to which the conflicting marks are applied, he may obtain registration. In *Seahorse Trade Mark* [1980] RPC 250, the question was whether the purchasers of marine engines exceeding 5,000 bhp were the same as purchasers of outboard motors with engines that were 115 bhp. The registration of 'SEAHORSE' for the former products was allowed even though 'SEA HORSE' was registered for the latter. The markets in which they operated were sufficiently separate so that no confusion would arise.

In considering the likelihood of confusion, factors such as the imperfect recollection of consumers, the type of products and the likely target consumer are relevant. In *Imperial Tobacco Ltd* v. *Berry Brothers & Ruud Ltd* (2001) (Opposition Number 47290), Patents Court, 31 October 2001, the respondents trade mark 'CUTTY SARK' was said to be a highly distinctive mark that must have had a significant reputation in the UK. Its opposition to the appellant's mark based on s.5(2)(b) was therefore upheld.

Section 5(3) states that an identical or similar mark will not be registrable if the earlier mark has gained a reputation, even in respect of different goods, if it would lead to taking unfair advantage of the earlier mark or would cause detriment to the earlier mark's distinctive character. So, for example, Rolls-Royce applied to burger bar services is unlikely to be allowed. Finally s.5(4) states that a mark will not be registered if its use could be prevented by passing off or the enforcement of some other earlier right, unless the proprietor's consent is obtained and there is no likelihood of confusion.

Oasis Store Ltd's Trade Mark Application [1998] RPC 631 concerned an application to register 'EVEREADY' for contraceptives and condoms. Ever Ready plc, the owner of numerous 'EVER READY' words and device marks for batteries, torches, plugs and smoke alarms, opposed this. Ever Ready claimed that use of the 'EVEREADY' mark on contraceptives and condoms was contrary to s.5(4)(a) of the Trade Marks Act 1994, on the ground that it would succeed in a passing off action against the applicant if the mark was put to use in relation to the goods for which registration was sought. It also opposed under s.5(3) that the mark would take unfair advantage of its reputation. It was held that the burden of establishing an earlier right under s.5(4)(a) rested on the opponent. The fact that the parties were trading in different fields added to the opponent's burden of establishing a real risk of confusion and deception. In this case the fields of activity were so far removed that it could not be assumed that even if a small amount of confusion did arise it would be damaging to the opponent. Thus the opposition under s.5(4)(a) failed. Opposition under s.5(3) also failed. Simply being reminded of a similar trade mark with a reputation for dissimilar goods did not necessarily amount to taking unfair advantage of the repute of that trade mark.

Contrast this with *CA Sheimer (M) Sdn Bhd's TM Application* [2000] RPC 484, where Visa International, the proprietor of the VISA financial services brand, successfully opposed an application to register VISA for condoms under s.5(3). According to Geoffrey Hobbs QC:

> 'The bringing to mind of the VISA mark for financial services, which had a strong distinctive character in the United Kingdom, when consumers were faced with the VISA mark on condoms was substantially detrimental to the distinctive character of VISA International's trade mark.'

Solicitors Rowe and Maw suggest that the difficulty for Ever Ready plc, in the earlier case, was that it is difficult to establish 'unfair advantage' when the mark consists of ordinary dictionary words (*Intellectual Property Newsletter*, Autumn/Winter 1999, at page 13).

See also *Inlima SL's Application for a 3-Dimensional Trade Mark* [2000] RPC

661, where the applicant's use of stripes similar to those used on Adidas sportswear was refused.

In *Intel Corporation* v. *Kirpal Singh Sihra* [2003] EWHC 17 (Ch), an application to register 'INTEL-PLAY' as a trade mark for toy puzzles was refused, since the applicant's intended use of it would take advantage of and be detrimental to the character and repute of INTEL's mark which was internationally recognised in the field of computer technology.

Finally, s.5(4) states that a mark will not be registered if its use could be prevented by passing off or the enforcement of some other earlier right, unless the proprietor's consent is obtained and there is no likelihood of confusion. See *Peter Byford* v. *Graham Oliver & Another* [2003] EWHC 295 (Ch), referred to earlier.

Sections 5(1)–(4) will not, however, prevent a mark being registered if the proprietor of the earlier mark, or other earlier right, consents to the registration (s.5(5)). This practice of letters of consent was introduced by the 1994 Act.

Currently, the Registrar can cite an earlier mark but s.8 allows the Secretary of State to make an order that a trade mark shall not be refused registration because of any of the grounds in s.5, unless objection is raised in opposition proceedings by the proprietor of the earlier mark, as is already the case in other European countries. This would place the onus on trade mark owners to study the *Trade Marks Journal* to make sure that marks that are identical or similar to theirs are not registered. For the moment, the discretion is still with the Registrar, as the Secretary of State cannot make such an order until ten years after the introduction of a working Community Trade Mark system.

Honest concurrent use

The principle of 'honest concurrent use' is maintained in the 1994 Act under s.7. It was introduced in the 1875 Act to cover a situation where two people are already using the same or similar marks in different parts of the country before one of them applies to register the trade mark. If the proprietor of the earlier unregistered mark is shown to have been an honest concurrent user, the Registrar cannot refuse the application because of the earlier use, unless an objection on that ground is raised in opposition proceedings by the proprietor of the earlier mark. See *Anheuser-Busch Inc.* v. *Budejovicky Budvar Narodni Podnik* [2000] RPC 906.

9.7 Maintaining Registration

If the application satisfies all the requirements in ss.1–7, the mark will be registered and the registration will last for a period of ten years (s.42(1)), and can be renewed indefinitely for further periods of ten years (s.43). After registration, a proprietor needs to take care to maintain the registration so that it does not lapse or is not open to challenge. As with patents, it is usual for a defendant in an infringement action to challenge the validity of the plaintiff's trade mark. Of course, a proprietor may decide of his own accord to surrender the trade mark in certain circumstances.

Under the 1938 Act, marks were registered in either Part A or Part B of the Register. Marks in Part A were protected from revocation (except on grounds of fraud) once they had been on the Register for seven years. When the 1994 Act came into force, the Register was consolidated for past and future marks. This means that all marks (including all Part A marks) are now open to revocation at any time.

Surrendering the trade mark

Section 45 allows the proprietor to surrender the trade mark in respect of some or all of the goods and/or services for which it is registered. It may be expedient to do this in the face of revocation or invalidity proceedings. If an identical Community Trade Mark registration has been obtained, there is no longer the need to retain the national registration so it may be surrendered by the proprietor.

Revocation and invalidity

Under ss.46 and 47, any person can apply to have a trade mark revoked or declared invalid.

Under s.46, there are three grounds on which a trade mark registration can be revoked.

The first is where the mark has not been used in the United Kingdom for a period of five years or more without good cause. A registration cannot be attacked under this provision before it is five years old (the period being counted from the date of registration, not the date of application) even if the proprietor never had a *bona fide* intention to use the mark and has never used the mark. Any use of the mark within three months before the application for revocation is filed will be disregarded, unless the proprietor can show that he had made preparations to make genuine use of the trade mark before he became aware that an application for revocation might be made. 'Genuine use' can be defined as 'substantial and genuine use judged by ordinary commercial standards'. See *Imperial Group Ltd* v. *Philip Morris & Co. Ltd* [1982] FSR 72.

A trade mark may also be challenged for non-use if the mark in question has been used in a way which differs in some essential element from the mark as registered. In the case of *United Biscuits (UK) Ltd* v. *Asda Stores Ltd* [1997] RPC 513, United Biscuits' registered marks of pictures of penguins were revoked for lack of use since the designs of penguins used on the Penguin packaging were different from those covered by the registration. As a result, the United Biscuits' claim of trade mark infringement against Asda for use of a representation of a puffin in relation to chocolate biscuits failed (although United Biscuits did succeed with their claim in passing off – see Chapter 11).

The second ground for revocation is where the mark has become generic. A trade mark can be challenged under s.46(1)(c) if it has become common 'in the trade' for the product or service for which it is registered by reason of the acts or inactivity of the proprietor. Famous examples include ASPIRIN and ESCALATOR. The party challenging must show that the mark has become 'generic' because of the proprietor's action or lack of action. To avoid marks becoming generic, proprietors should be vigilant and make good use of s.10 to stop the use of their mark on the same or similar goods as those for which the proprietor's mark is registered. Proprietors should also avoid using the trade mark as a noun to describe the product or service in question. For example, 'personal stereo' should be used instead of 'Walkman'. Rank Xerox have had to work against the peculiarly US practice of referring to 'xeroxing' instead of 'photocopying'.

The final ground for revocation is 'misleading use'. This is where the proprietor's use, or use with his consent, is likely to mislead the public as to the nature, quality or geographical origin of the goods or services to which the mark is applied.

In *Scandecor Developments AB* v. *Scandecor Marketing AV & Others* [2001] UKHL 21, the House of Lords had to consider among other things whether the use of two SCANDECOR trade marks used by two associated enterprises had become liable to mislead the public because of the use made of them. The proprietor of the mark was not the origin of the goods using the mark and had no quality control over goods bearing them. Their Lordships had to consider whether the grant of a bare exclusive licence was 'inherently likely to deceive potential customers'. Lord Nicholls of Birkenhead suggested that a trade mark should not be regarded as liable to mislead if the origin of the goods is a bare exclusive licensee. One of the major advantages of the 1994 Act over the 1938 Act is the provision made for licensing and sub-licensing. In the words of Bainbridge: His Lordship's opinion accords with 'modern business practices'. To decide otherwise would in our opinion be a step backwards.

A trade mark registration may be declared invalid under s.47 if the trade mark application should have failed under one or more of the absolute conditions listed in s.3, for instance, an application made in bad faith as in *Imperial* v. *Philip Morris* [1982] FSR 72. Once the registration is declared invalid, the mark is treated as though it had never been registered. In *British Sugar plc* v. *James Robertson & Sons Ltd* [1996] RPC 281, the mark 'TREAT', for dessert and ice-cream topping, was taken off the register after the owners brought an infringement action against the defendants for use of the mark in relation to their new spread. As a descriptive word, Jacob J was of the opinion that it should never have been allowed registration because it did not function as a trade mark.

Bearing in mind the apparently lax attitude of the Registry to some of the more ingenious trade mark applications, it is likely that a large number of trade marks will suffer the same fate if their owners ever try to exert their trade mark rights.

9.8 Special Marks

Collective marks

The collective mark was introduced by the Trade Marks Act 1994. Section 49 states:

> 'A collective mark is a mark distinguishing the goods or services of members of the association which is the proprietor of the mark for those undertakings.'

A collective mark is a mark that can be used by anyone who is a member of the association in whose name the mark is registered. It differs from other marks in that the proprietor is a body of persons rather than an individual or company.

The rules that apply to collective marks are set out in Schedule one of the Trade Marks Act 1994.

Certification marks

Certification marks guarantee that the goods to which they are attached have been certified as being of a particular material (such as the woolmark), method of manufacture, quality, accuracy or origin (s.50). Such marks are a testament to the quality or origin of the goods or services to which they are attached (see *Stilton Trade Mark* [1967] RPC 173). The rules that apply to certification marks are set out in Schedule two of the Trade Marks Act 1994. See also *Legal Aid Board's Application* (2114581) 3 October 2000.

Hot Topic . . .

THE REGISTRATION OF NON-TRADITIONAL MARKS

The enactment of the Trade Marks Act 1994 was met with a great deal of academic and professional excitement. Section 1(1) seemed to suggest that anything was possible, when it came to what could be registered. In her article 'Full Marks for the New Law?', Susan Singleton noted that distinctive packaging like the famous Coca-Cola bottle would be capable of registration for the first time (see *Solicitors' Journal*, 7 October 1994). Julian Gyngell, in 'Trade Marks – good news for business', stated that all manner of distinctive trade marks were eligible for registration and protection (*NLJ Practitioner*, 18 November 1994):

'. . . it may be now possible to register a distinctive sound . . ., a distinctive product design or packaging . . ., as well as the distinctive layout, arrangement or decoration of retail premises. It will also be easier to register colours. . . .'

In practice the registration of non-traditional marks has proved difficult because of the requirement for graphic representation as well as the ability of the mark to distinguish the goods. Indeed it could be argued that to allow the registration of shapes, sounds and smells, when the proprietor can register the name and symbols, is to allow an increase in the protection afforded, which may not be justified. But if proprietors have invested so much into creating goodwill in the colours, sounds or smells of their products and/services that they can attract common law protection, then it could be argued that proper registration should be permitted. The following case law on the Trade Marks Directive and the Community Trade Mark Regulation indicates that registration will not be straightforward:

▶ **Case C-273/00, *Ralf Sieckmann v. Deutsches Patent- und Markenamt* [2002] ECR I-11737**

Sieckmann wanted to register an olfactory mark at the German patent and trade mark office. The application contained a chemical formula and was accompanied by an odour sample of the scent. It was also described as 'balsamically fruity with a slight hint of cinnamon'. The ECJ stated that a smell would not be adequately graphically represented by a verbal description because it would not be 'sufficiently precise'. Depositing the sample was not sufficiently durable or stable; and the chemical formula would not be sufficiently clear or precise.

▶ **Case C-104/01, *Libertel Groep BV v. Benelux-Merkenbureau* [2003] ECR I-3793**

An attempt was being made to register the colour orange for telephone books. Attorney-General Leger was of the opinion that colours *per se* were not capable of graphic representation. Whilst the ECJ rejected that view, it stated that the colour sample was not sufficiently durable. The *Sieckmann* criteria would apply. The Court also suggested that an internationally recognised identification code (Pantone) may, in combination with a verbal description and colour sample, be acceptable.

▶ **Case C-49/02, *Heidelberger Bauchemie GmbH* [2004] ETMR 99**

Heidelberger Bauchemie brought proceedings against the German Patent and Trade Mark Office for its refusal to register the colours blue and yellow in respect of goods for the building trade. In its reference to the ECJ, the German Federal Patent Court referred the following questions:

(1) Are colours *per se* or other of their combinations distinctive for the purposes of Article 2?
(2) If so, under what circumstances?

The ECJ's response was that, for registration, colours would have to satisfy the following:

(1) must be a sign;
(2) must be capable of graphic representation;
(3) must be distinctive.

To meet the above criteria, the marks must be 'precise, unambiguous, and durable'. Abstract colours without contours would need to be 'systematically arranged by associating [them] in a predetermined and uniform way'. The mere juxtaposition of two or more colours without shape or contours would not satisfy the criteria.

▶ **Case C-283/01, Shield Mark BV v. Joost Kist (Trading as Memex) [2004] RPC 315**

This application was to register the first nine notes of *Für Elise* and the Dutch equivalent of the onomatopoeic sound cock-a-doodle-doo, said to be registrable in theory if the *Sieckmann* criteria are met. The problem was the linguistic differences in representing the sound of a cockerel across the European Union.

Summary

9.1 In theory, the Trade Marks Act 1994 makes it possible to register a range of matter as trade marks, provided they can be represented graphically and function as trade marks.

9.2 On receipt at the Registry, the application is examined, then published and registered if no reasonable objection has been raised within three months after publication.

9.3 Colours, shapes, sounds and smells are potentially registrable if they function as trade marks; the problem has been to find a suitable method to graphically represent non-traditional marks.

9.4 To obtain registration, the mark should be represented graphically and be capable of distinguishing the applicant's goods or services.

9.5 The grounds on which an application can be refused outright are listed in s.3. These are mainly linked to the fact that the mark lacks distinctiveness.

9.6 Under s.5, the Registrar can refuse a registration that interferes with a prior third party right unless the prior owner consents.

9.7 Even after registration the mark may be challenged as invalid under s.47 or revoked under s.46. A trade mark owner may also decide to surrender registration under s.45.

Further reading

Grant, *Bad Faith – Requirement of Dishonesty* [2005] EIPR 27(1), N14–15.

Middlemiss and Badger, *Nipping Taste Marks in the Bud* [2004] EIPR 26(3), 152–4.

Schulze, *Registering Colour Trade Marks in the European Union* [2003] EIPR 25(2), 55–67.

Chapter 10

Protection of Trade Marks

Key words

▶ **Comparative advertising** – the defendant advertises his goods and/or services by making distinctions between his goods and/or services and those of the claimant.

▶ **Infringement** – making use of the trade mark without the owner's authority.

▶ **Likelihood of association** – consumers are likely to think of the claimant's goods or services when they look at those produced or provided by the defendant.

▶ **Likelihood of confusion** – consumers are likely to purchase the defendant's goods or services in the mistaken belief that they are produced or provided by the claimant.

10.1 Rights of the Trade Mark Owner

Section 9 of the 1994 Act confirms the trade mark owner's exclusive rights. Exercise of those rights by anyone else, without his consent, amounts to infringement. In the case of co-owners, each owner is entitled to exercise the exclusive rights in relation to the trade mark without the other co-owner's consent. However, all co-owners must consent to the exercise of those rights by a third party. The rights of the owner date from the filing date of the trade mark application, but an action for infringement cannot be commenced until the registration has been granted. Section 14 provides the owner with the authority to sue, based purely upon ownership of the registered trade mark. Unlike passing off, there is no need to establish trade use or reputation.

Where a trade mark is owned by more than one person, any of the co-owners may commence proceedings for infringement, but cannot continue with the proceedings without joining with all the other co-owners as co-plaintiffs or defendants.

Licences of registered trade marks must be in writing and signed by the licensor. A licence may be general or limited, exclusive or non-exclusive. Section 29 defines an exclusive licence as one that authorises the licensee to use the trade mark to the exclusion of all other persons (including the licensor). Unless the licence states otherwise, it will be binding on any successor of the licensor. If the licence says so, the licensee will be entitled to grant sub-licences; this suggests that in the absence of an express right to sub-license, the licensee would not be entitled to grant sub-licences.

ion 30 sets out the rights of exclusive trade mark licensees in respect of infringements of the licensed trade mark. Broadly speaking, the licensee can, unless the licence says otherwise, call on the trade mark owner to bring infringement proceedings, and, if the owner refuses to do so, or fails to do so within two months of the request, the licensee may bring proceedings in his own name. The exact scope of the rights of an exclusive licensee are governed by ss.30 and 31, unless contractually varied.

10.2 When is the Trade Mark Infringed?

The activities that can amount to an infringement are covered in s.10 of the Trade Marks Act 1994 and Article 5 of the Directive. Infringement of a registered trade mark has been broadened by the 1994 Act to catch use of marks in relation to similar goods and services and, in some special cases, use in relation to dissimilar goods and services.

Section 10(1) states that it is an infringement of a registered trade mark to use, in the course of trade, an identical mark on the same goods or in respect of the same services for which that mark is registered. In *British Sugar plc* v. *James Robertson & Sons Ltd* [1996] RPC 281, Jacob J said that, if the defendant's use of the mark is in the course of trade, it does not need to be used in the trade mark sense to establish infringement. So it is possible to succeed in an infringement action, even if the claimant's symbol has not been used as a trade mark. The claimant needs only to prove that it was used in the course of trade. This contrasts with the position under the 1938 Act where infringing use meant use of the plaintiff's trade mark as a trade mark. In the case of *Unidoor* v. *Marks & Spencer* [1988] RPC 275, Marks & Spencer sold T-shirts with the words 'Coast to Coast' printed on them as a slogan. Unidoor had a registered trade mark for clothing of 'Coast to Coast'. The court held that because Marks & Spencer's use was not use as a trade mark, it did not constitute trade mark infringement.

'Course of trade' also means trade in the United Kingdom. In *Euromarket Designs Inc.* v. *Peters & Another* [2002] FSR 288, the claimant's trade mark was held as not being infringed by an advertisement in the UK magazine, or on a website, where the defendant's target market was in the Irish Republic rather than the United Kingdom.

The mark is used in the 'course of trade' if it can be said that such use takes place in a commercial context, with a view to economic advantage. See Case C-206/01, *Arsenal Football Club* v. *Reed* [2002] ECR I-10273.

A defendant may try to defend an infringement action under s.10(1) by adopting a narrow interpretation of the goods or services to which the claimant has attached trade marks. This was the case in *Thomson Holidays Ltd* v. *Norwegian Cruise Line Ltd* [2002] EWCA Civ 1828, where Norwegian

Cruise Line Ltd had offered a range of holiday services under the name 'FREESTYLE CRUISES'. Thomson was the registered proprietor of trade mark 'FREESTYLE', which it applied to a range of package holidays aimed at the 18–30 age group, which included cruises. The defendants argued that there had been no use of the claimant's mark on cruise holidays and that Thomson's use of the trade mark would be perceived as applied to land-based holidays, or holidays excluding cruises, so on that basis there was no infringement under s.10(1). The Court of Appeal rejected that argument. There was no evidence to show that there was a distinct category of holiday described as land-based. Although the tourism industry consisted of distinct segments, it did not follow that the claimant's services would not be referred to by a more general description, such as package holiday. On that basis, the defendant's use of the mark was in relation to services that were identical to those for which the claimant's mark had been registered.

What is 'identical'?

The protection provided in s.10(1) is stronger than that of s.10(2) in that there is no need to prove 'confusion'. But the claimant must show that the two marks are identical as are the goods or services to which they are applied. In *Reed Executive plc & Another* v. *Reed Business Information Ltd and Others* [2004] EWCA Civ 159, Jacobs LJ stated that the trade mark proprietor must show two things:

(1) use of a sign which is identical to his registered mark; and
(2) use for goods or services which are identical to those for which the mark is registered (para. 20).

The question is – to what extent would a slight variation take the action from s.10(1) to s.10(2)? In *Origins Natural Resources Inc.* v. *Origin Clothing Ltd* [1995] FSR 280, the addition of the letter 's' to the word 'Origin' was held not to be identical.

In Case C-291/00, *Société LTJ Diffusion* v. *Sadas Vertbaudet SA* [2003] FSR 34, the European Court of Justice had to consider this very question under Article 5.1(a). The dispute concerned two French companies. The claimant's mark was a device which consisted of the word 'Arthur' written in fancy script in the form of a signature. This was applied to clothing. The defendant operated a mail order business which included children's clothing under a range called 'Arthur et Félicie'. The defendant applied to register its mark as both a French trade mark and a Community trade mark. In addressing the claimant's opposition, the French court referred the following to the ECJ:

'Whether the prohibition in Article 5(1)(a) covered only identical reproduction, without addition or omission of the sign or signs constituting a mark or whether it could extend to
(1) Reproduction of the distinctive element of a mark composed of a number of signs?
(2) Full reproduction of the signs making up the mark where new signs were added?'

In response the ECJ stated:

'The criterion of identity of the sign and the trade mark must be interpretated strictly. The very definition of identity implies that the two elements compared should be the same in all respects (see paragraphs 50–51).'

This would appear straightforward. We suggest that on its own, this statement is clear. However the ECJ then went on to state that the perception of identity had to be made globally taking account of the average consumer, bearing in mind that the latter rarely had the opportunity to make a side-by-side comparison of the mark and the sign but must rely on his own imperfect recollection of them. That being the case, insignificant differences between the sign and the trade mark may go unnoticed by the average consumer. Thus the Court held:

'. . . the answer to the question referred must be that Article 5(1)(a) of the Directive must be interpreted as meaning that a sign is identical with the trade mark where it reproduces without any modification or addition, all the elements constituting the trade mark or where, *viewed as a whole, it contains differences so insignificant that they may go unnoticed by an average consumer.*' [our italics]

This reasoning has been described by Jacobs LJ as 'opaque' in *Reed Executive plc and Another* v. *Reed Business Information Ltd and Others* [2004] EWCA Civ 159. In *Reed*, the Court of Appeal held that Reed Business Information was not identical to the mark 'Reed'. The words 'Business Information' would not go unnoticed by the average consumer. See also *Compass Publishing SA* v. *Compass Logistics Ltd* [2004] EWHC 520; [2004] RPC 41.

Section 10(2) covers protection against the use of similar marks or identical marks attached to similar goods and states:

'A person infringes a registered trade mark if he uses in the course of trade a sign where because
(a) the sign is identical with the trade mark and is used in relation to goods or services similar to those for which the trade mark is registered, or
(b) the sign is similar to the trade mark and is used in relation to goods or services identical with or similar to those for which the trade mark is registered,
there exists a likelihood of confusion on the part of the public, which includes the *likelihood of association with the trade mark.*' [our italics]

This is where trade mark infringement has become broader, covering use of a trade mark on similar goods and services. Some commentators had said that because of this section, passing off will become an action of the past. This is not likely to be the case unless and until suppliers begin to register packaging and colour schemes more widely so as to have a registered trade mark that can be infringed in this broader sense. In the case of supermarket look-alike products, it is usually the overall colour scheme and get-up that are copied, and passing off is still, in most cases, the only available action.

The words 'likelihood of association' suggest a broader interpretation of s.10(2). In *Wagamama Ltd* v. *City Centre Restaurants plc* [1995] FSR 713, the plaintiffs operated a successful Japanese-style restaurant under the name WAGAMAMA. They also owned trade marks of that name. The defendants opened a restaurant, with an Indian theme, under the name RAJAMAMA. This was changed to RAJA MAMA when the plaintiffs objected but, in the plaintiffs' view, that also amounted to infringement. The plaintiffs claimed infringement in the classic sense, but also argued that the words at the end of s.10(2) suggested the introduction into English trade mark law of a new and enlarged basis for infringement. The plaintiffs argued that, as well as confusion in the classic sense, mere association between marks could amount to infringement, even if there was no possibility of a misunderstanding as to the origin of the goods or services in question. In other words, the mark would be infringed if, on seeing the alleged infringing sign, the registered trade mark would be called to mind.

The wording of s.10(2) comes directly from Directive 89/104/EEC to approximate the laws of the Member States relating to trade marks. The plaintiffs argued that the wording was introduced into the Directive on the insistence of the Benelux countries whose case law had developed to the extent that infringement included situations where there was mere association between marks, without confusion. Laddie J was not prepared to give s.10(2) such a broad interpretation. In his view, to do so would create a new type of monopoly, which related to the trade mark itself and not the proprietor's business. The defendants were, nevertheless, found liable for trade mark infringement on the narrower interpretation and in passing off.

The approach taken in *Wagamama* has been endorsed by the European Court of Justice in *Sabel BV* v. *Puma AG, Rudolf Dassler Sport* [1998] RPC 199. This concerned an application by a Dutch company to register in Germany its trade mark, which consisted of a spotted cheetah running above the word 'Sabel', for clothing, jewellery and various fashion accessories. The application was opposed by Puma, which had prior registration for two device marks consisting of a black silhouette of a puma respectively running and leaping without any words, registered for the same goods. Puma's opposition was partially successful in the German Trade Marks Registry and on appeal, the German Federal Court referred the following question to the ECJ:

'What is the significance of the wording of the Trade Mark Directive, according to which the risk of confusion includes the likelihood that a mark may be associated with an earlier mark?'

The Court stated that the reference to 'association' in Article 4(1)(b) could have been intended simply to make it clear that the concept of confusion is not limited to confusion in the narrow sense, that is, the consumer mistakes one product for another, but extends to confusion in the broad sense, that is, the mistaken assumption that there is an organisational or economic link between the undertakings marketing the two products. The 'association' had to be linked with confusion.

Thus the mere association which the public might make between two trade marks as a result of their analogous semantic content is not in itself a sufficient ground for concluding that there is a likelihood of confusion within the meaning of the provision. See also *Canon Kabushiki Kaisha* v. *Metro-Goldwyn-Mayer Inc.* [1999] FSR 332 and *Lloyd Schufabrik Meyer & Co. GmbH* v. *Klijsen Handel BV* (Case C-342/97) [1999] ETMR 690.

In *Lloyd Schufabrik Meyer & Co. GmbH* v. *Klijsen Handel BV* (Case C-342/97) [1999] ETMR 690, the European Court of Justice stated that the wording of Article 5(1)(b) of the Directive, from which s.10(2) is taken, shows that the perception of marks in the mind of the average consumer of the category of goods or services in question would play a decisive role (para. 25). It went on to add:

'the average consumer of the category of products concerned is deemed to be reasonably well informed and reasonably observant and circumspect.' (para. 26)

This certainly influenced the European Court in *Société LTJ Diffusion*, but note that the ECJ was interpreting Article 5.1(a) not 5.1(b). According to Isaac and Joshi (*What does Identical Mean?* [2005] 27(5) EIPR 184–7) the boundary between the two will become blurred.

To interpret s.10(2), Jacob J had suggested, in *Origins Natural Resources Inc.* v. *Origin Clothing Ltd* [1995] FSR 280 at page 284, that the court should assume that the plaintiff's mark is used in a normal and fair manner in relation to the goods for which it is registered, and then assess a likelihood of confusion in relation to the way the defendant uses the mark, discounting any added matter or circumstances.

Jacob J provided detailed guidance on the interpretation of s.10(2) in *British Sugar plc* v. *James Robertson & Sons Ltd* [1996] RPC 281. Here, the plaintiff's products included a syrup for pouring over ice cream and desserts called 'Treat'. Supermarkets usually placed the plaintiff's product in the sections for desserts and ice-cream topping. The trade mark was registered for desserts, sauces and syrups. The defendants used the mark 'Robertsons' for a range of jams and preserves. In 1995, they launched a new toffee-flavoured sweet spread in a jar labelled 'Robertson's Toffee Treat'. In supermarkets it was shelved with jams and preserves. The plaintiff took action for infringement.

Jacob J said that s.10(2) was asking two questions: whether the goods were similar and, if so, was there likelihood of confusion? In his view, merging the two questions together, without the need to prove similarity, meant that strong marks would attract protection for a wider range of goods than weaker marks. In order to judge whether the goods in question were similar, a number of factors should be taken into account (at pages 296–7):

(a) the respective uses of the respective goods or services;
(b) the respective users of the respective goods or services;
(c) the physical nature of the goods or acts of service;
(d) the respective trade channels through which the goods or services reach the market;
(e) if the goods are sold in a self-serve environment, their respective positions within that environment – in other words, whether they are shelved together;
(f) the extent to which there is competition between the respective goods or services.

Taking all of the above together, the court held that the spread should not be regarded as similar to the dessert and, therefore, there was no infringement.

In *European (The) Ltd* v. *The Economist Newspaper Ltd* [1998] FSR 283, the plaintiff published a weekly newspaper. The masthead featured its registered device mark incorporating the words 'The European'. The defendant's weekly newspaper used a masthead, which included the words 'European Voice'. The plaintiff sued under s.10(2) for use of a similar trade mark in relation to identical goods but disclaimed any monopoly in the word 'European'. The Court of Appeal was of the view that for infringement under s.10(2), the question was whether there was a likelihood of confusion because of the similarities between the defendant's sign and the plaintiff's registered trade mark. In this case there was no evidence of confusion. See also *Premier Brands UK Ltd* v. *Typhoon Europe Ltd & Another* [2000] FSR 767 and *DaimlerChysler AG* v. *Javid Alavi (t/a Merc)* [2001] RPC 813.

Section 10(3) deals with the unauthorised use of a mark with a reputation in the United Kingdom by use of an identical or a similar mark on totally different goods. It is an infringement if such use would harm, or take unfair advantage of, the original proprietor's trade mark. This section would clearly be available to marks such as Rolls-Royce, Microsoft or Virgin. In addition, under s.56 of the 1994 Act, the owner of a well-known mark (as defined under the Paris Convention) can obtain an injunction to prevent use of a mark that is the same as, or similar to, his mark, in relation to the same or similar goods where that use is likely to cause confusion. This section implements into English law the protection offered by the Paris Convention to well-known marks. This right is also available to persons who only carry on business or only have a registration outside the United Kingdom, provided that the reputation of the trade mark is known in the United Kingdom.

In some cases even where the goods on the face of it may seem dissimilar, the court will be influenced by the impression created. For example, in *Pfizer Inc.* v. *Eurofood Link (UK) Ltd* [2000] ETMR 187, the claimant's trade mark in VIAGRA for a pharmaceutical product to treat a form of impotence was held to be infringed by the defendant's use of the mark VIAGRENE on a herbal beverage. The court was influenced by the defendant's marketing of the drink, which suggested that it was an aphrodisiac. The claimant also succeeded under s.10(3), discussed below.

The availability of an action under s.10(3) appears to make up for the fact that the use of defensive registration is no longer possible under the 1994 Act. In *Eastman* v. *Griffiths* [1898] 15 RPC 105, the proprietors of the KODAK trade mark were able to stop the mark being used by another proprietor on bicycles in a passing off action because the court held that the trades in cameras and bicycles were similar. However, following that case (and a number of others) the Goschen Committee recommended the introduction of defensive registration for well-known marks so that in the Kodak situation a registration for the name could be obtained even in respect of goods in which the owner was not trading. Under the 1994 Act, Kodak would probably have a remedy under s.10(3) for unauthorised use of the Kodak name on other goods (including dissimilar goods).

Section 10(3) was considered in *Baywatch Production Co. Inc.* v. *The Home Video Channel* [1997] FSR 22. This case concerned the popular television programme *Baywatch* and a programme on an adult television channel called *Babewatch*. The plaintiffs, who were the producers of the *Baywatch* series and proprietors of the trade mark BAYWATCH in several classes, including Class 9, brought an action against the producer of the adult channel for trade mark infringement and passing off. The trade mark infringement claim was brought under ss.10(2) and 10(3). The plaintiff claimed that use of the name BABEWATCH was intended to take advantage of the reputation and distinctive character of the BAYWATCH mark and in addition would tarnish the reputation of the plaintiff's mark. In considering whether there had been s.10(3) infringement, the court considered the plaintiff's argument that confusion was not necessary to establish infringement. Section 10(3) applies where the goods or services of the plaintiff and defendant are not similar but where the mark used by the defendant is identical with or similar to the plaintiff's mark. The judge decided that 'the use of the concept of similarity in s.10(3) introduces in my judgment the ingredient of a likelihood of confusion on the part of the public'. As there was no evidence of actual or likely confusion between the two marks, the court dismissed the plaintiff's application. In passing, the judge referred to an unreported case *BASF plc* v. *CEP (UK) plc*, 26 October 1995, in which Knox J had commented that, in the absence of confusion, there was no basis for finding unfair advantage.

But in *Premier Brands UK Ltd* v. *Typhoon Europe Ltd & Another* [2000] FSR 767, Neuberger J pointed out that whilst the need for confusion is stated in s.10(2), it is not in s.10(3). He confirms that confusion is not a requirement for s.10(3). There the claimant held the trade mark Ty.Phoo for tea and other kitchen goods, which were usually given away as free gifts. They objected to the defendant's use of the mark 'TYPHOON' on kitchenware. Neuberger J stated that dilution could be by 'blurring' where the distinctiveness of a mark is eroded as illustrated in the passing off case of *Taittinger SA* v. *Allbev Ltd* [1993] FSR 641 or by the 'tarnishing' of the mark's reputation. The stronger the distinctive character and reputation of the mark the easier it would be to establish detriment. In this particular case the claimant had failed to demonstrate that either 'blurring' or 'tarnishing' would occur. See also *DaimlerChysler AG* v. *Javid Alavi (t/a Merc)* [2001] RPC 813.

Recent guidance from the ECJ also suggests that s.10(3) can be used against defendants attaching their signs to goods and services that are the same or similar. See Case C-292/00, *Davidoff & Cie SA* v. *Gofkid* [2003] 1 CMLR 35 and Case C-408/01, *Adidas AG* v. *Fitness World Trading Ltd* [2004] 1 CMLR 448. This would give the owners of such marks the possibility of using s.10(3) in combination with either s.10(1) or s.10(2). The added benefit being in the latter case of not having to prove confusion.

Other activities that amount to infringement include: affixing the mark to goods, importing and exporting trade-marked goods and using the mark on business papers or advertising (s.10(4)). A trade mark can also be infringed orally, for example in a radio advertisement criticising a rival product. Under s.10(5), persons other than the actual infringer can be liable. Those who apply a registered trade mark to material that is intended to be used for the labelling or packaging of goods, as business paper (for example, letter heads) or for advertising goods or services, will be treated as a party to infringement if they knew, or should have known, that use of the mark was not authorised.

10.3 Comparative Advertising

Comparative advertising is the practice of advertising by comparing the merit of the product or service being advertised with that of a rival, using the rival's brand name. Under the 1938 Act, use of a Part A mark in this way, no matter how truthful the comparison, amounted to infringement (as 'importing a reference'); see *News Group Ltd* v. *Mirror Group Ltd* [1989] FSR 126. Section 10(6) of the Trade Marks Act 1994 now appears to allow the practice. It states:

'Nothing in the preceding provisions of this section shall be construed as preventing the use of a registered trade mark by any person for the purpose of identifying goods or services as those of the proprietor or a licensee.

'But any such use otherwise than in accordance with honest practices in industrial or commercial matters shall be treated as infringing the registered mark if the use without due cause takes unfair advantage of, or is detrimental to, the distinctive character or repute of the trade mark.'

The question to ask is: who will decide whether an advertiser's use is 'otherwise than *in accordance with honest practices in industrial or commercial matters*'? Or whether the use '*without due cause takes unfair advantage of, or is detrimental to, the distinctive character or repute of the trade mark*'? [our italics] In the White Paper which preceded the 1994 Act, the Government stated that it was committed to allowing comparative advertising in the interests of better consumer awareness, provided advertisers and traders did not take a free ride on the back of the competitor's trade mark. Further, during the passage of the Trade Marks Bill, Lord Strathclyde, its sponsor, stated that the Government had been persuaded that there was no harm in comparative advertising, provided it made use of a competitor's registered mark for informing the public. Section 10(6) does not come from Directive 89/104/EEC, on which the rest of the Trade Marks Act 1994 is based. Rather the wording of s.10(6) is a combination of Article 10bis of the Paris Convention, which deals with unfair competition and Articles 4 and 5 of the Directive. Since the passing of the 1994 Act, there was a Directive on Comparative Advertising (Directive 97/55/EC), which the United Kingdom has since implemented (Control of Misleading Advertisements (Amendment) Regulations 2000, SI 914 of 2000).

The wording of s.10(6) was criticised by the courts for its lack of clarity. In *Barclays Bank plc* v. *RBS Advanta* [1996] RPC 307 at page 313, Laddie J said of the subsection:

'It is a mess. The first part of the subsection allows comparative advertising. Its meaning is clear. However the second half beginning with the words "But any such use . . ." is a qualifying proviso and its meaning is far from clear.'

However, Laddie J went on to decide, effectively, that the onus will be on the trade mark owner to establish that the use is not in '*accordance with honest practices in industrial or commercial matters'* [our italics]. The defendants, RBS Advanta, were launching a new credit card. They sent out pamphlets listing the 15 ways their card was allegedly better than other cards. On one of the pages, they listed the cards of six competitors, including that of Barclays. Barclays tried to obtain an injunction on the grounds that this use amounted to trade mark infringement. Laddie J held that, as the primary objective of s.10(6) was to allow comparative advertising, the proviso should not be construed in a way that would effectively prohibit all comparative advertising. The onus was on the plaintiff to demonstrate that the factors indicated in the proviso existed. In that case, the judge decided that Barclays had not shown that RBS's use fell within the proviso, because it was unlikely that any reasonable reader of the RBS advertisement would take the view that it was not honest when read as a whole. A similar decision was reached by the court in the case of *Vodafone Group plc* v. *Orange Personal Communications Services Ltd* [1997] FSR 34, where the defendant's claim in its advertising that 'On average, Orange users save £20 every month' was held to be objectively honest and not misleading to the ordinary reader. On comparative advertising see also *Macmillan Magazines Ltd* v. *RCN Publishing Co. Ltd* [1998] FSR 9 and *Cable and Wireless plc* v. *British Telecommunications plc* [1998] FSR 383.

A rather surprising interpretation of s.10(6) was adopted in *British Airways plc* v. *Ryanair Ltd* [2001] FSR 541. British Airways sued Ryanair for malicious falsehood and trade mark infringement, when the latter advertised their services and prices with the following headings: 'EXPENSIVE BA. . . . DS' and 'EXPENSIVE BA', making price comparisons which the claimants felt were unfair. The first advertisement was withdrawn after a complaint to the Advertising Standards Authority, however Jacob J held that the fact that the advertisement was offensive did not mean that it fell outside the proviso of s.10(6); although the defendant's claimed that the price of their flights to Frankfurt were five times cheaper than the claimants when they were in fact only three times cheaper. It was also claimed that like was not being compared with like as the defendant's flights were to a different airport in Frankfurt. Nevertheless, Jacob J held that the average consumer would not find the price comparison misleading. In his view the advertisements were true in substance and there had been honest use of British Airway's trade mark. It will be interesting to see whether a similar case would now be decided in the same way.

As already stated, the Directive on comparative advertising has now been implemented in the United Kingdom. Regulation 2(2A) defines comparative advertising as:

'an advertisement is comparative if in any way, either explicitly or by implication, it identifies a competitor or goods or services offered by the competitor or goods or services offered by a competitor.'

Regulation 4A then sets out the conditions under which comparative advertising will be permitted. The following is an outline:

(a) the advertisement should not be misleading;
(b) it compares goods and services meeting the same needs or intended for the same purpose;
(c) it objectively compares material;
(d) it does not create confusion;
(e) it does not discredit or denigrate the mark or trade name of the competitor;
(f) for products with designation of origin, it relates in each case to products with the same designation;
(g) it does not take unfair advantage of the reputation of a trade mark; and
(h) it does not present goods or services as imitations or replicas of goods or services bearing the protected trade mark or trade name.

We believe that even taking s.10(6) on its own, it is not fair and honest to state that your service is five times cheaper than a competitor's, when it is only three times cheaper. Hazel Carty suggests (see *Registered Trade Marks and Comparative Advertising*, [2002] EIPR 294) that the decision in *British Airways* v. *Ryanair* reflects the fact that consumers are seen as streetwise, 'aware of the hyperbole and massaging of facts in advertising'.

The European Court of Justice has held that the conditions laid down in the Comparative Advertising Directive should be interpreted in the way that is most favourable to comparative advertising. See Case C-112/99, *Toshiba Europe GmbH* v. *Katun Germany GmbH* [2002] FSR 39 and Case C-44/01, *Pippig Augenoptik GmbH & Co. KG* v. *Hartlauer Handelsgesellschaft GmbH* ECR I-3095 (see Case notes at end of this chapter).

See also *O2 Holdings Ltd (2) O2 (UK) Ltd* v. *Hutchinson 3G Ltd* [2006] EWHC 534 Ch, which concerned a comparative advertising campaign by the defendants which featured the use of bubbles, similar to those registered by the claimants and used in a variety of means in the claimants' advertisements. Lewison J held that whilst the claimants' trade mark was validly registered and infringed, the defendant's were covered by the defence under the Directive.

For a case on s.10(6) which does not concern comparative advertising, see *Primark Stores Ltd & Another* v. *Lollipop Clothing Ltd* [2001] FSR 637. Here the defendant had acquired clothing, which had been made for the claimant, from the claimant's supplier, bearing the claimant's trade mark. In response to an action for infringement, the defendant claimed s.10(6), namely that the mark merely identified the clothing as that of Primark. However, John Martin QC held that in order for the goods to be identified as the claimant's goods for the purposes of s.10(6), it was not enough that they were made to the claimant's specification; they must have been adopted by the claimant as its goods. Without that, the claimant could not be said to be the source of the goods for trade mark purposes.

10.4 Remedies

The general remedies for trade mark infringement are in s.14. These include damages, injunctions and an account of profits. A plaintiff cannot claim both damages and an account of profits. As with actions in tort, the purpose of damages is to place the plaintiff in the position in which he would have been had the wrong not been committed. The court will, therefore, take into consideration revenue from lost sales. If infringement is proved, the defendant is liable to pay damages even if the act was committed innocently (see *Gillette UK Ltd* v. *Edenwest Ltd* [1994] RPC 279). If the plaintiff claims an account of profits, the defendant has to hand over all the profits made from infringement. Account of profits is an equitable remedy, which means it will only be granted at the judge's discretion and is not available in cases of innocent infringement. An injunction prohibiting further use of the trade mark may also be granted. This is also an equitable remedy and where the plaintiff is seeking an interlocutory injunction, the conditions set out in *American Cyanamid Co.* v. *Ethicon Ltd* [1975] AC 396 apply.

Courts are also given the discretionary power under s.15 to order that an infringing sign be erased, removed or obliterated from any infringing goods (defined in s.17). Under s.16 an infringer can be ordered to deliver up to the trade mark owner any infringing goods, materials or articles. This must be specifically requested by the trade mark owner. Under s.19, the trade mark owner can apply to have the goods destroyed on delivery. The court must consider other remedies, and should take into account the interests of others in relation to the goods, for example, a person who has an interest under a retention of title clause or an interest in other intellectual property rights comprised in the infringing goods (for example, copyright or patent rights).

10.5 Exceptions and Defences

An effective defence will remove the defendant's liability. The general defences are outlined in s.11. First of all, it is not an infringement to use the same mark as that of the claimant, if the defendant's mark is also registered. This is a form of statutory honest concurrent use. However, this should be read in the light of s.47 (discussed in Chapter 9), where the latter mark can be declared invalid if it should not have been registered in the first place because of the presence of the earlier mark.

The use of a person's name or address is not an infringement under s.11(2)(a), provided such use is consistent with 'honest practices in industrial or commercial matters'. In *Scandecor Developments AB* v. *Scandecor Marketing AV & Others* [2001] UKHL 21, Lord Nicholls has suggested that a limited company can be a person for this purpose. This was followed in *Euromarket Designs Inc.* v. *Peters & Another* [2002] FSR 288 and confirmed by Jacobs LJ in *Reed Executive Plc* v. *Reed Business Information Ltd* [2004] EWCA Civ 159 at para. 116. However in *Asprey & Gerrard Ltd* v. *WRA (Guns) Ltd* [2001] EWCA Civ 1499; [2002] FSR 30, the Court of Appeal held that the own name defence is not available to a new company. So a Mr Paul Smith would not get away with opening a shop called 'Paul Smith' selling designer menswear. This subsection also allows the use of a trade mark to indicate the kind, quality or origin of goods, as well as use to indicate the purpose of the goods or service in question. So, for example, if a supplier is selling goods that have been manufactured using a material that is produced and sold by another supplier under a trade mark, the first supplier can state that his goods are made from the other supplier's material and use the other supplier's trade mark in doing so. And if a trader's goods are intended for use with the claimaint's goods (for example, as accessories), the trader can use the claimant's trade mark to indicate that connection. However, all these uses must be in accordance with honest practices to fall within s.11(2).

Where a defendant can show that he had an established reputation in respect of his use of the mark in question in a particular locality predating the claimant's registration, he can benefit from the defence in s.11(3). 'Locality' is not defined. To have such an 'earlier right', the right must be capable of protection by some other rule of law (including passing off).

One particular defence, discussed in more detail in Chapter 24, is the exhaustion of rights defence which is set out in s.12. This section provides that, once goods bearing the claimant's trade mark have been legitimately put into circulation in the European Economic Area, the use of the trade mark in relation to those goods cannot be prevented elsewhere in the European Economic Area by means of a claim of trade mark infringement. There is an exception to this, namely, where the goods have subsequently been tampered with in a way that could impair their quality.

It is also not an infringement of a trade mark to use only a part of the trade mark that is the subject of a disclaimer. A disclaimer is given for any part of a trade mark that does not satisfy the requirements of registrability and is necessary to ensure that the trade mark owner is not given a monopoly over a common word or other identifier. Under the 1938 Act, disclaimers had to appear on the face of the registration – this is not the case under the 1994 Act. A first step for any defendant should be to check whether any part of the infringed trade mark is disclaimed.

10.6 Groundless Threats

The 1994 Act introduced a remedy for defendants in receipt of groundless threats of infringement (s.21), which is along the same lines as the corresponding section in the Patents Act 1977. This remedy is not, however, available to anyone who has actually applied the trade mark to goods or packaging, or who has imported the goods so trade-marked, or who is supplying services under the mark. The aim of this section is to protect traders who have not themselves instigated the act of trade mark infringement but who are just trading in goods or in some other way involved in dealing in the marked goods or services so that they might be targeted by a plaintiff. Attacking others in the chain of supply is a tactic often used by claimants when trying to reach the true primary infringer.

10.7 Criminal Offences

There are a number of criminal offences under the 1994 Trade Mark Act. First, to catch those persons who make a business of blatantly producing and selling counterfeits, s.92 makes it a criminal offence to commit any of the acts that amount to trade mark infringement with a view to gain for the offender or with intent to cause loss to another person. However, *R* v. *Johnstone* [2002] EWCA Crim 194, *The Times*, 12 March states that for a successful prosecution under s.92, the Crown must prove that the defendant's acts amounted to civil infringement of the trade mark in question. Specific enforcement rights are given to the local weights and measures authority (that is, Trading Standards Officers).

Other offences under the Act include:

(a) falsifying an entry on the Register of Trade Marks;
(b) falsely representing a trade mark as being registered when it is not (by including the ® against the mark before it is registered – ™ should be used instead);
(c) falsely representing that a registered mark is registered in respect of goods or services for which it is not registered; and
(d) unauthorised use of Royal arms in such a way that suggests that such use has been duly authorised.

As with the Copyright, Designs and Patents Act 1988, where a company is found guilty of an offence, any officers with whose consent or connivance the offence was committed will also be guilty of an offence (s.101).

Sections 89–91 give trade mark owners the right to give notification to Customs and Excise of expected importation of infringing goods so that Customs and Excise can seize such goods on the point of entry. Customs and Excise only have power to seize goods but they can pass on information to the relevant weights and measures authority to enable any offences to be prosecuted.

10.8 Dealings in Trade Marks

A registered trade mark is capable of assignment or transmission and may also be charged like other personal property to provide security for, say, a loan.

Under the 1938 Act, special procedures had to be followed if a registered trade mark was to be assigned without the goodwill relating to the mark. Under the 1994 Act there are no such requirements, but if the trade mark is split from the business and goodwill to which it relates, there is a risk of the mark opening itself up to a possible challenge if the mark becomes deceptive. Registered trade marks may also be assigned in respect of only some of the goods covered by the registration or in respect of a particular locality only.

To be effective, an assignment must be in writing and signed by the assignor. All transactions in registered trade marks can be entered on the Register at the request of the person interested. If a transaction is not registered, a subsequent acquirer of interests in that mark who is not aware of the transaction would be entitled to treat the transaction as if it had not taken place. Failure to register a licence means the licensees do not have the rights in respect of infringements of the trade mark which are otherwise conferred by ss.30 and 31 of the 1994 Act. Someone who becomes the owner or licensee of a trade mark should register the transaction within six months, otherwise, in any infringement action, he will not be able to claim for an account of profits for the period between the transaction and registration of the transaction. These provisions concerning assignment of registered trade marks also apply to applications for trade marks. The position on unregistered trade marks is that, as they arise as a result of the generation of goodwill, they can only pass with the associated goodwill (normally as part of a business sale).

Hot Topic . . .

IS COMPARATIVE ADVERTISING FAIR?

What is comparative advertising?
As previously stated, comparative advertising is the practice of advertising by comparing the merit of the product or service being advertised with that of a rival, using the rival's brand name. Regulation 2(2A) of Control of Misleading Advertisements (Amendment) Regulations 2000, SI 914 of 2000, defines comparative advertising as:

'an advertisement is comparative if in any way, either explicitly or by implication, it identifies a competitor or goods or services offered by the competitor or goods or services offered by a competitor.'

The main argument in favour of this practice is that in an open market, consumers should have all the available information and that comparative advertising facilitates this. The main argument against is that the advertiser will be selective in the way in which the products or services are compared in order to portray his own goods and/or services in the best possible light. According to Cornish and Llewelyn (para. 17.103):

'Some argue that no comparative advertising by one trader against another [. . .] can be regarded as an honest practice . . . Those who take this view either treat it as self-evident or else claim that the advertising will evitably be selective in content (and so distortive) so as to favour the advertiser.'

The above is certainly the view of some Members of the European Union. In Germany and the Benelux countries, comparative advertising was prohibited prior to Directive 97/55/EC. In France, only comparisons of price were permitted. And in Denmark, advertisers had to make comparisons between all the relevant features, not just those favourable to the advertiser.

In the United Kingdom, the activity is regulated in a number of areas. For example, there is the British Code of Advertising which is administered by the Advertising Standards Authority, a self-regulatory system. According to Bentley and Sherman: 'the Code is based on the premise that comparative advertising should be allowed in the interests of vigorous competition and public information' (page 922). The interpretation of s.10(6) of the Trade Marks Act 1994 also reinforces the view that there is a liberal attitude in the United Kingdom, in contrast to Germany which is perhaps more paternalist, believing its citizens to be in need of consumer protection. According to Jacobs J (as he was), German unfair competition law is protective of 'even the stupid or careless' (*British Airways plc* v. *Ryanair Ltd* [2001] FSR 541 at page 552). British consumers, on the other hand, are regarded as somewhat streetwise in their attitude towards advertisements. According to Hughes, the decision in *British Airways* v. *Ryanair*, discussed in section 10.3, 'highlights the view that the general public are used to the ways of advertisers and that they expect hyperbole . . .'.

Cases where the ECJ have responded to references on the interpretation of Directive 97/55/EC suggest that a more liberal approach is to be encouraged within the internal market.

Case notes

▶ **Case C-112/99,** *Toshiba Europe GmbH* **v.** *Katun Germany GmbH* **[2002] FSR 39**

Katun had placed the reference numbers that Toshiba used for Toshiba's products alongside Katun's own product codes.

This was done to allow consumers to identify the equivalent Toshiba products. The EJC was asked:

(1) Was Katun's use of Toshiba's product numbers to be regarded as comparative advertising?

(2) If so, did the display of Toshiba's code alongside Katun's constitute a permissible comparison of goods?

In responding to the questions, the Court took account of the objectives as stated in the Preamble to the Directive. This indicated the importance of advertising in the establishment and furtherance of the internal market and the need to stimulate it. It therefore responded that the new Directive should be interpreted in the way that was most favourable to comparative advertising.

▶ **Case C-44/01,** *Pippig Augenoptik GmbH & Co KG v. Hartlauer Handelsgesellschaft GmbH* **ECR I-3095**

Hartlauer ran an advertising campaign in which leaflets directly compared Pippig's prices for frames with Zeiss lenses with Hartlauer's prices in respect of the same frames but with Optimed lenses. Television and radio broadcasts featured the same price comparison but did not state that the lenses were different brands and showed a Pippig shopfront. The questions referred to the European Court concerned whether a distinction could be made between those parts of the advertisements which could be considered comparative and those that could be considered non-comparative, with the latter being subject to national law on misleading advertisements. As with *Toshiba*, the Court was of the opinion that the new Directive should be interpreted in the way that was most favourable to comparative advertising. Further as the objective is the 'exhaustive harmonisation' of the conditions under which comparative advertising is deemed lawful, the ECJ ruled that the new Directive precludes national legislation governing misleading advertising from applying to comparative advertising 'as far as the form and content of the comparison is concerned' (para. 56).

▶ **Case C-50/05,** *Siemens AG v. VIPA Gesellschaft für Visualisierung und ProzeBautomatisierung mbH*

Siemens manufactures and distributes programmable controllers under the name 'Simatic'. In 1983 it introduced a system of order numbers of the controllers and their add on components, which consists of a combination of capital letters and numbers. VIPA manufacture and sell components that are compatible with 'Simatic' controllers. Since 1988 it used an identification system that was almost identical to that used by Siemens, replacing the first group of characters of the Siemens' order number with VIPA, for example 6ES5 928-3UB21 became VIPA 928-3UB21. In its catalogue it added:

> 'Please check the order number of the memory modules you require in the handbook for your module or call us. The order numbers correspond to those of Siemens' programmable modules.'

Siemens claimed VIPA was taking unfair advantage of the reputation of its products. According to the ECJ:

> 'An advertiser cannot be regarded as taking unfair advantage of the reputation of the distinguishing marks of his competitor if effective competition on the relevant market is conditional upon a reference to those marks' (para. 15).

> 'Comparative advertising is designed to enable consumers to make the best possible use of the internal market, given that advertising is a very important means of creating genuine outlets for all goods and services throughout the Community' (para. 22).
>
> 'The purpose of comparative advertising is also to stimulate competition between suppliers of goods and services to the consumers' advantage' (para. 23).
>
> The European Court went on to hold that VIPA did not take unfair advantage of Siemens' reputation.

Summary

10.1 A trade mark is infringed if a person other than the owner makes use of it without his consent. Licensees also have a right to protection against infringement, which they can enforce if the trade mark owner fails to do so.

10.2 Whereas it is obviously infringement to apply the same or a similar trade mark to the same or similar goods, it is also an infringement to apply a trade mark to dissimilar goods if the mark in question has acquired a reputation.

10.3 Judges appear to be adopting a liberal interpretation of s.10(6) and Directive 97/55/EC to allow comparative advertising.

10.4 Section 11 outlines a number of defences that remove the defendant's liability.

10.5 A number of criminal offences have been introduced to stop the production and sale of counterfeit goods.

Futher reading

Bainbridge, *Intellectual Property Law*, 5th edn, Longman, pages 606–8.

Bentley and Sherman, *Intellectual Property Law*, 2nd edn, OUP, pages 916–23.

Cornish and Llewelyn, *Intellectual Property Law*, 5th edn, *Sweet & Maxwell*, para. 17.103.

Fletcher, Fussing and Indraccolo [2003] EIPR 25(12), 570–4.

Hughes, [2001] Ent LR 12(4), N34–5.

Stephenson, [2006] EIPR 28(3), 182–91.

Chapter 11

Passing Off

- ▶ **Confusion** – claimants must show that customers were misled because of confusion.
- ▶ **Damage** – it is necessary to be able to quantify the harm suffered by the claimant.
- ▶ **Goodwill** – goodwill is a combination of the reputation built up for goods and services and customer loyalty.
- ▶ **Misrepresentation** – the claimant's customers are misled into purchasing the defendant's goods and/or services in the belief that they come from the claimant.

11.1 Introduction

The practice of passing off involves one trader giving consumers the impression that his goods are those of another trader who has an established goodwill. It also occurs where one trader indicates that his goods are of the same quality as those of another trader or where one trader creates the impression of association with another trader. Where an existing trader has a reputable and popular product or service, another trader will hope to take advantage of the goodwill that has been established in that product or service, by confusing consumers into purchasing his goods instead of those of the first trader. The first trader suffers lost sales as consumers buy goods from the trader who is passing off, believing them to be the same (or of the same quality) as those of the genuine trader. Where the second trader's goods are not of the same standard, there is added damage as consumers will assume that the substandard goods come from the first trader. There is, therefore, a loss of sales coupled with a loss of reputation.

Honest traders are protected against such activities by the law of passing off. Passing off is a tort. It provides common law protection of brand names and get-up. This form of action is used either where the mark is an unregistered mark, or where the mark is unregistrable. For registered marks, the proprietor can bring an action for passing off as well as trade mark infringement. In court, the issues will be the same, namely, there must be a balance between protecting the proprietor's goodwill, while protecting the interests of other legitimate traders. The interests of consumers must also be considered.

11.2 The Difference between Trade Mark Infringement and Passing Off

Once a trade mark is registered, protection against infringement is automatic. Trade marks are a form of personal property and their use by another without the proprietor's authority is interference with his property right. The proprietor need prove nothing more. On the other hand, the plaintiff in a passing off action must demonstrate the presence of goodwill in order to have a right of action. The common law protects the goodwill of a business associated with a trade name or get-up, while trade mark legislation protects rights in the actual name. The protection provided in passing off is potentially broader. Business goodwill can cover the name of the goods or services in question, business methods, get-up and marketing styles.

Two cases sum up the difference in the protection provided. In *Coca-Cola Trade Mark Applications* [1986] 2 All ER 274, the House of Lords refused to allow the registration of the shape of the famous Coca-Cola bottle, because it was concerned about the creation of a monopoly in containers. Yet the same court, in *Reckitt & Colman Products Ltd* v. *Borden Inc. (No. 3)* [1990] 1 All ER 873, restrained the defendant's use of a plastic container resembling the plaintiff's plastic lemon in a passing off action. Registration of shapes as trade marks is now allowed under the Trade Marks Act 1994.

By way of further example, the registration of single colours was refused in *Wyeth (John) Coloured Tablet Trade Mark* [1988] RPC 233, but in *White Hudson & Co. Ltd* v. *Asian Organisation Ltd* [1964] 1 WLR 1466, the plaintiff was able to claim protection in passing off for red cellophane sweet wrappers. Again, single colours are now being passed for registration under the Trade Marks Act 1994 (for example, BP has applied for a trade mark of the colour green in relation to petrol station services). So the protection given in passing off would appear to be wider, although it has proved difficult to use for protecting advertising campaigns (see *Cadbury-Schweppes Ltd* v. *Pub Squash Co. Ltd* [1981] 1 All ER 213).

11.3 Historical Background

The traditional form of passing off is where the defendant gives the consumer the impression that the goods sold are actually those of the plaintiff. In other words, where the defendant passes off his goods as those of the plaintiff. A defendant may also be found to be passing off one quality of the plaintiff's goods as goods of another quality. In *Spalding (A.G.) & Bros.* v. *Gammage (A.W.) Ltd* (1915) 84 LJ Ch 449, the plaintiffs manufactured 'Orb' footballs. They applied their mark to two types of ball, and sold the inferior type to waste rubber merchants. The defendant bought these inferior products and sold them in such a way as to imply that they were the higher quality 'Orb' footballs. It was held that, as the plaintiffs had established a reputation in the quality of their footballs, the defendants were passing off the plaintiffs' goods of inferior quality as those of the higher quality.

In *Bollinger* v. *Costa Brava Wine Co.* [1960] Ch 262, the producers of French champagne took action against the producers of 'Spanish champagne'. The plaintiffs argued that they were the only people entitled to use the word 'champagne' as it was the name of a product from a particular region. This argument succeeded on the basis that use of the word in this way could lead to dilution of the word 'champagne'. See also *Taittinger SA* v. *Allbev Ltd* [1993] FSR 641. Further, passing off can be used to ensure that goods are manufactured to the quality indicated by the name. In *Erven Warnink Besloten Vennootschap* v. *J. Townend & Sons* (Hull) Ltd [1979] AC 731, the plaintiff made a high quality spirit-based drink called advocaat. The defendant produced 'egg flip' made from dried egg powder and fortified wine and called it 'Keeling's Old English Advocaat'. The defendant's product was an inferior, but cheaper, drink, which took away some of the plaintiff's custom. The plaintiff's main objection was that, in making the product incorrectly, a misrepresentation was being made to customers. Using the name 'advocaat' should mean that the drink was made to the same high quality as the plaintiff's product.

However, once a defendant has established goodwill in his own product using the plaintiff's name, it will be very difficult to restrain him. In *Vine Products Ltd* v. *Mackenzie & Co. Ltd (No. 3)* [1969] RPC 1, Spanish producers of sherry tried to stop the use of the sherry name on wines produced from regions other than the Jerez region in Spain. However, producers in other countries were able to show that they had already established goodwill in their 'sherry'. As a result, the court held that they were entitled to continue to use the name, with the country of origin as a prefix. In each of these drinks cases, the goodwill in the relevant name was shared between any number of producers of the legitimate product.

11.4 The Requirements of a Passing Off Action

Traditionally, the minimum requirements for a successful action in passing off were laid down by Lord Diplock in *Erven Warnink Besloten Vennootschap* v. *J. Townend & Sons (Hull) Ltd* [1979] AC 731 at page 742. These were:

> '(1) a misrepresentation, (2) made by a trader in the course of trade, (3) to prospective customers of his or ultimate customers of goods or services supplied by him, (4) which is calculated to injure the business, or goodwill, of another trader (in the sense that it is a reasonably foreseeable consequence) and (5) which causes actual damage to the business or goodwill of the trader by whom the action is brought or (in a *quia timet* action) will probably do so.'

These five requirements were reduced to three in *Reckitt & Colman Products Ltd* v. *Borden Inc. (No. 3)* [1990] 1 All ER 873, by Lord Oliver as: (a) the existence of plaintiff's goodwill, (b) a misrepresentation, and (c) damage (or likely damage) to the plaintiff's goodwill or reputation. This test was adopted in *Consorzio del Prosciutto di Parma* v. *Marks & Spencer plc* [1991] RPC 351.

11.5 The Claimant's Goodwill

The claimant must establish goodwill associated with the goods or their get-up. Goodwill has been defined in *Trego* v. *Hunt* [1895] AC 7 as:

> 'The whole advantage, wherever it may be, of the reputation and connection of the firm which have been built up by years of honest work or gained by lavish expenditure of money.'

In other words, it is the likelihood that consumers will continue to return, because of the quality and reputation of the goods or service provided by the trader. This suggests a reputation built up over time, so a claimant who has just started trading is unlikely to succeed in a passing off action. However, in *Stannard* v. *Reay* [1967] RPC 589, three weeks was held to be sufficient time to build up goodwill in the name 'Mr Chippy' for a mobile fish and chip van.

Each case will depend on the circumstances. If, for example, there has been an intensive advertising campaign, goodwill can be acquired in a relatively short period of time, even if the goods or services to which it relates are not yet available, as happened in *Elida Gibbs Ltd* v. *Colgate Palmolive Ltd* [1983] FSR 94.

Although goodwill suggests trade, passing off can be used to protect non-commercial activities. In *British Diabetic Association (The)* v. *The Diabetic Society* [1996] FSR 1, the plaintiff charity was able to restrain the defendants (another charity) from using the name 'Diabetic Society'. The court was convinced that, as a result of the likely confusion, charitable contributions and support intended for the plaintiff charity might be diverted to the defendant.

In *Richard Burge & Another* v. *John Bernard Haycock & Another* [2001] EWCA Civ 900, members of the 'Countryside Alliance', a pressure group set up to pursue the interests of those living in the countryside, successfully restrained a former member of the British National Party from standing in an election under a 'Countryside Alliance' banner.

The claimant will need to prove that the goodwill existed at the time that the defendant commenced his activity rather than at the time of the action. See *Inter Lotto (UK) Ltd* v. *Camelot Group Plc* [2003] EWCA Civ 1132; [2004] RPC 9.

How long can goodwill last? See *Kevin Floyd Sutherland & Others* v. *V2 Music Ltd & Others* [2002] EWHC 14 (Ch).

Goodwill and geographical considerations

Goodwill can be localised. For example, a hairdresser in Derby, operating under the name 'Clippers', may not be able to stop another hairdresser using the same name in Reading. However, if the business has a national or international reputation, then a successful action in passing off is more likely. In *Sheraton Corp. of America* v. *Sheraton Motels* [1964] RPC 202, Sheraton had a successful chain of hotels, but there were none in the United Kingdom. Despite this, the court held that there was a tangible connection, as it was possible to walk into a travel agent in the United Kingdom and book a room in a Sheraton anywhere in the world. In *Maxim's Ltd* v. *Dye* [1977] 1 WLR 1155, the plaintiff owned a restaurant in Paris known as 'Maxim's'. The defendant opened a restaurant in Norwich calling it 'Maxim's'. As the plaintiff may have wanted to open a restaurant in the United Kingdom using the same name, it was held that he should be able to rely on the goodwill he had acquired in connection with that name to prevent the defendant from trading under that name.

The above cases contrast with *Bernadin* v. *Pavillion Properties* [1967] RPC 581, where the owners of the 'Crazy Horse' nightclub in Paris were unable to stop the defendants using the name for a club in London. In *Anheuser-Busch Inc.* v. *Budejovicky Budvar* [1984] FSR 413, the fact that the plaintiff's beer had only been made available in the United Kingdom to US diplomats and servicemen meant that it had not established sufficient goodwill in the United Kingdom, even though it had a good reputation and goodwill in the United States from where there had been spill-over advertising.

The position of foreign plaintiffs was considered by the High Court in *Jian Tools for Sales Inc.* v. *Roderick Manhattan Group Ltd & Another* [1995] FSR 924. Jian Tools had established goodwill in the United States for the 'BizPlan Builder' software for the preparation of business plans. The defendants introduced a product performing the same functions called the 'BusinessPlan Builder'. The plaintiff claimed ownership of both 'BizPlan Builder' and 'BusinessPlan Builder' and sought an injunction for passing off. Both parties accepted that a foreign plaintiff, suing in passing off, had to establish goodwill in the United Kingdom. Sales of the 'BizPlan Builder' in Britain had reached 127 units. A number of sales were the result of advertising in American publications that were available in the United Kingdom, others were the result of recommendations from American friends or colleagues. Two advertisements were placed in British publications and those generated ten sales. Knox J felt that this provided the plaintiff with an arguable case for passing off. It was established that the plaintiff had customers in the United Kingdom. The purchases in the United Kingdom were not to be disregarded simply because they were generated from foreign sources, unless they were purchases that no member of the general public would make.

Medgen Inc. v. *Passion for Life Products Ltd* [2001] FSR 496 concerned a passing off dispute in relation to a natural health care product to prevent snoring, 'Snorenz'. The claimants had developed the product in the United States, and appointed PFL as its exclusive distributors in the UK. PFL, who marketed the product for eighteen months, had designed the product's packaging which carried its own name and not that of Medgen. When the parties could not agree terms on which to renew the exclusive distributorship, PFL developed a similar product, which it marketed under its registered trade mark 'Snoreez'. The packaging used was practically the same as that used for 'Snorenz'. It was common ground that 'Snorenz' and its packaging had established a substantial goodwill, but the question was to whom did that goodwill belong? The marketing and sales of 'Snorenz' had been undertaken by PFL in its own name. Wholesalers, retailers and ultimately consumers would only have known PFL as the source of the product. Medgen did not operate in the UK and there was no reference to Medgen on the product's packaging. Thus on the evidence, the goodwill was said to belong to PFL.

11.6 Misrepresentation

The misrepresentation need not be intentional for a passing off action to succeed, and innocence of a misrepresentation is no defence. However, the defendant's state of mind may influence the remedy awarded by the court.

The misrepresentation may be in respect of the origin of the goods, their quality, or even the way in which they are made. Most of the cases concern misrepresentation as to origin and quality. In *Coombe International* v. *Scholl* [1977] RPC 1, the plaintiff manufactured insoles called 'Odor Eaters', which contained activated charcoal. The defendant, who was a well-known manufacturer of footwear, also produced odour eaters. These were packaged in the same way. An injunction was granted on the basis that there was a misrepresentation as to the origin of the defendant's product, which was found to be inferior. *Spalding (A.G.) & Bros.* v. *Gammage (A.W.) Ltd* (1915) 84 LJ Ch 449 is an example of misrepresentation as to the quality of the goods. *Wilkinson Sword Ltd* v. *Cripps & Lee Ltd* [1982] FSR 16 is another. The defendants imported blades from the United States called 'Wilkinson blades'. The plaintiffs had an established reputation in the United Kingdom for their blades under the name 'Wilkinson Sword'. The imported blades were inferior. When the defendants brought the inferior goods into the United Kingdom market they created a false impression as to their quality. The defendants had applied to strike out the plaintiffs' claim as having no reasonable cause of action but the court held that the plaintiffs did, indeed, have a reasonable cause of action.

Misrepresentation and confusion

Case law would indicate that the misrepresentation should lead, or be likely to lead, to confusion on the part of consumers. This is illustrated by *Morning Star* v. *Express Newspapers* [1979] FSR 113, where the defendant intended to publish a newspaper called the *Daily Star*, a tabloid that would be sold through newsagents. The plaintiff was the publisher of the *Morning Star*, a weekly paper of the Communist Party. Foster J was of the opinion, having looked at the two papers side by side, that there would be no confusion as to the origin of the newspapers. His view was that 'only a moron in a hurry!' would confuse the two. This suggests that the test is that of the 'reasonable consumer'. However, there is no uniform standard. In *Reckitt & Colman Products Ltd* v. *Borden Inc. (No. 3)* [1990] 1 All ER 873, Lord Oliver was of the opinion that customers have to be taken as found: it is no argument to suggest that they would not have been deceived had they been 'more careful, more literate or more perspicuous'. The case of *United Biscuits (UK) Ltd* v. *Asda Stores Ltd* [1997] RPC 513 relied on the statement in *European (The)* v. *The Economist Newspaper* [1996] FSR 431 that, in a case of this kind, the judge should form his own view and decided that the judge's 'judicial first impression [was] of some importance' on the issue of confusion.

In *Alan Kenneth McKenzie Clark* v. *Associated Newspapers Ltd* [1998] RPC 261, the plaintiff, Alan Clark, was a well-known Member of Parliament who had published his '*Diaries*'. A deal to contribute articles in the form of diary entries to one of the defendant's newspapers, *The Evening Standard*, did not materialise. Instead the newspaper published a weekly spoof of Alan Clark's diaries based on what the journalist imagined Alan Clark would record in his diary. The column was headed 'Alan Clark's Secret Political Diaries' and included a picture of Alan Clark. The journalist was identified as the author below as well as on what the basis for the column was. The defendant was held liable for both passing off and false attribution of authorship under copyright law. To be actionable as passing off, the deception had to be more than momentary and inconsequential. In cases where they were mixed messages, the dominant message is what matters and it is not sufficient to claim that a careful sensible reader would not have been misled.

If the likelihood of confusion is marginal, claimants will need actual evidence of confusion. This was confirmed by the Court of Appeal in *Neutrogena Corp. & Another* v. *Golden Ltd & Another* [1996] RPC 473. The plaintiffs sold a range of hypoallergenic products for the skin and hair under the name NEUTROGENA. The defendants started marketing a similar, but narrower, range of skin and hair products under the name NEUTRALIA. The plaintiffs argued that use of the prefix 'NEUTR' led to confusion. At trial, they brought varied evidence of confusion. This included complaints received about a NEUTRALIA advertisement, which the complainants had taken to be for NEUTROGENA, members of the public who had been interviewed having picked up the products from shops that had advertised a special offer for NEUTROGENA and the staff at the plaintiffs' solicitors who had responded to an internal e-mail asking whether they had heard of or used NEUTRALIA products. The Court of Appeal held that the legal test on the issue of deception was whether, on a balance of probabilities, a substantial number of members of the public would be misled into purchasing the defendants' product in the belief that it was the plaintiffs'. The court felt that the evidence produced (in particular the complaints about the advertisement) demonstrated confusion caused by the defendants' mark.

In *Kimberly-Clark* v. *Ford Sterling* [1997] FSR 877, the judge stated that in a case concerning consumer products in a highly competitive market, damages were bound to follow deception and could almost be assumed. In this case, the manufacturers of Nouvelle toilet paper offered customers, who were not satisfied with the Nouvelle product, a free pack of Andrex toilet paper (Andrex being the product made and sold by one of Kimberly-Clark's competitors). The reference to the Andrex product on the Nouvelle packaging in order to publicise this offer was held to constitute passing off.

Confusion and common fields of activity

Traditionally, there was a need for the claimant and defendant to be in the same field of business activity before it was considered likely that there would be confusion leading to injury to goodwill. This qualification has prevented some individuals from stopping the unauthorised use of their name. In *McCulloch* v. *May* [1947] 2 All ER 845, the plaintiff was a well-known children's broadcaster who used the name 'Uncle Mac'. The defendant sold cereal under the name 'Uncle Mac', alluding to some of the plaintiff's characteristics, without his permission. The plaintiff failed in his action in passing off because he was not involved in the making or marketing of cereals. According to Wynn-Parry J, there had to be a 'common field of activity' in which, however remotely, both plaintiff and defendant are engaged. If the plaintiff and defendant are operating in dissimilar trades, it is thought unlikely that consumers will be misled in a way which would harm the plaintiff.

In *Stringfellow* v. *McCain Foods* [1984] RPC 501, the plaintiff owned a nightclub called 'Stringfellows'. He took action against the manufacturers of oven chips, who had named one of their brands 'Stringfellows' because of their long thin appearance. Their advertising campaign included young people dancing in the kitchen as if in a discotheque. The Court of Appeal considered whether there would be confusion because the plaintiff also served food, and, if so, whether the plaintiff had suffered, or was likely to suffer, damage. The court found that even though some evidence of confusion was shown, this was unlikely to result in any damage to the plaintiff. By contrast, in *Annabels (Berkeley Square)* v. *Schock* [1972] RPC 838, the court felt that there was a possibility of confusion between a night club and an escort agency operating under similar names because both could be considered night-time activities.

If the plaintiff has an outstanding reputation, nationally or internationally, then passing off can be shown even where the plaintiff and the defendant are involved in different fields of activity. This is illustrated by *Lego Systems A/S* v. *Lego M. Lemelstrich Ltd* [1983] FSR 155. The plaintiff made coloured plastic construction bricks for children. The defendant used the plaintiff's name (LEGO) on plastic irrigation and gardening equipment outside the United Kingdom and planned to use it in the United Kingdom. The House of Lords held that the plaintiff's bricks had become so well known in the United Kingdom, as had the name LEGO, that confusion was extremely likely merely as a result of use of the same name. However, in *Harrods Ltd* v. *Harrodian School* [1996] RPC 697 there was said to be no confusion where the defendants called their preparatory school 'The Harrodian'. They had purchased the premises from Harrods, who had previously used it as a sports club for their staff. It had been known as 'The Harrodian' since 1929. The Court of Appeal did not accept the plaintiff's argument that the defendants were seeking to take advantage of a perceived connection with Harrods. Kerr LJ dissented. In his view, if the sports club had been called 'The Harrods Club' and the defendants had called their school 'The Harrods School', an injunction would not have been refused.

The need for a common field of activity to prove damage has had a detrimental effect on the commercial practice of character merchandising, as well as preventing well-known personalities from controlling the use of their names and images as indicated by the 'Uncle Mac' case. This is where the names or pictures of famous characters, whether real or fictional, are applied to everyday goods to make them more marketable. In *Lynstad* v. *Anabas Products Ltd* [1977] FSR 62, the members of the pop group ABBA were unable to stop their pictures being applied to T-shirts because they were in the entertainment business and not in the same field as manufacturers of clothing. However, the courts have been moving away from this strict approach in the field of character merchandising. See, for example, *Mirage Studios v. Counter-Feat Clothing Co. Ltd* [1991] FSR 145 and *Edmund Irvine & Another v. Talksport Ltd* [2002] EWCH 367 (Ch).

Certain fields of activity may have been traditionally distinct but in the minds of consumers there is a trade connection and the courts are beginning to appreciate this. In *NAD Electronics Inc. v. NAD Computer Systems Ltd* [1997] FSR 380, Ferris J held that the fields of audio hi-fi and computers were converging and were not sufficiently distinct to negate confusion in the minds of the public.

11.7 Damage

The claimant must show damage or a probability of damage. The damage need not necessarily be tangible. For example, in *Taittinger SA v. Allbev Ltd* [1993] FSR 641, the Court of Appeal accepted that use of the word 'champagne' by those not entitled to use it would diminish the goodwill associated with that name. In *Chocosuisse Union des Fabricants Suisse de Chocolat & Others v. Cadbury Ltd* [1998] RPC 117 the defendants were the United Kingdom's leading chocolate confectionery manufacturers. They produced a new range of chocolate bars called 'Swiss Chalet'. The claimant successfully argued that the exclusivity of the designation 'Swiss Chocolate', descriptive of chocolate made in Switzerland, would suffer. Laddie J accepted that while the number of people confused into thinking that the defendant's product belonged to a group of products made in Switzerland was smaller than the number for whom there was no confusion, those confused were still likely to have been a substantial number. This was affirmed by the Court of Appeal ([1999] RPC 826).

Certain products associated with particular places are also protected by EC Regulations. For example, Council Regulation 1576/89/EEC restricts the use of geographical names for spirits such as whisky. In *Gloag (Matthew) & Sons Ltd v. Welsh Distillers Ltd* [1998] FSR 718, the defendant bought Scotch whisky and marketed it under the name Welsh whisky. Laddie J held that there had been an arguable case for passing off and the plaintiff also had a private right under the regulation.

Case C-108/01, *Consorzio del Prosciutto di Parma v. ASDA Stores Ltd* [2002] FSR 37, concerned Council Regulation 2081/92/EEC, which restricts designations of origin and geographical indications for agricultural products and Parma ham which comes from the Parma region of Italy. ASDA were selling ham that was sliced and packaged outside the region. The lower courts had found in ASDA's favour. The High Court had decided that as Council Regulation 2081/92/EEC did not directly refer to the slicing and packaging, the defendants were not in contravention. Differing views were expressed in the House of Lords. Lord Hoffman was of the opinion that a valid Community right that was directly enforceable in a domestic court was being infringed. Lord Scott on the other hand was of the view that the consortium's supervisory role to ensure that only the genuine product was sold as Parma ham was discharged once the product left the local processors or packers. In its response to the House of Lords' reference, the ECJ agreed with Lord Hoffman. The ECJ was of the opinion that in order to maintain the quality and reputation of Parma ham, it should only bear that name if it has been sliced and packed in Parma itself under the supervision of members of the consortium.

In *Harrods Ltd* v. *Harrodian School* [1996] RPC 697, the Court of Appeal did not accept that use of the word 'Harrodian' by the school would dilute the good name of Harrods.

A claimant may employ a range of methods to prove confusion leading to lost sales or dilution of reputation. One method is the use of surveys. However, the courts are not usually impressed by this as a means of obtaining evidence. If surveys are used they should be properly carried out otherwise the results may be discredited by the court. Guidance on this was provided in *Imperial Group Ltd* v. *Philip Morris & Co. Ltd* [1982] FSR 72. The plaintiff made John Player Specials (JPS) cigarettes, which were packaged in black with gold lettering and a gold monogram. The defendant used black and gold packets for 'Raffles' cigarettes. The plaintiff used surveys to show that there was a high degree of association between the colours black and gold and the JPS cigarette.

In considering the results of the survey, Whitford J set the following guidelines:

(a) persons interviewed must be selected to represent a relevant cross-section of the public;
(b) the sample size must be statistically significant;
(c) the survey must be conducted fairly;
(d) all surveys carried out must be disclosed in full (that is, warts and all);
(e) all answers given must be disclosed and made available to the defendant;
(f) no leading questions must be asked of interviewees;
(g) interviewees must not be led to embark on a field of speculation they would not otherwise have considered;
(h) instructions to interviewees must be disclosed;
(i) if the answers are to be coded for computer input, the coding instructions must also be disclosed.

Therefore, good statistical methods must be coupled with openness and disclosure. Plaintiffs can also make use of trap orders. This is where they place orders for genuine goods in the hope that defendant will supply other goods instead.

11.8 Domain Names

These are the Internet addresses registered by users of the Internet to enable e-mails to be sent to them or their websites to be accessed. Ideally, for businesses, the domain name should indicate who they are and in that respect they perform similar functions to trade marks. However, the domain name system is far less flexible than that for the registration of trade marks. Each name given is unique so there is little scope for having the same name for a number of differing businesses, all of whom may legitimately wish to use it. There can, for example, be only one BBC.com although it is also possible to have BBC.co.uk. The system is not yet as comprehensively regulated as that for trade marks, thus leaving it open to abuse by speculators registering domain names they have no intention of using. This is discussed in more detail in Chapter 25 but is relevant here because the courts have shown a willingness to allow actions for passing off and trade mark infringement under s.10(3). In *British Telecommunications plc* v. *One in a Million Ltd & Others* [1999] FSR 1, the defendant had registered a large number of domain names comprising the names or trade marks of well-known enterprises without their consent. None were in use as active sites. The defendants had registered them with a view to making a profit either by selling them to the owners of the goodwill or to collectors. Among the brands concerned were Marks & Spencer, Sainsbury, Ladbrokes, Virgin and British Telecom, and all these companies sued the defendants alleging passing off and trade mark infringement. In Marks & Spencer's case, the Court of Appeal were of the opinion that the registration of the domain name made a false representation that the defendants were associated or connected with Marks & Spencer plc. The other cases were slightly different in that there were people called 'Sainsbury' and 'Ladbroke', and there were other companies with the name 'Virgin' and also people or firms with the initials BT. However Aldous LJ believed that for the same reasons expressed in the Marks & Spencer action, passing off and threatened passing off had been demonstrated.

On the trade mark issue, the domain names were registered to take advantage of the distinctive character and reputation of the marks. This was unfair and detrimental. It therefore amounted to infringement under s.10(3) of the Trade Marks Act 1994. See also *Phones 4U Ltd (2) Caudwell Holdings Ltd* v. *(1) Phone4U.co.uk Internet Ltd (2) Abdul Heykali (3) New World Communications Ltd* [2006] EWCA Civ 244.

11.9 Injurious Falsehood

In-between the torts of defamation and passing off, there is injurious falsehood. The action is sometimes referred to as malicious falsehood or trade libel. It is linked to passing off because it is another form of protection for a trader's goodwill. And it is a form of defamation because the defendant has allegedly libelled the business of another trader.

Injurious falsehood actions can be brought by legally aided plaintiffs whereas defamation actions cannot. Where there is overlap, it is perfectly acceptable for the claimant to found his action in injurious falsehood and thus benefit from legal aid. See *Joyce* v. *Sengupta* [1993] 1 WLR 337; [1993] All ER 897.

To succeed, the plaintiff must show that the defendant maliciously made false statements about the plaintiff's goods or services, which were calculated to cause damage. Mere advertising puffs, suggesting that the defendant's product is slightly better than the plaintiff's product, are not usually sufficient.

Falsehood

If the defendant's statement about the plaintiff's goods is true, there is no action; the onus is on the plaintiff to prove that the statement is false. We already know that selling one quality of the plaintiff's goods as those of another quality amounts to passing off as illustrated by *Spalding (A.G.) & Bros* v. *Gammage (A.W.) Ltd* (1915) 84 LJ Ch 449. This can also amount to injurious falsehood. In *Wilts United Dairies Ltd* v. *Thomas Robinson Sons & Co. Ltd* [1958] RPC 94, the Ministry of Food sold off quantities of the plaintiff's old condensed milk on condition that it should not be used for human consumption, because it had been kept during the Second World War and had deteriorated with age. The defendants obtained large quantities of the milk and sold it for human consumption. The defendants were held to have passed off one class of the plaintiff's goods as another and their activities amounted to injurious falsehood as they harmed the plaintiff's reputation.

The action has also been used on the whole unsuccessfully where a defendant has engaged in comparative advertising. In *McDonald's Hamburgers Ltd* v. *Burger King (UK) Ltd* [1986] FSR 45, Burger King advertised its hamburger, the 'Whopper', by referring to McDonald's 'Big Mac'. The injurious falsehood action failed but the advertisement was said to have led to confusion and the defendants were therefore liable in passing off.

In *British Airways plc* v. *Ryanair Ltd* [2001] FSR 541, the claimants had sued for injurious falsehood as well as trade mark infringement. Jacob J stated that a higher standard of liability was required.

According to Carty (*Registered Trade Marks and Comparative Advertising* [2002] EIPR 294), it would appear that the action would only really succeed where the attack on the claimant is a personal one that affects their economic interest – see *Joyce* v. *Sengupta* [1993] 1 WLR 337; [1993] All ER 897.

Damage

Traditionally the plaintiff had to prove special damage, such as a fall in trade. Proof of a significant fall in turnover was enough. In *Ratcliffe* v. *Evans* [1892] 2 QB 524, the defendant suggested in its local weekly newspaper that the plaintiff had gone out of business. The plaintiff, whose business was within the area of the paper's circulation, suffered a fall in trade. The court held that this amounted to injurious falsehood. In *Timothy White* v. *Mellin* [1895] AC 154, the plaintiff's infant foods were sold with labels attached to the wrappers that indicated that another product was more nutritious and healthier. The court in that case held that there was no evidence that the statement was false or that it had caused special damage.

The need to show special damage has been modified by s.3 of the Defamation Act 1952. There is no need for the plaintiff to show special damage if the defendant's statement was calculated to cause pecuniary damage to the plaintiff and was published in writing or another permanent form or was calculated to cause pecuniary damage to the plaintiff in respect of any office, profession, calling, trade or business held by the plaintiff at the time of the publication.

11.10 Remedies

Damages are available in a passing off action. These are usually based on the actual loss suffered as far as that can be calculated. Damages may also be calculated on a royalty basis, in other words, the amount that the defendant would have paid if he had applied for a licence to use the plaintiff's name or mark. In practice, the plaintiff would prefer an injunction to restrain the defendant's activities and the most effective type of injunction is an interlocutory injunction (in other words, an injunction applied for before the main issues are decided). If this is the case, the court will follow Lord Diplock's guidance from *American Cyanamid Co.* v. *Ethicon Ltd* [1975] AC 396 on interlocutory injunctions. See also *Macmillan Magazines Ltd* v. *RCN Publishing Co. Ltd* [1998] FSR 9.

Hot Topic . . .

CHARACTER MERCHANDISING AND PERSONALITY ENDORSEMENT

Character merchandising involves attaching the name or image of a popular character to otherwise mundane everyday products. Examples would include U2 on T-shirts, or bedding featuring any of Walt Disney's animated princesses. Personality merchandising is: '. . . the practice whereby celebrities use their names and images to endorse and associate themselves with products and services . . .' (Bentley and Sherman). Both character and personality merchandising are multi-million pound activities.

In theory such activities take place with the authority of the personality or the owner of the character concerned, usually in the form of a licence agreement. However in many cases characters are attached to merchandise without such agreements and the images of well-known personalities used without their authority. Traders who fail to obtain such licences avoid paying the fees and can, therefore, afford to sell their goods at a lower price than licensed traders. The result is a possible loss of custom for those trading legitimately. Further, unlicensed traders will not have any responsibilities as regards quality. Consumers, therefore, risk being supplied with inferior goods.

Legal protection against the unauthorised use of characters is haphazard to say the least. In passing off, protection has been hampered by the need to establish a common field of activity between the owner of the character and the person using it. Judges were only prepared to grant protection on the basis that members of the public were aware of this form of commercial exploitation. Whereas the judges tended to deny that such public awareness existed, it was argued that the public were aware of character merchandising. They simply did not know it by that phrase (see Bainbridge).

Defamation

In some cases, a real person can stop unauthorised use of their character by suing in defamation. An example of such an action is that of *Tolley* v. *Fry* [1931] AC 333. The plaintiff was an amateur golfer. His picture was used by the defendants to advertise their chocolate without his consent. They were sued for libel. The plaintiff successfully claimed that anyone seeing his picture would think that he had compromised his amateur status by accepting money from advertising. Tolley was only able to succeed because the defendants had published '*a false statement which lowered him in the estimation of right thinking members of society*' [our italics]. The advertisement suggested that he had compromised his amateur status and so fell within the standard definition of defamation.

Members of the public are now fully aware that personalities allow their names to be used to endorse all manner of goods and services and this is generally accepted. Defamation would only be a viable action if the name has been used to endorse something undesirable. Otherwise publication is unlikely to lower the esteem of a personality in the eyes of right-thinking members of society, so we cannot see how a real character would succeed. In *Sim* v. *H.J. Heinz Co. Ltd* [1959] 1 All ER 547, the defendants used the voice of one actor to mimic that of another actor, who was the plaintiff. It was held that there was no evidence of damage to the plaintiff's reputation.

Copyright

Copyright offers some protection. Section 1(1)(a) of the Copyright, Designs and Patents Act 1988 states that copyright subsists in 'original literary, dramatic, musical or artistic works'. So the owners of a character can protect its image, under the Act, as an artistic work. Under s.4, photographs and drawings are included as artistic works. Anybody making a copy of the work, or issuing copies of it to the public without the copyright owner's permission, is guilty of infringement according to ss.17 and 18. So putting an unauthorised copy of a cartoon onto a T-shirt would amount to infringement, as would selling the T-shirt bearing the copy of that cartoon. Further, a two-dimensional artistic work can be infringed by a three-dimensional representation. In *King Features Syndicate Inc.* v. *O & M Kleeman Ltd* [1941] 2 All ER 403, Popeye dolls and brooches were held to infringe the plaintiff's copyright in the comic-strip character.

Copyright does have its limitations. There are difficulties where only the name of the character is used, as there is no copyright in names or titles, no matter how distinctive (see *Exxon Corporation & Others* v. *Exxon Insurance Consultants International Ltd* [1982] RPC 69. Even if a picture of a character is used, the copyright owner must show that the representation is an exact or substantial copy, as copyright protects the expression of an idea and not the idea itself (see *BBC Worldwide Ltd & Another* v. *Pally Screen Printing Ltd & Others* [1998] FSR 665). However, in *Mirage Studios* v. *Counter-Feat Clothing Co. Ltd* [1991] FSR 145, the defendant took the concept of humanoid turtles and produced its own designs. Browne-Wilkinson VC, nevertheless, took the view that there was an arguable case of copyright infringement. Where the representation is a photograph of a real personality, the personality will only be able to use copyright to protect his image if the copyright in the photograph has been assigned to him, since the copyright in a photograph usually belongs to the person taking it. In *Lynstad* v. *Anabas Products Ltd* [1977] FSR 62, the defendants obtained a licence from the copyright owners of photographs of the group ABBA. When such photographs were reproduced on T-shirts, the group could not sue for copyright infringement and so sued in passing off and failed for reasons we discuss later. An interesting attempt to use copyright to protect a personality's 'features' is the case of *Merchandising Corp. of America* v. *Harpbond* [1983] FSR 32. This case concerned the pop group Adam and the Ants and, in particular, the distinctive face make-up worn by the lead singer (Adam Ant). The plaintiff sued the defendants for reproducing pictures of Adam Ant with his distinctive make-up, claiming that the make-up was a copyright work (that is, a painting). This argument was rejected by the court.

Registered Trade Marks

Registering the name of the personality or character is also a possibility but not without its problems. The Elvis Presley case (*Elvis Presley Trade Marks* [1999] RPC 567) has made some interesting observations in this field. In particular, Laddie J had said that in his view the name 'Elvis' did not satisfy the requirements of distinctiveness necessary to satisfy the test of registrability under ss.9 and 10 of the Trade Marks Act 1938. In fact the more famous the celebrity or character the less likely they are going to be to establish distinctiveness. In *Linkin Park LL's Trade Mark Application* (unreported, 7 February 2005), the application by the rock group Linkin Park to register their name in respect of printed matter, posters and poster books was refused as devoid of distinctive character. Although the word was an invented word, by the date of the application it had become so well known as to be descriptive of the subject matter, that is the goods to which it would be applied. This paradox appears to be endorsed by the opinion of Attorney-General Colomer in *Picasso* v. *Office for Harmonisation in the Internal Market* (Case C-361/04), 8 September 2005. He advised that although a famous person may have a reputation in a certain area, this would not afford enhanced distinctiveness where the mark is applied for or licensed for different goods or services typically because the marks would not be seen as designating the commercial origin of the goods or services. If this is the case, how can the decision in *Arsenal Football Club* v. *Reed* (Case C-206/01) [2002] ECR I-10273 be reconciled? The difference between *Arsenal* and *Linkin Park* appears to be that Arsenal had already registered their mark for the merchandise concerned and the decision concerned infringement. In *Linkin Park*, reference was made to *Tarzan Trade Mark* [1970] FSR 245, which had been refused registration under the 1938 Act. Had Tarzan and Linkin Park been registered before they became well known, they would not have become descriptive of the goods to which they were attached. So what can personalities and owners of characters do? Macleod and Wood suggest that personalities can try to create an *alter ego* or something surrounding their most famous exploits. The examples quoted include the registration by jockey Frankie Dettori of a stylised drawing of himself jumping in the air, or David Beckham's registration of a stylised logo of himself taking a free kick. (See Macleod and Wood, *The Picasso Case, Famous Names and Branding Celebrity* [2006] Ent LR 17(1), 44–6).

Passing off

The use of passing off as a form of protection has been hindered by Wynn-Parry J's statement in *McCulloch* v. *May* [1947] 2 All ER 845, that there has to be a 'common field of activity' in which both the plaintiff and defendant are engaged. In *Lynstad* v. *Anabas Products Ltd* [1977] FSR 62, ABBA were unable to stop the unauthorised use of their photographs on T-shirts and souvenirs because they were in the business of making records, even though they were involved in the marketing of goods with their image.

This need for a 'common field of activity' failed to take account of the fact that character owners will not be in the same field as those taking advantage of the character. The Beatles made music, not T-shirts. More importantly, it failed to take account of the fact that character merchandising existed as a distinct commercial activity. Bainbridge points out that the law was failing to recognise that well-known personalities, in particular, may license others to manufacture products bearing their names. This failure to recognise the practice is illustrated in a number of cases.

Wombles Ltd v. *Wombles Skips Ltd* [1977] RPC 99 concerned the Wombles, who were fictitious animals from a television series and were well known for cleaning up litter. The plaintiff owned the copyright in the books and in the drawings of the Wombles. Its main business was to grant licences in respect of the characters. The defendant formed a company to lease builders' skips and, recalling the Wombles' reputation for tidy habits, decided to call the company 'Wombles Skips Ltd'. It was argued that such use of the name would give the impression that the defendant's business was connected with the plaintiff in some way. A 'common field of activity' was claimed because the plaintiff had granted a licence to reproduce the Wombles on wastepaper baskets. The court disagreed. There was no common

field of activity. The similarity between marketing wastepaper baskets and hiring out builders' skips was simply not strong enough.

Taverner Rutledge v. *Trexapalm Ltd* [1977] RPC 275 concerned the famous television detective 'Kojak', known for sucking lollipops. The plaintiff made lollipops similar in shape to those used by the character and called them 'Kojakpops'. It quickly established goodwill in the name for the products, yet had not sought a licence from the television company responsible for the series. The defendant company started making similar lollies called 'Kojak lollies', under a licence agreement from the owners of the rights in the television series. The plaintiff sued for passing off. Although it was argued that the defendant's licence, with its terms on quality control, illustrated a connection in the course of trade between the defendant and the owners of the name, in other words a common field of activity, this argument, and with it the defence, failed because there was no actual or potential common field of activity between the owners of the television series and the defendant's business, there being no evidence of any exercise of quality control by the owners of the television series. According to Walton J, the defendant would have to show that the practice of character merchandising had become so well known that as soon as anybody in the street realised that a product was licensed by the owners of some series, like 'Kojak', he would say to himself not only 'this must have been licensed by them', but also 'and that is a guarantee of its quality'. In the event, the plaintiff's

lollies were of better value and quality and the defendant's product would have harmed the plaintiff's reputation.

The reference to quality control indicates a way to get around the 'common field of activity' problem. Stricter quality control exercised through the terms of a licence would indicate an active interest in the type of goods being produced and thereby form the necessary connection in the course of trade. An Australian decision indicates that this is a solution. In *Children's T Workshop Inc.* v. *Woolworths (NSW) Pty Ltd* [1981] RPC 187, a licence agreement for soft toys of Muppet characters incorporated detailed quality control provisions. This was enough to establish a connection in the course of trade.

The decision in *Mirage Studios* v. *Counter-Feat Clothing Co. Ltd* [1991] FSR 145 illustrates judicial recognition that the public are well aware of the practice of character merchandising. The plaintiff created the 'Teenage Mutant Ninja Turtle' characters. They also made and marketed cartoons, films and videos containing these characters. Part of the plaintiff's business involved licensing the reproduction of the characters on goods sold by licensees. Without the plaintiff's permission, the defendant made drawings of humanoid turtle characters, which were similar in appearance to the plaintiff's characters but were not exact reproductions. The defendant licensed these drawings to garment manufacturers to reproduce on T-shirts and other goods. In granting an injunction against the defendant, Browne-Wilkinson VC adopted the classic passing off test from *Erven Warnink* v. *Townend* [1979] AC

731. A misrepresentation had taken place because there was evidence to show that a substantial number of the buying public expected, and knew, that where a famous cartoon or television character was reproduced on goods, that reproduction was the result of a licence granted by the owner of the copyright or owner of other rights in that character. The defendant had, therefore, misrepresented that the goods bearing their turtles were produced under licence from the plaintiff:

'Since the public associated the goods with the creator of the characters, the depreciation of the image by fixing the Turtle picture to inferior goods and inferior materials might seriously reduce the value of the licensing rights.' (at page 156)

The decision has been welcomed by practitioners and academics alike. It is obviously welcomed by honest traders. Does it affect the decisions in the Wombles, Kojak or Abba cases? We believe it is distinguishable because only a name was involved in those cases, not a drawing. Further there was, according to Browne-Wilkinson VC, an arguable case of copyright infringement in *Mirage Studios*. However, *Mirage* finally establishes that judges are aware of character merchandising and, more importantly, that they know that members of the public are aware of it, which assists in satisfying the 'course of trade' requirement. For further reading, see Chong and Maniatis [1991] EIPR 7, 253.

It is yet to be seen whether this approach will be applied to cases of personality merchandising. In *Stringfellow* v. *McCain Foods* [1984] RPC 501, Peter Stringfellow failed to convince the court that use of his name by the defendants was actionable by him. In the case of *Elvis Presley Trade Marks* [1999] RPC 567, the estate of Elvis Presley did not argue their case on the grounds of personality merchandising, but the court made the interesting observation that, in its view, the purchaser of souvenirs bearing a particular personality's name or likeness 'was likely to be indifferent as to its source'.

In *Edmund Irvine & Another* v. *Talksport Ltd* [2002] EWCH 367 (Ch), Laddie J distinguished *Elvis* from cases which suggest that a sports (or other) personality has expressly endorsed a product or service in exchange for payment. This compares with *Tolley* v. *Fry*, where, as stated, the personality concerned sued in defamation. No doubt that option was also open to the Formula One racing driver popularly known as 'Eddie Irvine', whose photograph had been altered to make it appear that he was enjoying and thereby endorsing the defendant's radio programme. His Lordship also appeared to reject the 'common field of activity' as a requirement. (Note that Irvine's appeal against the damages awarded was also successful in the Court of Appeal, see [2003] EWCA Civ 423.)

Law of confidence and human rights
It is also suggested that following the decision in *Douglas* v. *Hello* [2005] EWCA Civ 595, the law of confidence incorporating aspects from the Human Rights Act 1998 could also be used by personalities to control the use of their images.

Summary

11.1 Passing off is the practice of giving consumers the impression that goods or services of one trader come from another trader who has established goodwill.

11.2 Goodwill is the likelihood that customers will return.

11.3 The plaintiff must show that the defendant's misrepresentation will damage, or is likely to damage, his goodwill.

11.4 Recent cases suggest that the defendant's misrepresentation must lead, or be likely to lead, to customer confusion about the source of the goods or services.

Summary cont'd

11.5 The plaintiff must prove damage or probability of damage.

11.6 Character merchandising involves attaching popular names or images to products.

11.7 The Trade Marks Act 1994 has made it easier to register character names and images as trade marks.

11.8 The tort of passing off has been of limited use because judges in the United Kingdom do not, on the whole, appreciate public awareness of character merchandising.

Exercises

11.1 Outline the elements required for a passing off action.

11.2 Consider whether the following have goodwill:

(a) *A* Bros, who have had the same market pitch in Leicester market for 25 years;

(b) *B* Co. Ltd, which owns a string of hotels on the French Riviera;

(c) 'Josie the talking elephant', a children's toy launched in the shops seven days ago and sold out in all major toy shops.

11.3 In January 1995, *A* wrote a children's book called *Josie in the Jungle*. The main character is a gentle elephant called Josie who teaches her friends to protect themselves against evil ivory hunters. The book is now an international best seller and has been turned into a full length cartoon film, which is also a success.

The rights in Josie have been assigned to *B* Ltd, who intends to exploit the characters in Europe.

C, a well-known Spanish stationery company, has acquired the first licence from *B* Ltd and has made preparations to market Josie stationery in the United Kingdom. To date, no sales have taken place.

B and *C* have discovered that two companies are using 'Josie' in the course of their business. One is a company calling itself 'Josie's Tissues' which produces and sells paper tissues. Its packaging has a picture of a fierce-looking elephant. The other is *D* Co. Ltd, which is manufacturing and selling children's T-shirts with the words 'I'm a friend of Josie' printed in bold letters.

Advise *B* and *C*.

Chapter 12

Trade Marks – International Provisions

Key words

- **Base registration** – registration of the mark in the applicant's home country.
- **Community trade mark** – a trade mark that applies throughout the European Union.
- **Examination period** – the twelve-month period during which an objection can be raised against registration.

12.1 Introduction

Trade marks, like all other intellectual property rights, are national rights. This means that a trade mark, once registered, only offers protection against unauthorised use by third parties within the country of registration. Unlike copyright, there is no automatic extension of a national trade mark to other countries.

There are, however, a number of international conventions and arrangements that give some international recognition to national trade marks. These are the Paris Convention, the Madrid Agreement and the Protocol to the Madrid Agreement (commonly known as the Madrid Protocol). There is also a Community Trade Marks System that creates a trade mark that gives rights throughout the European Community.

12.2 Paris Convention

The Paris Convention was established in 1883 to create some interaction and recognition between various countries of each other's national intellectual property rights. For all intellectual property rights of a registerable nature, this was achieved by the concept of priority.

Priority recognises the first filing date for a particular intellectual property right in any Convention country as the filing date for all other filings in any Convention country in respect of the same intellectual property right by the same proprietor made during the priority period. The period of priority differs from intellectual property right to intellectual property right, but in the case of trade marks the period is six months. This has given a level of international protection for trade marks, because the first to file a trade mark application is, in most countries, the person with the better claim to a trade mark.

This is not the case in the United Kingdom, because rights in passing off can be built up through sufficient use of a trade mark without registration, and those rights can act as an obstacle to any subsequent application to register the trade mark by a third party.

Another provision of the Paris Convention relevant to trade marks is Article 6bis, which gives international protection to 'well-known' trade marks. A person can own a 'well-known' mark in registered or unregistered form even in countries where the action of passing off does not exist. Ownership of a well-known mark will prevent a third party from applying to register the same or a very similar mark in any other Convention country that has implemented Article 6bis into its national laws and allows cancellation of an existing registration for such an identical or similar mark during the first five years after registration on the application of the owner of the well-known mark to the relevant authority.

This international recognition of national trade marks is of limited application because it only applies to trade marks that have become 'well-known' in other Convention countries. The Paris Convention gives no definition of the phrase 'well-known' and therefore countries of the Paris Union have devised their own guidelines from case law. The World Intellectual Property Organisation (WIPO) has commented that this is unsatisfactory for a provision having international effect.

12.3 Madrid Agreement

In 1891, the Madrid Agreement was implemented to simplify the procedure for filing trade mark registrations in many countries. Up until that point, anyone wanting to obtain trade mark registrations in, say, ten countries, had to file ten separate applications at the ten separate national trade mark registries in accordance with the ten different procedural requirements.

The Madrid Agreement allows anyone established or domiciled in a Madrid Agreement country, with a trade mark registration in his or her country of establishment or domicile, to file one international application that can be extended to one or more other Madrid Agreement countries as specified. The central international application is filed with WIPO in Geneva, designating to which countries it is to be extended. WIPO then takes responsibility for passing the application on to each of the designated national registries, where the application proceeds according to the national laws and procedures of each country.

The United Kingdom did not sign the Madrid Agreement and so this method of filing registrations is not available to anyone who is established or domiciled only in the UK (or only in countries that are also not party to the Madrid Agreement).

The UK did not sign the Madrid Agreement because the procedures that the Trade Marks Registry would have had to apply in dealing with Madrid Agreement applications are in conflict with the established procedures used by the Trade Marks Registry. The particular areas of dispute were (1) the need for a base registration, (2) the 12-month examination period and (3) the concept of central attack.

Base registration

In order to be able to file an international application with WIPO under the Madrid Agreement, an applicant must have an existing registration of the trade mark in its 'home country'. 'Home country' means the country where the trade mark owner is a national, or is domiciled, or has a real and effective industrial or commercial establishment.

This requirement has favoured trade mark owners of countries which have less stringent examination procedures (for example, countries with so-called deposit systems, where there is little or no examination of prior rights). The UK Trade Marks Registry carries out a thorough examination of trade mark applications both to see whether the mark is inherently registrable and to see whether there are existing conflicting rights. As a consequence, obtaining a registration in the United Kingdom can take much longer. The examination countries also disliked the possibility of their Registries being affected by loss of a registration in another country (because of central attack – see below).

Examination period

Under the Madrid Agreement, once an international application has been filed by WIPO at each designated national registry, each registry has 12 months within which to raise an objection. If no objection is raised in that period, the application will automatically proceed to registration. In the United Kingdom, the examination procedure used to take up to 12 months. Thereafter, a trade mark application is advertised in the *Trade Marks Journal* so that third parties with prior rights can raise an objection. These parties have three months from advertisement in which to raise an objection. The 12-month time limit imposed by the Madrid Agreement would have required the Trade Marks Registry to adapt its procedure to accommodate the shorter period for examination and advertisement; at the time this was not considered acceptable by the United Kingdom. In fact, the examination procedure in the United Kingdom is now generally around two to three months.

Central attack

When filing international applications under the Madrid Agreement, an applicant must have an existing registration in a Madrid Agreement country (the base registration). If the base registration is cancelled within five years after the date of the registration, all the dependent applications/ registrations are automatically cancelled. As a result of the likelihood of base registrations being sought and obtained in countries with speedier registration procedures (most notably, countries that do not operate a detailed examination system), the United Kingdom saw this as resulting in an uncertain system.

12.4 Madrid Protocol

As a number of key countries (for example, the United Kingdom, the United States, Canada, South Africa) had been unwilling to sign the Madrid Agreement, discussions began in the mid-1980s (around the time of the discussions on general harmonisation of trade mark laws in the European Community) on how to make the Madrid Agreement system more palatable. The result was the Protocol to the Madrid Arrangement which was adopted in 1989. At the date of writing there are 54 signatories to the Protocol (including the United Kingdom). (See www.itma.org.uk for up-to-date information about the signatories to the Protocol.)

The Protocol is based on essentially the same structure as the Madrid Agreement. It is open to anyone with a pending application in a Protocol country which is their home country. This is the first advantage of the Protocol system over the Madrid Agreement system – namely, the possibility of filing an application and immediately filing a Protocol application with WIPO to extend the protection to designated Protocol countries. The other differences, which have led to the United Kingdom signing up, are that:

(1) the examination period can be extended at each country's choice to 18 months; and
(2) although central attack still applies, all cancelled applications/ registrations can be refiled nationally with the same priority date as the original Protocol application.

12.5 Community Trade Mark System (CTM)

Although classed as an international registration system, the CTM operates very differently from either the Madrid Agreement or the Madrid Protocol. It is more like the national systems, in that it is a means of filing an application for one trade mark at one trade mark registry to obtain one registration under one set of laws and procedures. The only real difference is that the area covered by the registration is a collection of countries, namely, the European Union, rather than one country.

The CTM is legislated for in Council Regulation 40/94, with amendments from Council Regulation 422/2004 and Commission Regulation 1042/2005. Each Member State is required to implement the Regulations into national law. An application can be filed direct with the Office for the Harmonisation of the Internal Market (Trade Marks and Designs) (OHIM) in Alicante, Spain, or at the national trade mark office in any EC country which will pass the application to the Community Trade Mark Office.

Once filed, the application will be examined to make sure that it meets all the basic conditions of registrability. These conditions will be similar to those applied in most of the national trade mark offices of the EU. Appeals against a refusal to register can be made to one of the Boards of Appeal. From there, further appeals on the interpretation of the Regulation will go to the European Court of First Instance (CFI), and ultimately to the European Court of Justice (ECJ). In *Swizzels Matlow Ltd's Application for a 3-Dimensional Trade Mark* [1999] RPC 879, Simon Thorley QC stated that decisions of the OHIM were persuasive but not binding. We suggest that decisions from the CFI and the ECJ concerning matters such as graphic interpretation and distinctiveness should be treated as highly persuasive if not binding. So decisions such as that of *Procter & Gamble* v. *Office for Harmonisation in the Internal Market (Trade Marks and Designs)* (Case C-383/99P), 20 September 2001, discussed in Chapter 9, will be of great significance.

Even though the trade mark laws of nearly all EU countries have been harmonised in line with the trade mark harmonisation Directive (89/104/EEC), because of the differences in registry practices there are still going to be situations where a trade mark that is not accepted as registrable in an individual country might be accepted by the OHIM.

Further, meeting the conditions for registration of a trade mark in one or more Member States does not guarantee a successful application for a CTM. See *Ford Motor Company* v. *Office for Harmonisation in the Internal Market* (Case T-91/99), 30 March 2000.

Once a Community Trade Mark application has satisfied the conditions of registrability, searches will be conducted of the Community Trade Marks Register and of the national registers of all countries other than Italy, Germany and France (which have opted out of the search procedure). The applicant will be told of any prior rights found on any registers, but it can choose to ignore them and the application will not be prevented from proceeding just because prior conflicting rights exist. The OHIM will tell owners of prior CTMs of the conflicting application and, if such owners challenge the application, it will not be allowed to proceed unless the proprietors can agree to some form of co-existence. Owners of prior conflicting national trade marks will not be told of conflicting CTM applications.

Once a CTM registration has been granted, it can still be revoked on the application of an owner of a prior conflicting right (CTM or national) for up to five years after the owner of the prior right becomes aware of the use of the CTM, and also by anyone on grounds of non-use (after five years of non-use) or by anyone at any time if the mark becomes generic or misleading. Since a CTM can be maintained by use in any part of the EC, it is clearly possible for the owner of a prior national right to be unaware of a conflicting CTM for many years. Since the existence of a CTM will be a matter of public record, the test of awareness may develop into a concept of constructive awareness – in other words, in future it may be held that if a CTM is on the Register, third parties will be fixed with constructive knowledge of its existence.

If a CTM is challenged and removed from the CTM Register, the owner of the CTM can refile national applications in all EC countries other than the country or countries in respect of which the challenge was made. These national applications will have the same application date as the CTM application.

Proposals have been put forward for the European Community (as distinct from its Member States) to sign and ratify the Madrid Protocol. This will make it possible for a CTM to be applied for as part of a Madrid Protocol international application. It will also mean that a CTM application could be used as the base application for a Protocol international application.

Businesses that already have trade mark registrations in Member States but wish to apply for a CTM (to save costs and administration on renewals) can allow the national registrations to lapse once the CTM is in place. In such situations, the CTM will acquire the seniority of the national registrations. What this means is that, if there is a corresponding existing United Kingdom trade mark registration with a priority date of 1 January 1990, and the proprietor relinquishes the United Kingdom registration and decides to rely on its corresponding CTM, then in any action, defence or opposition in the United Kingdom, the CTM will be treated, in the United Kingdom, as dating from 1 January 1990. If there are several existing national registrations being replaced by a CTM, the CTM will be accorded several different seniorities in respect of the various countries. If a CTM with such various seniorities is subsequently challenged and the owner has to refile national applications in unaffected countries, as well as these national applications having the same application date as the CTM, any seniorities will also be reflected in the 'revived' national applications.

Despite the unitary nature of a CTM, infringements will occur country by country and the enforcement of the CTM will be dealt with in specially designated Community Trade Mark Courts in each country of the EC. In dealing with CTM infringement claims, the Community Trade Mark Courts are to apply the provisions of the Community Trade Mark Regulation. However, in relation to any matters not covered by the Regulation, the national law of the country of the courts where the case is proceeding will apply. National rules of procedure will also be applied in relation to any questions of procedure not covered by the Regulation. Once an infringement has been proved, the court can issue an order to stop the infringing activity and use whatever measures are available under the relevant national law to enforce that order. Any other sanctions for infringement available under the national law can be used by the Community Trade Mark Courts.

If an infringement occurs, the action must be brought in the country where the infringer is domiciled or has an effective establishment. If that is not in the EC, then the action will be brought in the country where the owner of the CTM is domiciled or has an establishment. If that is not in the EC, the action must be brought in the Spanish courts. There will be the possibility of forum shopping in situations where the defendant or the plaintiff have establishments in several EC countries; the availability of injunctive relief and criminal sanctions, and the possibility of commencing actions on the basis of an application, vary from country to country.

The Agreement on Trade Related Aspects of Intellectual Property Rights 1994 (TRIPs)

This sets out requirements for trade mark registration and protection that are similar to those found in the legislation of the United Kingdom and the European Union. Section 2, Articles 15–21 of the Agreement deal with trademarks. Although the TRIPs Agreement cannot be said to have direct effect, it was confirmed in Case C-245/02 *Anheuser-Busch Inc* v. *Budejovicky Budvar Narodni Podnik* [2000] RPC 906 that since the EC is a party to the Agreement, it is under an obligation to interpret trade mark legislation, so far as possible in the light of the wording of the Agreement (para. 42).

Summary

12.1 The various international registration systems are intended to reflect the need for transnational protection of trade mark rights.

12.2 The Madrid Agreement and its Protocol still work on the basis of separate national rights but facilitate the method for obtaining such rights. Their advantage over the CTM is that there is greater flexibility for dealings in the rights in different territories and the countries covered by these arrangements are actually, in the case of the Agreement, and potentially, in the case of the Protocol, far more numerous than the countries covered by the CTM.

12.3 The CTM is aimed at consolidating the single market from a trade mark perspective. The unitary nature of the right is intended to support the free movement of goods doctrine and is intended to work against the creation of national borders.

12.4 The CTM will only be available in the European Union but, with the ratification of the Madrid Protocol, it can form part of a broader international registration programme.

Exercises

12.1 What is the best way to achieve international protection of trade marks?

12.2 Explain how the English common law may affect the application of the rule of priority.

12.3 Examine whether the United Kingdom was justified in refusing to sign the Madrid Agreement.

12.4 Is there any significant difference between the Madrid Agreement and the Madrid Protocol?

12.5 Outline the application procedure for a Community Trade Mark.

12.6 Discuss whether the Trade Marks Act 1994 satisfies the United Kingdom's international obligations.

Part III

Copyright and Designs

Chapter 13

Copyright

Key words

▶ **Broadcast** – a transmission by any electronic means which is transmitted either for simultaneous reception by members of the public or for presentation to members of the public at a time determined solely by the person making the transmission (but there is an exception for most Internet transmissions).
▶ **Copyright** – the right to prevent others from reproducing a work.
▶ **First published** – when copies of the work made with the permission of the copyright owner are issued to the public.
▶ **Qualifying person** – includes a British citizen or subject, an EU citizen or a citizen of another Convention country, or a company incorporated in such a country.

13.1 What is Copyright?

As the word suggests, copyright is the right to prevent others from copying, or reproducing, your work. A distinction that is often discussed in the context of copyright is the distinction between ideas and expression. Copyright protects the expression of an idea, not the idea itself. If I have an idea for a story, that idea, while still in my head, or communicated to someone else in speech, will not be a copyright work; once it is committed to paper or some other fixed form, whether by me or someone else, it becomes a work in which copyright can subsist.

If I have copyright in a written expression of my idea, what can I stop others from doing? I can stop anyone from directly or indirectly copying the whole or a substantial part of my copyright work. I cannot stop someone from borrowing my idea and I cannot stop someone who, independently, and without reference to my work, produces an extremely similar or identical work. However, the courts have acknowledged that it is difficult to draw the line between protecting ideas and expression (see, for example, *University of London Press Ltd* v. *University Tutorial Press Ltd* [1916] 2 Ch 601; *Plix Products Ltd* v. *Winstone (Frank M) (Merchants)* [1986] FSR 608; *Designers Guild Ltd* v. *Russell Williams (Textiles)* [2001] FSR 11). If an idea is expressed in detail in the work, then copying the idea may involve copying the expression; in such cases, copyright will, in effect, protect copying of the idea as well as the expression (*Ibcos Computers Ltd* v. *Barclays Mercantile Highland Finance Ltd* [1994] FSR 275).

Copyright is a right that arises automatically upon the creation of a work that qualifies for copyright protection. There is no registration process. This means that there is no registration certificate to prove ownership of copyright. To prove ownership, the author will need to produce original and, preferably, dated evidence of the creation of the work and proof of authorship. The author will also need to show that he is a qualifying person or that the work was first published in a Convention country. To be a qualifying person (s.154 of the Copyright, Designs and Patents Act 1988) the author must have been, at the material time, a British citizen, subject or protected person, a British overseas territories citizen, a British National (Overseas) or a British Overseas citizen or must have been resident or domiciled in a Convention country at the material time. In addition, a body incorporated under the law of a part of the United Kingdom or another Convention country can also be a qualifying person. The material time is when an unpublished work was created or when a published work was first published (if the author dies before publication, the material time is just before his death). A Convention country is any country that is a signatory to either the Universal Copyright Convention or the Berne Copyright Convention. Broadly speaking, this covers most countries of the world. A work is first published when copies of the work, made with the permission of the copyright owner, are issued to the public.

The works that may qualify for copyright protection are defined in s.1 of the 1988 Act. These are (a) original literary, dramatic, musical and artistic works, (b) sound recordings, films and broadcasts and (c) typographical arrangements of published editions. Although the broad categories of copyright work in the 1988 Act are the same as those in the Copyright Act 1956, the definitions of the specific works that fall within each of those categories have changed. This change has partly come about because of technological developments and also to reflect decisions reached by the courts over the period between 1956 and 1988. A further recent change introduced by the Copyright and Related Rights Regulations 2003, SI 2003/2498 (referred to in this book as the New Copyright Regulations) is the removal of cable programmes as a distinct category of copyright work and the redefinition of a broadcast to mean a transmission by any electronic means (not just wireless telegraphy) which is transmitted either for simultaneous reception by members of the public or is transmitted for presentation to members of the public at a time determined solely by the person making the transmission. The new definition of broadcast excludes Internet transmissions other than those comprising live transmissions or transmissions of recorded material scheduled by the person responsible for making the transmission or those which are being transmitted simultaneously on the Internet and by other means.

Historical Background

Copyright has its roots in the sixteenth century. Initially the courts recognised a need for some form of protection for books. In the 1550s, a compulsory system of registration of books with the Stationers' Company was established with the aim of affording protection for authors. This registration system became optional after the 1911 Act. If an author registered a book with the Stationers' Company, it purported to give them a perpetual right to reproduce the book and, consequently, prevent reproduction by anyone else. It was argued by publishers that there existed a common law right of copyright, but it is far from clear whether such a law existed. However, the first copyright Act adopted by Parliament was known as the Statute of Anne 1709, and was introduced following calls for greater protection of authors. This gave an exclusive printing right of 14 years, followed by a further period of 14 years to be enjoyed by the author, if living. In 1734, the Engraving Copyright Act was passed, which gave copyright protection to engravings. Gradually, over the next 150 years, a number of Acts were passed extending copyright protection to musical, dramatic and artistic works. By the 1800s, there were around 14 copyright-related Acts on the statute books. A consolidating Act was needed to pull all the strands together.

In 1875, a Royal Commission looked into the position and recommended that a clear and consistent approach to all the various forms of copyright protection be incorporated into one Act. This did not happen, however, until after Great Britain had signed the Berne Copyright Convention in 1885. The Berne Copyright Convention provided for international protection of copyright for the works of nationals of all countries who signed the Convention. It required each Member Country to extend minimum standards of protection to nationals of all other Member Countries. At that time, the law of the United Kingdom did not meet these minimum standards and so the United Kingdom was forced to implement the 1911 Copyright Act, which repealed and replaced a number of the existing Acts and abolished common law copyright which had previously extended an indefinite term of copyright for unpublished literary works.

Further changes to the Berne Copyright Convention in 1951 again prompted the United Kingdom to amend its copyright law and to introduce the Copyright Act 1956. This Act brought copyright law to a point very close to where we find it today. A number of amending statutes then followed that were necessary to reflect the technological advances being made, in particular in the field of computers and microchip technology.

In 1973, the Whitford Committee was appointed to review the state of copyright law. The Committee reported in 1977 suggesting changes to the law to deal with technological advances and recommending that the United Kingdom legislate to implement various changes to copyright law as required by the international Conventions to which it was party. The result was a Green Paper in 1981, 'Reform of the Law Relating to Copyright, Designs and Performers' Protection' (Cmnd 8302), and subsequently the White Paper 'Intellectual Property and Innovation' (Cmnd 9712), which led to the 1988 Copyright, Designs and Patents Act, which consolidated the amendments made by legislation subsequent to the 1956 Act and implemented changes in the law that, according to a number of case decisions, were long overdue.

Since the Act came into force, on 1 August 1989, there have been a number of amending Regulations dealing with matters such as implementation of EC Directives on rights to reproduce copyright software as is necessary for lawful use, protection of semiconductor chip topography rights, harmonisation of copyright duration and, most recently, the introduction of several new rights such as the communication to the public right under the New Copyright Regulations. These Regulations came into force on 31 October 2003 to implement the Copyright Directive 2001/29/EC on the harmonisation of certain aspects of copyright and related rights in the information society. The Copyright Directive's aim was to bring national copyright laws into the twenty-first century so that they could deal adequately with the challenges presented by multimedia, digitisation and the Internet, and to achieve harmonisation of copyright protection across the European Union.

Another influence on UK copyright law is the Agreement on Trade Related Aspects of Intellectual Property Rights (TRIPs), which was signed on 15 April 1994. One of the basic principles of TRIPs is to establish minimum standards for protection and enforcement of intellectual property rights (including copyright). In broad terms, TRIPs follows the Berne Convention as a starting point and builds on it. Article 9.1 of TRIPs states that members should comply with Articles 1–21 of the Berne Convention, which deal with copyright. Article 10 of TRIPs extended copyright protection to computer programs in object code or source code form. This is now reflected in both UK and EU legislation. Protection of databases and rental rights may also be attributed to TRIPs.

13.3 The Need for Change?

Prior to implementation of the New Copyright Regulations, in theory, the existing law of copyright was probably already capable of dealing with the new developing information technology world. The digitisation of artistic and literary works does not mean that they cease to be copyright works and the transmission of images, data and sound across the Internet still constitutes reproduction that requires the same licences as any other form of reproduction or transmission of those copyright works. The real problem was that, as it became easier to reproduce these works and spread unlawful copies across the world, and as it became more and more difficult to trace the source of such copies, enforcement of existing copyright law was becoming almost impossible. It is hoped that the New Copyright Regulations will go some way to easing this situation although the solution to the problem may, in fact, be in further technological advances such as encryption, 'watermarking' and other anti-copying devices.

Hot Topic . . .
CREATIVE COMMONS

The proliferation of content on the Internet has caused concern for copyright owners and users alike and has highlighted the issue of what should be protected by copyright and what should be free for everyone to use. Copyright owners are usually keen to maintain some measure of control over the exploitation and use of their copyright protected content, while users may be uncertain as to if and how they can use such content. The Creative Commons is a worldwide organisation which was established in the United States in 2001 and is designed to provide 'middle-ground' solutions between, on the one hand, full copyright control with all rights reserved and, on the other hand, no copyright control with no rights reserved.

The United Kingdom adopted a Creative Commons scheme in 2003. From the beginning of 2005 the UK scheme was 'replaced' with a scheme for Scotland and a separate, although similar, scheme for England and Wales. A further scheme for Northern Ireland is anticipated. Under the scheme, copyright owners can select one of four freely available public licences

to use in conjunction with their work/content. Each of the licences defines the conditions under which the copyright owner's works may be used by others. The first licence is described as the 'attribution' licence which permits others to copy, distribute, display and perform the work and derivative works based upon it only where they give the owner credit. The second licence is described as the 'non-commercial' licence which permits others to do the same acts but only for non-commercial purposes. The third licence is described as the 'no derivative works' licence which permits others to copy, distribute, display and perform only exact copies of the work and not derivative works based upon it. The fourth licence is described as the 'share alike' which permits others to distribute derivative works only under a licence identical to the licence that governs the owner's work/content. Of course, it remains open to copyright owners to allow unrestricted use of their works which, for practical purposes, is similar to putting the work into the public domain. With the exception

of the 'no derivative works' and the 'share alike' licences (which are inherently incompatible), these licences can be combined in relation to the same work.

A copyright owner may elect to use one of the four available licences because they feel it will result in an increase in the distribution of their work, or because they want to maximise the exposure of the work. The scheme is stated to be operated for the benefit of teachers, scholars, scientists, writers, photographers, filmmakers, musicians, graphic designers, Web hobbyists, artists and other content developers, and it is anticipated that the licences can be used anywhere in the world. Clearly, whilst the licences have been drafted to ensure, as far as possible, that they will be enforceable in a multitude of jurisdictions, it cannot be stated unequivocally that they will be enforceable in all jurisdictions.

The Creative Commons scheme was generally well received in the year or so following its inception in 2001, although it has subsequently been subjected to various criticisms including those made by the content industries suggesting that the scheme undermines copyright.

Summary

13.1 Copyright is an automatic right that entitles the owner to prevent others from copying their work.

13.2 The works protected by copyright are original literary, dramatic, musical and artistic works, sound recordings, films, broadcasts and typographical arrangements of published editions.

13.3 Whilst each country will have their own copyright law, attempts have been made over the years to harmonise the laws to some degree through international conventions such as the Berne Convention.

Exercises

13.1 How does an individual obtain copyright in their work?

13.2 What is the idea/expression dichotomy?

13.3 Why is the nationality of the person creating the work so important?

Chapter 14

Subsistence (1)

Key words

▶ **Artistic work** – a graphic work, photograph, sculpture or collage irrespective of artistic quality, a work of architecture being a building or a model for a building or a work of artistic craftsmanship.

▶ **Dramatic work** – includes a work of dance or mime.

▶ **Literary work** – any work, other than a dramatic or musical work, which is written, spoken or sung.

▶ **Musical work** – a work consisting of music, exclusive of any words or action intended to be sung, spoken or performed with the music.

14.1 The Subject Matter Protected

As we have already seen, copyright protects expression, rather than ideas, but the dividing line is blurred. A further complication to this area is that a single item may be protected by a number of copyrights, which can sometimes be owned by different people.

A song comprises words and music and each of these will have its own copyright protection. It is quite possible that those elements will have been written by two or more different people. If that song is recorded, the resulting sound recording will be protected by copyright and the underlying copyright in the words and music will continue to be protected separately as copyright works. The sleeve of a compact disc will probably have a photo or design on it that will be a protected artistic work, and any written commentary about the music or song will be a literary work (as well as there being separate copyright protection for the typographical arrangement of the printed words).

Understanding the different rights that may exist in something such as a compact disc requires an understanding of what can be protected as a copyright work.

14.2 Literary Works

A literary work is defined in the 1988 Act as 'any work, other than a dramatic or musical work, which is written, spoken or sung'. The Act goes on to say that this includes a table or compilation, a computer program and preparatory design material for a computer program and a database. The inclusion of computer programs is as a result of consolidation of the Copyright (Computer Software) Amendment Act 1985, which implemented into law what the courts had begun to indicate, namely, that a computer program, being something that is initially written down in a programming language, is a literary work. In *Thrustcode* v. *W.W. Computing Ltd* [1983] FSR 502, the court had already held under the 1956 Act that computer programs were capable of protection as literary works. The inclusion of preparatory design material for a computer program is as a result of the Copyright (Computer Programs) Regulations 1992 (SI 1992 No. 3233), which implemented Council Directive 91/250/EEC on the legal protection of computer programs into United Kingdom law. The former copyright treatment of databases was changed by the introduction of the Copyright and Rights in Databases Regulations 1997 which amended certain sections of the 1988 Act (see Chapter 19 for a more detailed discussion about the protection of databases).

'Literary' is, perhaps, an unfortunate word to use as a description of the type of work protected because it suggests that the work must have some literary merit. Books, magazines, articles and poems are all obvious literary works, but less obvious examples have also been considered by the courts to merit copyright protection as literary works, provided that they satisfy the condition of originality. For example, a football coupon (*Ladbroke (Football) Ltd* v. *William Hill (Football) Ltd* [1964] 1WLR 273), rules for a game (*Caley (A.J.) & Son Ltd* v. *Garnett (G.) & Sons Ltd* [1936–45] Mac. CC) and instructions on the packaging for weedkiller (*Elanco Products Ltd* v. *Mandops (Agrochemical Specialists) Ltd* [1980] RPC 213 – an interim injunction application).

Tables and compilations are perhaps strange examples of literary works – is a table written or drawn? If a table is drawn, does it cease to be a table and become a graphic work (which is part of the definition of an artistic work), or can it be both? A compilation is not defined in the 1988 Act but the dictionary definition is 'that which is compiled. A literary work or the like formed by compilation', and to compile is defined as 'to put together and collect' and 'to construct (a written or printed work) out of materials collected from various sources'. As there is no corresponding category within the definition of artistic works, the courts have considered the possibility of a compilation of drawings or photographs being treated as literary works. In *Express Newspapers* v. *Liverpool Daily Post and Echo plc* [1983] FSR 306 the court held that a grid and set of five letter sequences (as appearing on a scratch card) qualified as a literary work, being a compilation. A significant factor was the skill and labour that had been employed in producing these works.

A particularly complex example of overlapping of literary and artistic works arises in relation to circuit diagrams. This interrelationship was considered in the case of *Aubrey Max Sandman* v. *Panasonic UK Ltd & Another* [1998] FSR 651. As this case was just an application to strike out, a final decision was not reached on whether infringement had taken place but Pumfrey J made the point that there was 'a surprising lack of law in relation to copyright in circuit diagrams', although he did refer to the case of *Electronic Techniques (Anglia) Ltd* v. *Critchley Components Ltd* [1997] FSR 401. Whilst the question of infringement was not decided in this case, Pumfrey J felt there was no reason why both artistic and literary copyright could not exist in the same work (namely a circuit diagram).

Although literary works include works that are spoken or sung, s.3(2) of the 1988 Act says that copyright will not subsist in a literary work (or indeed in a dramatic or musical work – see below) until it has been recorded, in writing or otherwise. If I recite a poem of my own composition, which I have never previously recorded in any permanent form, the poem will not attract copyright protection until it is recorded (either by me or someone else). If it is recorded, the poem will, at that point, attract copyright protection as a literary work and the recording will itself attract copyright protection as a sound recording. The question of who owns the two copyrights (which were both triggered by the same event (that is the recording) and have the same subject matter) is dealt with in Chapter 18.

The word 'original' appears as a qualification to literary, dramatic, musical and artistic works, whereas it does not for sound recordings, films, broadcasts or typographical arrangements of published editions. The relevant sections concerning sound recordings, films and typographical arrangements do state that copies are not protected, and the sections concerning broadcasts state that no copyright will subsist in a broadcast which infringes the copyright of another broadcast. What is intended by the word 'original' is that the work should not be a pure copy of another work. The threshold is very low – provided that the work was not copied from a previous work, it can attract its own copyright protection, even though there may be other works already in existence which are very similar to it.

In *University of London Press Ltd* v. *University Tutorial Press Ltd* [1916] 2 Ch 601, the defendants issued a publication that reproduced certain examination papers in which the claimant claimed copyright. In considering the claim, the court expanded on the meaning of originality for the purposes of copyright. The idea expressed in the work need not be original; it is the expression which must be original. If independent skill and labour have been applied in creating a work, this will suggest a new work that attracts copyright protection even if an existing work has been used as a reference point. In *Sawkins* v. *Hyperion Records Ltd* [2005] EWCA Civ 565, Mummery LJ found that Dr Sawkins, the editor of four fragmented and incomplete works by the French composer Lalande (1657–1726), had employed such considerable 'effort, skill and time' in rendering the works capable of performance that (as the High Court had already held) he owned the copyright in the resulting scores as original musical works. However, pure copying, even if it involves considerable skill and labour, will not satisfy the test of originality.

Apart from originality, there is another qualification that a written, spoken or sung work must meet in order to be a literary work. Although nothing is said in the 1988 Act, the courts have for some time made it clear that a literary work must impart some instruction, information or pleasure (*Hollinrake* v. *Truswell* [1894] 3 Ch 420). Using this reasoning the courts are not prepared to extend copyright protection to single words (as was shown by *Exxon Corporation & Others* v. *Exxon Insurance Consultants International Ltd* [1982] RPC 69) or to titles of books or films (*Francis, Day & Hunter Ltd* v. *Twentieth Century Fox Corp. Ltd* [1940] AC 112) although in *Ladbroke (Football) Ltd* v. *William Hill (Football) Ltd* [1964] 1 WLR 273 there was found to be sufficient skill, judgment and labour in the selection and presentation of bets in the form of a football betting coupon, including in particular the headings, to attract copyright protection.

14.3 Dramatic Works

Original dramatic works are not defined save that they include 'a work of dance or mime'. The courts have expanded on the statutory provision by deciding that the word 'dramatic' requires an element of performance accompanied by action.

One recent case to consider the definition of 'a dramatic work' was *Norowzian* v. *Arks Ltd (No. 2)* [2000] FSR 363. This concerned the Guinness advertisement called 'Anticipation', featuring a man performing a jerky dance while waiting for his pint of Guinness to settle. Mr Norowzian, a film director, complained that this advertisement infringed copyright in his film known as 'Joy'. The two films appeared similar to the viewer in that they both made use of distinctive 'jump cutting' techniques although the steps and the context of the two films were different. In the High Court, the judge held that 'Joy' was not a dramatic work because the dance in question was not capable of being performed. However, the Court of Appeal overturned that decision by deciding that the film could itself be protected as a dramatic work, defining such a work as 'a work of action with or without words or music which is capable of being performed before an audience' – since the film could be performed before an audience, it was entitled to protection as a dramatic work. In the event, however, it was held that the defendant had not copied a substantial part of 'Joy' and Mr Norowzian's appeal therefore failed. This definition was applied by the Judge in *Nova Productions Ltd* v. *Mazooma Games Ltd & Others* [2006] EWHC 24 when he had to consider whether the screen displays on a coin-operated video game could constitute a dramatic work. He concluded that it was not a dramatic work because, since it was a game, the sequence of images would change from game to game as it was played, so that it was not capable of performance.

In *Brighton* v. *Jones* [2005] FSR 16, it was decided that the director of a play was not a joint author of the play by virtue of suggestions that she had made during rehearsals to changes in the script and how it would be performed. These amounted to contributions to the interpretation and theatrical presentation of the dramatic work, rather than to its creation.

A recital of a poem or the singing of a song without action and the impromptu 'gags' of a performer (for instance, in a game show) will not be dramatic works (although they may be performances of literary or musical works). To attract copyright protection, a dramatic work must be recorded in some form – the mere performance (without a record) will only be protected by performance rights (see Chapter 20).

14.4 Musical Works

An original musical work is defined as 'a work consisting of music, exclusive of any words or action intended to be sung, spoken or performed with the music'. The dictionary definition of 'music' as given in the *Oxford English Dictionary* is the 'art or science of combining vocal and/or instrumental sounds to produce beauty of form, harmony, melody, rhythm, expressive content, etc.'. Again, the musical work must be recorded in some fixed form for copyright to subsist. In *Lawson* v. *Dundas* (Ch D, 12 June 1985, unreported) the four bars of the Channel 4 'Signature' were held to merit protection as a musical work – either the musical notes (as opposed to the words to a song) must be recorded in some final form or the music recorded. The definition of music was considered in *Sawkins* v. *Hyperion Records Ltd* [2005] EWCA Civ 565. There it was found that the sound produced by the musicians when playing the musical score created by the claimant was influenced by the performing indications, tempo and performance practice indicators which he had added to his new edition of an old musical composition, and that his skill and effort in producing the new edition were sufficient to attract copyright protection.

There has even been a copyright dispute relating to a piece of 'music' called 4′33″ by John Cage. The whole piece is simply silence, but when Mike Batt included a track on The Planet's album called *A Minute's Silence*, he settled a legal dispute with John Cage's publishers by paying them a sum of money.

14.5   Artistic Works

Artistic works are defined as being 'a graphic work, photograph, sculpture or collage irrespective of artistic quality, a work of architecture being a building or a model for a building or a work of artistic craftsmanship'. 'Graphic work' is further defined as *including* 'any painting, drawing, diagram, map, chart or plan and any engraving, etching, lithograph, wood cut or similar work' (note that this definition is not exhaustive). The Act makes clear that a still from a film is not a 'photograph' and will instead be protected as a film.

'Sculpture' includes a cast or model made for the purposes of sculpture. In *Wham-O Manufacturing Co.* v. *Lincoln Industries Ltd* [1985] RPC 127, a plastic frisbee, displaying concentric ridges, was held to be a copyright work on the basis that it was an engraving. In that case, the court was not prepared to say the resulting frisbees produced from injection moulding were sculptures, but the original wooden models used to create the moulds were sculptures. In another case, *Breville Europe plc* v. *Thorn EMI Domestic Appliances Ltd* (1985) [1995] FSR 77, the court found that the plaster shapes of toasted sandwiches created to form the mould for a toasted sandwich maker could be protected as artistic works (being casts for a sculpture). And even the pattern of the underside of a rubber car mat has been protected from copying by relying on the copyright found to subsist in metal plates used to make the mats, and in the resulting mats, as engravings – *Hi-Tech Autoparts Ltd* v. *Towergate Two Ltd* [2002] FSR 254; [2002] FSR 270. However, in *Metix (UK) Ltd & Another* v. *G.H. Maughan (Plastics) Ltd & Another* [1997] FSR 718, the Patents Court in an interim hearing said that a mould produced as a means for making a functional article should not be treated as a work in which sculpture copyright subsists. So the position regarding the protection of moulds and the resulting products made from them is somewhat uncertain.

Another difficult area is what constitutes an artistic work which is protected as a work of artistic craftsmanship, because a subjective judgment is often involved. Items of furniture have been brought before the courts to determine whether they are works of artistic craftsmanship. In *Hensher (George) Ltd* v. *Restawile Upholstery (Lancs)* [1976] AC 64, the court was not convinced that a prototype for a suite of furniture was a work of artistic craftsmanship. Originality is one hurdle that has to be overcome, but even if original, in order to qualify for protection, the work must also be of artistic value. The courts have indicated that the intention of the 'craftsman' or creator is an important factor. In *Merlet* v. *Mothercare* [1986] RPC 115, the intention of the claimant in making the baby hood was to serve a practical purpose, and the style and design of the hood was of secondary consideration, so the design did not qualify as a work of artistic craftsmanship.

Hot Topic . . .

IS FASHION ART?

A particularly interesting issue in this area is whether *haute couture* or designer dresses can constitute works of artistic craftsmanship. In a case concerning a dress design, *Burke and Margot Burke Ltd v. Spicers Designs* [1936] 1 Ch 400, the designer of a one-off dress design had shown her sketch to her seamstresses who made a dress to the design. The Court found that the dress was not protected as a work of artistic craftsmanship because the artistic qualities came from the designer, whereas the craftsmanship came from the seamstresses. Since almost all fashion designers work in the same way, if this decision was followed, it would suggest that none of their designs would be protected by copyright. However, in a later case also concerning dress designs, *Radley Gowns Ltd v. Costas Spyrou* [1975] FSR 455, the judge said that he did not consider the decision in *Burke v. Spicers* to be conclusive on the point regarding separate contributions towards the craftsmanship and artistic elements. He was also not convinced that just because a dress was mass-produced meant that it could not be a work of artistic craftsmanship. Two further cases, one in Australia and one in New Zealand, decided that there was no problem where the artist and the craftsperson were different people, so it is hoped that that position will be adopted in future

cases in the United Kingdom. For a review of all the cases concerning works of artistic craftsmanship up to 2000, see Clark, 'What is a work of artistic craftsmanship?', *Copyright World*, November 2000. In the first instance case of *Guild v. Eskandaar Ltd* [2001] FSR 38, which concerned the design of three fashion garments (a shirt, a sweater and a cardigan), all being 'very wide, unstructured garments inspired from ethnic or "peasant" dress', the court decided that such garments did not qualify as works of artistic craftsmanship (and only the design right issue was appealed to the Court of Appeal). The court reached this decision because the garments were machine-made as prototypes for mass production (which meant that they could not reasonably be regarded as works of craftsmanship) and there was no evidence that the designer intended to create works of art or saw herself as an artist.

The most recent case to consider copyright in clothing designs is the Court of Appeal decision in *Lambretta Clothing Co. Ltd v. Teddy Smith (UK) Ltd* [2005] RPC 6. Lambretta had brought copyright infringement proceedings against both Next and Teddy Smith for selling alleged copies of a track suit top. The top was of a generic shape, but Lambretta relied on copyright in its design drawing showing the positioning of the colour segments

on the top (namely, red sleeves and blue body, with a white zip). Before this case, it had been widely considered that the three-dimensional shape (if original) would be protected by unregistered design right, and the surface decoration (the colour layouts and any pattern on the fabric) would be protected by copyright in the design drawing showing them, in exactly the same way that copyright protects paintings, drawings, photographs and other works of a two-dimensional nature. However, the Court of Appeal held that there was no copyright protection in the colour patterns in the Lambretta top. It was a majority decision, with two of the three judges concluding that copyright protection is not available for any surface decoration elements of a design drawing for an article which features any three-dimensional aspects in the design drawing, as a result of the wording of s.51 of the 1988 Act. In this case, the outline shape of the top was shown on the design drawing which also showed the positioning of the colours. This case could effectively remove copyright protection for most designs which are a combination of two-dimensional and three-dimensional aspects, such as fashion and furniture designs (although protection may be available for more recent designs under the Community design right – see Chapter 22).

The first category of artistic works (that is, graphic work, photograph, collage or sculpture) is capable of protection 'irrespective of artistic quality'. This means that a very simple drawing will be protected by copyright, provided it is original. The case of *Kenrick & Co.* v. *Lawrence & Co.* [1890] 25 QBD 99 reminds us that it is expression and not idea that is protected. In that case, a work in question was a very simple drawing of a hand pointing to the voting box on a polling card. The Court held that if copyright did protect such a drawing, it would only have prevented others from making a virtually identical copy of it – it would not have prevented anyone from creating their own drawing using the idea of a hand as an indicator of where a voter should put their cross.

Other such artistic works (arguably devoid of artistic quality) that have been protected as copyright works are the design of a trade mark (*Karo Step Trade Mark* [1977] RPC 255), dress and knitting patterns (*Bernstein (J.) Ltd* v. *Sidney Murphy Ltd* [1981] RPC 303 and *Lerose Ltd* v. *Hawick Jersey International Ltd* [1973] FSR 15) and, in an unreported case in 1977, a signature.

In *Antiquesportfolio.com plc* v. *Rodney Fitch* [2001] FSR 23, the court addressed the question 'is a photograph of a static object protected by copyright?' The judges found that there was no direct authority on this point, so they looked initially to certain commentaries, including US works, for guidance. The conclusion the court reached was that almost all photographs will qualify as copyright works because of the photographer's skill in the selection of subject matter, lighting, positioning and camera angle. In that case, the photographs were of three-dimensional objects and had been taken in such a way as to exhibit certain colours and qualities of the objects – so the court concluded that they were copyright works. The case left open the possibility that a purely representational photograph (for example of another photograph or picture) might not qualify as a copyright work.

Summary

14.1 The 1988 Act protects a range of works from literary works to sound recordings.

14.2 Literary works include football coupons, instructions on weedkiller and compilations, as well as such matter as novels and magazines.

14.3 'Original' in the context of copyright works means that the work originates from the author and has not been copied.

14.4 A dramatic work includes a work of dance or mime.

Summary cont'd

14.5 A musical work consists of music without lyrics.

14.6 Artistic quality is not a criterion for copyright protection of an artistic work unless the claimant is claiming copyright for a work of artistic craftmanship.

Exercise

See end of Chapter 15.

Chapter 15

Subsistence (2)

Key words

> ▶ **Film** – a recording on any medium from which a moving image may by any means be produced.
> ▶ **Published edition** – a published edition of the whole or part of any literary, dramatic or musical work.
> ▶ **Sound recording** – a recording of sounds from which the sounds may be reproduced; or a recording of the whole or any part of a literary, dramatic or musical work, from which sounds reproducing the work or part may be produced.

15.1 Sound Recordings

A sound recording is defined as 'a recording of sounds from which the sounds may be reproduced; or a recording of the whole or any part of a literary, dramatic or musical work, from which sounds reproducing the work or part may be produced' regardless of the medium on which the recording is made or the method by which the sounds are reproduced or produced.

Although there is no 'originality' requirement for sound recordings, the Copyright, Designs and Patents Act 1988 specifically says that a sound recording, which is just a copy taken from a previous sound recording, will not be protected by copyright. This means that in the case of mass production of a CD, only the original recording will be a copyright work. However, if anyone copies any of the CDs that are sold, this would be an indirect infringement of the original sound recording (see Chapter 16).

The Duration of Copyright and Rights in Performances Regulations 1995 amended s.5 of the 1988 Act so that the soundtrack accompanying a film is now to be treated as part of the film and will be protected as part of the film, where the film is a copyright work. However, where the sound recording is played separately from the film, it will be protected as a sound recording. This avoids double protection for soundtrack rights when the soundtrack is really just part of the film performance and would be protected as such. Sound recordings will cover music recordings, soundtracks of films (when played separately from the film) and audio CDs (such as language courses and narrated stories). It is sound, and not just music, which is the subject matter of a sound recording.

Hot Topic . . .

DURATION OF COPYRIGHT PROTECTION FOR SOUND RECORDINGS

The British music industry, backed by Sir Cliff Richard, is currently campaigning for the extension of the duration of copyright in sound recordings. The Copyright, Designs and Patents Act 1988 states that copyright in these recordings will expire at the end of the period of 50 years from the end of the calendar year in which they were made. Alternatively, the copyright will expire 50 years from the end of the calendar year in which the recording was released.

This means that performers in the UK can receive royalties for 50 years until one of the trigger events referred to above has occurred. Once that period has expired, the performer, or usually their record company, will lose the exclusive right to exploit the recording.

However, if a songwriter writes a piece of music, the 1988 Act protects the copyright for the life of the songwriter plus 70 years, which means that the songwriter continues to have exclusive rights to the music in the song and to collect royalties for a much longer period than the artist who performed the song on the recording. For example, Sir Cliff Richard said that he was sometimes fed up of having performed his big hit, Living Doll, since 1959, and that had he not done so, the song would not have provided royalty earnings for the writer of the song, which will continue to accrue long after Sir Cliff's own rights as the recording artist have expired.

The British Phonographic Industry represents the record companies by campaigning for an equality between song writer and performer. In fact, it goes so far as to suggest that the United Kingdom should have the same system as the United States where the same copyright is protected for 95 years. The United States is not alone in having extended periods of copyright either – it is 60 years in India and 70 years in Australia and Brazil.

A review of copyright and intellectual property policies is currently underway in the United Kingdom by Andrew Gowers, but it remains to be seen whether any changes will result in the duration of protection of copyright in sound recordings.

15.2 Films

A film is defined as 'a recording on any medium from which a moving image may by any means be produced'. A film will cover video, television and movies. It will also include 'stills' that are produced from a moving film, even though they appear to be photographs; stills are specifically excluded from protection as artistic works. The digitisation of artistic works on computer in a way that enables moving images to be produced will constitute a film.

15.3 Broadcasts

A broadcast is any non-interactive 'electronic transmission of visual images, sounds or other information' that is either transmitted for simultaneous public reception in such a way that the public can lawfully receive it (for example, by means of legitimate decoding equipment if the transmission is encoded) or at a time determined solely by the broadcaster for presentation to the public. Prior to the New Copyright Regulations, the 1988 Act dealt with broadcasts and 'cable programmes' as distinct categories of work, the former being concerned only with transmission by wireless telegraphy, the latter with transmission by telecommunications systems other than wireless telegraphy. The new definition of broadcast does away with both of the old terms, although it clearly does not encompass all types of transmission, particularly 'on-demand' services. As mentioned in section 13.1, Internet transmissions (other than live webcasts and simulcasts or transmissions starting at times scheduled by the broadcaster) are excluded from the definition of broadcast on the basis that the works transmitted in such a service are themselves adequately protected as copyright works (for example, literary works, artistic works, music, sound recordings, films and so on). Furthermore, owners of rights in such works would have a remedy in case of infringement over the Internet by virtue of the two new rights granted by the New Copyright Regulations to both copyright owners and performers enabling them to prevent the communication of a work to the public (see Chapters 16 and 20).

The Broadcasting Acts of 1990 and 1996 impose specific requirements in relation to both digital and analogue broadcasting, covering satellite broadcasts, terrestrial television and radio.

15.4 Published Editions

Section 1 of the Act provides that copyright may subsist in 'the typographical arrangement of published editions'. 'Published edition' is defined in s.8 as a published edition of either the whole or part of any literary, dramatic or musical work. The typographical arrangement is made up of various elements: the style of the printed letters, their size, and the way in which they are laid out on the page. The typographical arrangement of a published edition will only be protected by copyright if it is new. If it simply reproduces the typographical arrangement of the previous edition of the work then copyright will not subsist in it. The section is intended to protect the effort expended in setting out the literary, dramatic or musical work; there is no such effort where a publisher is simply reproducing an old edition. The practical consequence of s.8 is that if you photocopy an extract from a book, you may be infringing at least two copyrights – copyright of the author of the text (if it is still within copyright) and the publisher's copyright in the typographical arrangement of the text.

Summary

15.1 Sound recordings need not be original to attract copyright protection but should not simply be a copy taken from another sound recording.

15.2 Copyright in sound recordings, generally speaking, lasts for 50 years whereas copyright in the underlying musical works lasts for the life of the songwriter plus 70 years.

15.3 The definition of 'film' covers video, television and movies.

15.4 The definition of 'broadcast' covers any 'electronic transmission of visual images, sounds or other information' which is transmitted for simultaneous reception at a time determined solely by the broadcaster.

15.5 Since the New Copyright Regulations, cable programmes are no longer considered as a distinct category of work from broadcasts.

15.6 Transmissions on the Internet and other on-demand services are subject to new rights to prevent the making available to the public of certain copyright works by electronic transmission.

15.7 The typographical arrangement of a literary, dramatic or musical work is also protected by copyright.

Exercise

State whether the following are protected by copyright, and the level of protection given:

(a) the latest CD by a popular band;
(b) the first showing on British television of the latest *King Kong* film;
(c) a politician's speech at their party's annual conference;
(d) a recording of a child's first words;
(e) the handouts prepared by a college tutor;
(f) a photograph of a boy band taken by a fan;
(g) *Agnes Grey* by Anne Brontë;
(h) Microsoft Word;
(i) a Girls Aloud doll;
(j) *Later with Jools Holland*;
(k) a passport photograph of a child carried in his mother's purse;
(l) the movements from *Dancing On Ice*.

Chapter 16

Infringement

Key words

- ▶ **Copying** – (in relation to a literary, dramatic, musical or artistic work) reproducing the work in any material form, including storing the work in any medium by electronic means.
- ▶ **Doing an act restricted by copyright** – doing an act in relation to the work as a whole or any substantial part of it.
- ▶ **Performance** – any mode of visual or acoustic presentation.
- ▶ **Rental** – making a copy of the work available for use, on terms that it will or may be returned, otherwise than for direct or indirect economic or commercial advantage.
- ▶ **Technological measures** – any technology, device or component which is designed, in the normal course of its operation, to protect a copyright work other than a computer program.

16.1 Introduction

The owner of copyright in a work has the exclusive right to do certain specified acts in respect of that work. This means that the owner has the right to prevent others from doing those acts. The owner can either grant a licence (or permission) to a third party to perform those acts or bring an action for infringement against any unauthorised performance of those acts.

The acts which the copyright owner can control in this way in respect of his copyright work are copying, issuing copies to the public, renting or lending the work to the public, performing, showing or playing the work in public and communicating the work to the public. These restricted acts extend to any adaptation of the work. An adaptation will itself be protected as an original copyright work. There are also various acts known as secondary infringements, all of which are subject to an additional knowledge requirement. These are discussed later in this chapter.

The restricted acts will only constitute infringement if they are done in relation to the whole or a substantial part of the protected work, but will be caught whether committed directly or indirectly. It is irrelevant, in the case of indirect infringement, whether the intervening act infringes copyright. If *A* writes a book in which *A* owns copyright, and licenses *B* to produce a French translation of that book (this would be an adaptation and would be an infringement of *A*'s work if done without *A*'s permission), *B*'s translation will not be an infringement. However, if *C*, without *A*'s permission, uses *B*'s French translation (with *B*'s permission) to write a Spanish translation, *C*'s work (or adaptation) will be an infringement of *A*'s copyright (done indirectly through *B*'s work) (*King Features Syndicate Inc.* v. *O & M Kleeman Ltd* [1941] 2 All ER 403). So for example, if a photographer uses an existing photograph as a reference point from which to set up a substantially similar or identical 'shoot' reproducing the particular composition of features selected and photographed by the photographer of the original work, his photograph may well be an infringement of the original photograph even though taken independently. In the case of *Baumann* v. *Fussell* [1978] RPC 485, the claimant had photographed two cockerels, but since their positioning in the photograph was a matter of 'luck', the defendant's copy of the subject matter (as distinct from the photograph) did not infringe.

In a case involving the band Oasis (*Creation Records Ltd* v. *News Group Newspapers Ltd* [1997] EMLR 444), an attempt was made to claim copyright in the scene featured in the photograph to be used on the cover of their *Be Here Now* album, in order to prevent *The Sun* from printing an unauthorised photograph taken at the photoshoot. However, it was held that the actual arrangement of the members of the group by a swimming pool did not constitute a copyright work. The scene was not a work of artistic craftsmanship because there was no craftsmanship, and it was not a collage because it only existed for a few hours and did not involve sticking anything. This is to be compared with the situation regarding somebody using an existing photograph (which is a copyright work) to recreate a specific arrangement as photographed for the purposes of taking a separate photograph and thereby possibly indirectly infringing copyright in the original photograph.

Many infringement cases will not involve reproduction of the entire copyright work but just a substantial part. This means working out what constitutes a substantial part. This should not be confused with finding that a substantial part of the infringed work comprises a part of the original work. Even if the defendant has added a great deal of material so that the copied work only forms a small proportion of the defendant's work, it will still be an infringement of the claimant's work if a substantial part of the claimant's work has been reproduced in the small section of the defendant's work. Substantiality is to be judged qualitatively and not just quantitatively. There is no general test and the facts of each case will determine the final decision (the test that you can make five changes to avoid infringement often quoted, is pure myth). In *Hawkes & Son (London) Ltd* v. *F Service Ltd* [1934] Ch 593, twenty eight bars of a musical piec(be a reproduction of a substantial part of that musical piece l twenty eight bars were so recognisable. In the case of *Designers Guild Ltd* v. *Russell Williams (Textiles) Ltd* [2001] FSR 11, the House of Lords provided some guidance as to how to decide whether a substantial part of a copyright work has been copied, although with four of the five Law Lords giving separate judgments, it is far from clearcut. The case involved a copy of a fabric design which featured a background of two different coloured stripes, overlaid with several impressionistic-style flowers scattered across the design. The trial judge found that there had been copying, and this issue was not appealed to the Court of Appeal, who therefore only had to decide whether a substantial part of the original design had been copied. The Court of Appeal concluded that the copy fabric adopted the same ideas and some of the techniques as the original, but that the resulting visual result was different, and so there was no infringement. The House of Lords overturned this decision, unanimously finding that a substantial part had been copied (although not all for the same reasons). Lord Millet said that the first stage was to identify those features which had been taken from the original and reproduced in the copy. When this list of elements had been compiled, there was no longer any need to consider the copy, but rather to ask whether that list of elements, taken together, amounted to an important part of the original design. If it did, then a substantial part had been copied. This means that it is possible for an infringing copy to appear quite different from the original design, provided that an important part of the original has been reproduced in the copy.

Infringing works will themselves only be copyright works if skill and effort have been expended, but not if they are just slavish copies. So, if *B* copies *A*'s work slavishly, *B*'s work will be an infringement of *A*'s work but will not be a copyright work in itself. If *C* then copies *B*'s work, that will not be an infringement of *B*'s work (because *B* had no copyright) but it would be an indirect infringement of *A*'s work.

It is also an infringement for someone, without permission of the copyright owner, to authorise another to do an infringing act. In *Moorhouse* v. *University of New South Wales* [1976] RPC 151 (HC Australia), photocopying machines were available in the university library for use by students and other library users, and one such user made two copies of a story from the claimant's book. The decision turned on whether or not the university could be said to have authorised students to copy literary works without licence and whether, therefore, the university authorised an infringement. Notices in library guides and on the photocopiers were held not to be adequate warnings against unlawful copying as they were not a clear enough statement. However, in the case of *CBS Songs Ltd* v. *Amstrad Consumer Electronics plc & Another* [1988] 2 All ER 484, Amstrad was found not to have authorised the making of infringing copies by advertising and selling twin-deck double speed tape recorders. In that case, it was relevant that the tape recorder did have a number of lawful, as well as unlawful, uses and that Amstrad could not be said to have any influence or control over the activities of those who purchased, and subsequently used, the tape recorders. In this context, in *CBS Inc.* v. *Ames Records & Tapes Ltd* [1982] Ch 91 it was said that authorisation 'can only come from someone having or purporting to have authority, and . . . an act is not authorised by someone who merely enables or possibly assists or even encourages another to do that act, but does not purport to have any authority which he can grant to justify the doing of the act'.

16.2 Copying

Copyright infringement by 'copying' applies to all types of copyright work but clearly the scope for reproduction of different works varies. In relation to artistic, literary, dramatic and musical works, copying means reproduction in any material form (including by storing in any medium by electronic means – so scanned images or digitised sound will be copies for these purposes). One common misconception is that reproduction in any material form includes carrying out the instructions in a literary work. To make a recipe from a recipe book is not reproduction of that recipe as a literary work (*Davis (J. and S.) (Holdings) Ltd* v. *Wright Health Group Ltd* [1988] RPC 403), nor is knitting a jumper to a knitting guide reproduction of that guide (*Brigid Foley Ltd* v. *Ellott* [1982] RPC 433). However, a design drawing for an intricate jumper could be infringed by the knitting of a jumper that reproduced that intricate pattern. This issue was considered in the case of *Jo-Y-Jo* v. *Matalan Retail Ltd & Another* [2000] ECDR 178, where the defendants had produced jumpers which the claimant claimed infringed copyright and design right in the drawings of the claimant's garments. Since the allegedly infringing garments did not reproduce any of the embroidery on the original garments, the copyright claim failed. However, as we saw in Chapter 14, the decision in the *Lambretta* case has now thrown doubt over the extent to which copyright can be enforced in the design drawings for a garment.

Artistic works may be infringed by reproducing a two-dimensional work in three dimensions and vice versa (s.17(3) of the 1988 Act) – however, in Chapter 17 we shall see that there are some specific acts within this category that are now not actionable as copyright infringement. In the case of architects' plans, it is an infringement to copy the plan by reproducing the plan or by building the building, and it will be infringement of a work of architecture to make another work of architecture to the same design. However, it is not an infringement to make a graphic two-dimensional work (drawing or photograph) of a building or of a sculpture, a model for a building or a work of artistic craftmanship in a public place, because s.62 of the Act specifically states so.

It is worth remembering that a dramatic work is defined as including 'a work of dance or mime' and that it is distinct from any literary or musical work that may be performed in the dramatic work. This is important for the question of infringement – a dramatic work may be infringed even if the language and/or the music is not copied.

Copying films or broadcasts is said by the 1988 Act to include photographing any image in these works. Copying a typographic arrangement of a published edition means making a facsimile copy, by which is meant not a transmission via a fax machine but rather, as the *Oxford English Dictionary* defines facsimile, making 'an exact copy, counterpart or representation'. The Act provides that a reduced or enlarged copy will also constitute a facsimile copy. In the House of Lords' decision in the case of *Newspaper Licensing Agency Ltd* v. *Marks & Spencer plc* [2003] 1 AC 551, the court held that Marks & Spencer had not infringed copyright in typographical arrangements by virtue of making further copies and circulating newspaper cuttings received from a press cuttings agency. The court held that in the case of a typographical arrangement, 'nothing short of a facsimile copy would suffice' for infringement purposes and that in order for there to be copying of a substantial part of a published edition, nothing less than reproduction of a layout of a page of a newspaper would be sufficient. Since Marks & Spencer's cuttings did not reproduce whole pages but merely articles, Marks & Spencer were found not to have infringed the typographical arrangement of the published newspapers concerned.

In cases concerning infringement of computer programs, determining copying has been made more difficult by the possibility of programmers using different computer languages to write programs, thus making a direct comparison difficult. In *Ibcos Computers Ltd* v. *Barclays Mercantile Highland Finance Ltd* [1994] FSR 275, copying was proved by the existence of marked and unexplained similarities between the claimant's and the defendant's code – for instance, spelling mistakes and unused lines of code. The judge set out the test of copyright infringement in a case of non-literal copying as being: (a) is there a work?; (b) is it original?; (c) has there been copying?; and, if so, (d) was this of a substantial part? He said that it was not only right to consider 'literal similarities' but also the program structure and design features.

Transient and/or incidental copying which is an integral and essential part of a technological process and the sole purpose of which is to enable either transmission of the work in a network (for example, on the Internet) or lawful use of the work and which has no independent economic significance no longer constitutes an infringement, following the implementation of the New Copyright Regulations.

Hot Topic . . .

THE DIFFERENCE BETWEEN COPYING IDEAS AND THE EXPRESSION OF THOSE IDEAS

We have already considered the idea/expression divide in relation to deciding what is protected by copyright. The distinction is equally important when considering copyright infringement. Even where it is obvious that a third party has copied an idea, this will not necessarily be a copyright infringement unless the form of expression of the idea has also been copied.

Determining whether someone has copied the idea, or the expression of the idea, can sometimes be difficult. The *Designers Guild* case involved the reproduction of a striped fabric with impressionistic-styled flowers scattered over the stripes. The Court of Appeal had considered that all that the defendant had taken from the claimant's fabric was the same techniques and ideas which it used when creating its own fabric (that is, the paint techniques and the idea of flowers scattered over the stripes). However, the House of Lords overturned the Court of Appeal's decision, finding that on the application of the proper qualitative (rather than just quantitive) test for copying, which concentrated on the similarities rather than the differences between the two designs, the

defendant's design *was* sufficiently similar for it to amount to an infringement. The defendant had taken more than just the ideas and techniques, but had also copied the way in which they had been expressed in the form of the claimant's design. The case of *Navitaire Inc.* v. *easyJet Airline Co. Ltd* [2004] EWHC 1725 concerned the issue of whether a software program which produced a very similar looking online flight booking system as the original program infringed copyright. The judge referred to the recitals from the Software Directive which say that only the expression of a computer program is protected and that ideas and principles which underlie its interfaces are not protected by copyright. He therefore found that easyJet had not infringed the copyright in the main software for its online flight bookings program which had been written for it by the claimant, when easyJet commissioned another software company to write a new program which, although it did not copy the source code of the original program, produced a system which looked very similar to and worked in a very similar way to the original program. It was therefore possible for two completely different

computer programs to produce an identical result without infringing copyright, because copyright protected the embodiment of the functional effects in the software, rather than the functional effects themselves.

The latest case to consider this issue was *Baigent and Leigh* v. *The Random House Group*, 7 April 2006, Smith J, where the co-authors of *The Holy Blood and the Holy Grail* ('HBHG') claimed that Dan Brown's novel *The Da Vinci Code* copied the 'central theme' of HBHG which tied together the facts and ideas of the book. HBHG was described by the authors as historical conjecture. The judge therefore had to decide whether the ideas expressed in the central theme of HBHG, as identified by the authors, were capable of being protected by copyright. The judge was critical of the 'central theme' as defined by the authors, and described it as an 'artificial contrivance' designed to create an illusion of a central theme in order to establish copyright infringement. He found that the central theme was nothing more than a series of generalised ideas and facts which were not capable of being protected by copyright. The decision suggests that it is harder for authors of factual books or documents to protect the use of the results of their research by others than it is for authors of fictional works. Copyright will only protect the structure or 'architecture' of the work, rather than the facts and ideas contained in it.

16.3 Issuing Copies, Performances in Public and Communicating to the Public

All copyright works may be infringed by the issue of copies to the public. 'Issuing' means putting into circulation copies of a work not previously put into circulation anywhere in the EEA. This means that once a copy work has legitimately been put into circulation in any country within the EEA (either by the copyright owner or with the copyright owner's permission) the copyright owner cannot prevent subsequent circulation (whether by sale, loan, hire or distribution) of that copy. However, the copyright owner still has the right to prevent the making of other copies of that one legitimately circulated copy.

Even though the copyright owner cannot prevent the sale or other issue of any legitimately made copies, he can prevent the unauthorised rental of copies of such works to the public (this is discussed further below).

Performing, showing and playing of works in public are also acts of infringement if done without licence. Performance, which means 'any form of visual or acoustic presentation', relates to literary, dramatic and musical works, and showing or playing relates to sound recordings, films and broadcasts. The performance must be in public to be an infringement. What constitutes 'in public' will be a question of fact and degree (and common sense) but examples of what have been held to comprise public performances are music played over a loudspeaker system to workers in their place of work (*Ernest Turner etc. Ltd* v. *Performing Right Society Ltd* [1943] Ch 167) and playing of music by a shop that is trying to sell the records being played (*Performing Right Society* v. *Harlequin Record Shops* [1979] FSR 233).

In each of these cases, when the performance or playing or showing is done by means of an apparatus for receiving the images or sounds, the sender of the images or sounds and the performers will not be guilty of infringement; the person responsible for operating the relevant apparatus is the primary infringer.

It is also an infringement of most copyright works to communicate the work to the public by electronic transmission including by broadcasting and by inclusion in an on-demand or other interactive service (that is, 'in such a way that members of the public may access it from a place and at a time individually chosen by them').

16.4 Adaptation

This act of infringement only relates to literary, dramatic and musical works. 'Adaptation' means a translation of a literary or dramatic work, the conversion of a dramatic work into a non-dramatic form (and vice versa), the reproduction of a literary or dramatic work in a form whereby the story is conveyed by pictures suitable for inclusion in a book, magazine or periodical and, in relation to a musical work, means an arrangement or transcription. Adaptation also includes conversion of a computer program from one computer language to another (from object code to source code, or from FORTRAN to COBOL). As a result of the EC Software Directive, implemented into English law by ss.50(A)–(C) of the 1988 Act, a lawful acquirer of software has an implied licence to copy to the extent necessary for lawful use of the software.

16.5 Rental Right

The 1988 Act provides that the rental of a literary, dramatic or musical work, an artistic work other than a work of architecture or applied art, a film or a sound recording is an infringement if done without the copyright owner's consent. 'Rental' is defined as an arrangement where, for payment, use is allowed on terms that the copy of the work will, or may, be returned. 'Rental' and 'lending' do not include, among other exceptions, making available for public performance, playing, showing or communicating to the public.

16.6 Secondary Infringement

All of the acts referred to above are instances of 'primary' infringement (although not labelled as such in the Act). Acts of secondary infringement are dealt with in ss.22–26 and are the acts committed by persons dealing in infringing copies. The secondary infringer is one step removed from the act of unlawful reproduction or performance. There must already have been an act of 'primary' infringement in order for an act of secondary infringement to be committed.

Another precondition of secondary infringement is that it should be done in the course of business or for profit or gain and that there is some level of knowledge or reason to believe that the works dealt in are infringing.

The acts of secondary infringement are: importing into the United Kingdom (otherwise than for private and domestic use); possessing, exhibiting or distributing in the course of a business; selling, letting for hire or offering for sale or hire; and distributing other than in the course of a business to an extent that will prejudicially affect the owner of a copyright (so if a private individual distributes copies of infringing software over the Internet as freeware, this will not be in the course of a business, but will prejudicially affect the copyright owner who is licensing the software for a licence fee commercially).

Sections 24, 25 and 26 are concerned with the actions of providing the means or the premises or the apparatus to enable an infringing act to be committed. Section 24(1) prohibits the making, importing, possessing in the course of business or the selling, or hiring or exposing for sale or hire of any item that is designed or adapted for making copies of a particular copyright work, if the person believes, or has reason to believe, that the item will be used to make infringing copies of that work. The position on copying works by faxing them or transmitting them by means of a telecommunications system (otherwise than by communication to the public) to a machine where a copy will be produced for the recipient is specifically covered by s.24(2). The person instigating the transmission must have the requisite knowledge.

What level of knowledge or suspicion is required for secondary infringement was addressed in the case of *Hutchison Personal Communications Ltd* v. *Hook Advertising Ltd* [1995] FSR 365. In that case, knowledge of allegations of infringement, the facts of which had yet to be proved, was held not to be sufficient to constitute knowledge of infringement for the purposes of secondary infringement. However, in the case of *Vermaat and Powell* v. *Boncrest Limited* [2002] FSR 21, the judge stated that for there to be sufficient knowledge for secondary infringement, the defendant must have reason to believe that there is an infringement rather than just a suspicion. The judge expanded on this by stating that the person must have notice of the facts, with sufficient information identifying the copyright work (with a copy of the work or access to view the copyright work) and that such information must be given sufficiently in advance so that he can have time to 'evaluate the facts and convert them into a reasonable belief'.

The question of when an alleged infringer will have the requisite knowledge or reason to believe was considered in the case of *Nouveau Fabrics Ltd* v. *Voyage Decoration Ltd and Dunelm Soft Furnishings Ltd* [2004] EWHC 895. In that case, Voyage, an importer and distributor of fabrics, was accused of importing and selling an infringing copy of Nouveau's fabric design which was protected by copyright. Voyage denied that it was aware at the time it began importing the fabric that it might infringe Nouveau's copyright and that it did not have reason to believe until Nouveau made its first complaint that the fabric might be infringing. It also relied upon evidence from its Italian supplier of the fabric of the independent creation of the fabric design by the supplier as a reason for defending Nouveau's infringement claims. It was held that Voyage ought to have known that the fabric had been copied from Nouveau's design when it became clear, after pressure from Nouveau to disclose this information, that the Italian supplier could not provide satisfactory evidence of the origin of the allegedly infringing fabric design. Accordingly, it is possible to be found to have the requisite reason to believe by not taking sufficient steps to discover the true origins of an allegedly infringing article having been made aware of a potential infringement.

16.7 Copy Protection Devices, Electronic Rights Management Information and Decoders

In an effort to prevent acts of infringement, devices are constantly being devised to make unlawful copying more difficult. Copy protection devices can, of course, be overridden or incapacitated and therefore if the legal protections offered by the 1988 Act against infringements are to be effective, these devices need to be offered protection under the law.

Under s.296 of the 1988 Act, if someone issues or communicates to the public (with the permission of the copyright owner) a computer program which is protected by some form of copy protection device or system, they will have the same rights as the copyright owner has against infringers, against anyone who makes, imports, distributes, sells, hires etc. means to get around the copy protection device or who publishes information enabling someone to get around the copy protection device. Originally, s.296 applied to all copyright works but the New Copyright Regulations amended it so that it now applies just to computer programs, and then added further provisions (ss.296ZA–296ZD) to offer equivalent protection for all other copyright works to which effective technological measures have been applied. An effective technological measure is: 'any technology, device or component which is designed, in the normal course of its operation, to protect a copyright work other than a computer program' from infringement and which is controlled by the copyright owner through some means such as 'encryption, scrambling or other transformation of the work'. It is now a criminal offence to make, import, sell, hire, offer or expose for sale or hire, advertise, possess in the course of business or distribute (whether in the course of business or otherwise to such an extent as to prejudice the copyright owner) any 'device, product or component which is primarily designed, produced or adapted for the purpose of enabling or facilitating the circumvention of effective technological measures'. Equally, it is a criminal offence to provide, promote, advertise or market any service the purpose of which is to enable or faciliate the circumvention of effective technological measures. It is, however, a defence that the defendant did not know or have reason to believe that the device or service could enable avoidance of effective technological measures.

Section 296ZE provides for a situation where certain permitted acts in relation to copyright works are being prevented by an effective technological measure. This applies to all copyright works other than computer programs. In such a case someone who wishes to exercise one of the permitted acts in relation to that copyright work may serve a notice of complaint on the Secretary of State who will then require the copyright owner or exclusive licensee to provide the required access (unless there are already arrangements in place, such as a licensing agreement, allowing such access). The complaint notice route is not available where the copyright work in question is available via an on-demand service or where the complainant has already obtained the copyright work unlawfully.

The New Copyright Regulations also introduced protection for electronic rights management information – this is information concerning the identity of the author, the work, and terms and conditions of use of the work. Anyone who 'knowingly and without authority, removes or alters electronic rights management information' or who 'distributes, imports for distribution or communicates to the public copies of a copyright work from which electronic rights management information ... has been removed or altered without authority' when they know or have reason to believe that by doing so an infringement will be committed or concealed or made easier, will be open to an action for infringement by the copyright owner or exclusive licensee of the work to which the electronic rights management information relates.

There are also provisions in the 1988 Act concerning reception of broadcasts where recipients avoid payment of charges applicable to the reception, and concerning distribution, manufacture and possession of unauthorised decoders (that is, devices which unscramble any form of encryption, password and so on which is intended to prevent viewing of broadcasts unless appropriate payments have been made).

The case of *R* v. *Mainwaring* [2002] FSR 20 concerned a criminal prosecution for breach of s.297 of the 1988 Act (as amended by the Conditional Access (Unauthorised Decoders) Regulations 2000). The court stated that 'unauthorised' in relation to a decoder meant that the decoder allowed an encrypted transmission to be received in intelligible form without payment of the fee which the broadcaster usually charges. In this case, the broadcast in question was not intended to be received in the United Kingdom and so the broadcaster had not made arrangements to collect fees from potential recipients. But the court said that this made no difference, otherwise the legislation (which emanates from a Directive) could be avoided merely by selling decoders in countries other than the country where the broadcast was intended to be received. This would defeat the purpose of the European Directive aimed at removing geographic barriers.

Additional provisions allowing for search warrants and forfeiture of unauthorised decoders were added by the Copyright, etc and Trade Marks (Offences and Enforcement) Act 2002 which came into force on 20 November 2002.

16.8 Infringing Copy

Obviously, an infringing copy is any copy of a copyright work that has been made without the permission of the copyright owner. It also includes copies of works that were made legitimately outside the United Kingdom (for example, with the permission of the owner of the copyright in another country, who may be a different person from the copyright owner in the United Kingdom) but were then imported or proposed to be imported into the United Kingdom, when the making of such copy in the United Kingdom would have been an infringing act or a breach of an exclusive licence agreement (s.27).

This provision of the 1988 Act is subject to the operation of EC competition law. In particular, s.27(5) protects any enforceable community right (such as freedom of movement of goods). This conflict between competition law and the exercise of copyright is considered in more detail in Chapter 24.

16.9 Remedies

The remedies available to a copyright owner (and to an exclusive licensee) for copyright infringement are to bring a civil action (for damages or an injunction, and delivery up or destruction of the copies, disclosure of the names of suppliers and sometimes customers, legal costs and interest) and/or to prompt a criminal prosecution either privately or by the enforcement authorities (commonly, Trading Standards) for one or more of the criminal offences under the 1988 Act. In addition s.100 of the 1988 Act gives the copyright owner or a person authorised by him the right to seize and detain infringing copies which are openly on sale, subject to certain conditions.

In a case of infringement, a claimant may wish to apply for an interim injunction, because the continued reproduction of infringing articles pending a full hearing could put the copyright owner out of business or be highly prejudicial in some other way to the copyright owner. The matters that must be proved for the grant of an interim injunction were established in the case of *American Cyanamid Co.* v. *Ethicon Ltd* [1975] AC 396 and more recently endorsed in *Series 5 Software Ltd* v. *Philip Clarke & Others* [1996] FSR 273.

In the case of *Microsoft Corp.* v. *Plato Technology Ltd* [1999] FSR 834, the innocence of the defendant, who was found to have been dealing in counterfeit copies of Microsoft software, was found by the court to be a justification for limiting the scope of the injunction granted to the claimant.

An exclusive copyright licensee will have the same rights as the copyright owner in respect of an infringement committed after the granting of his licence. Except for the application for interim relief, which the exclusive licensee may bring on his own, all other infringement actions brought by the exclusive licensee must also involve the copyright owner. Either the claimant licensee will get the copyright owner's agreement to be joined as co-claimant or the exclusive licensee will join the copyright owner as a second defendant. In the latter case, the copyright owner is not liable for any costs awarded in the case unless he takes part in the proceedings.

A non-exclusive licensee now has the right to bring an action for copyright infringement where the infringing act was directly connected to a prior licensed act of the licensee – s.101A, introduced by the New Copyright Regulations. As with an exclusive licence, it must be in writing and signed by the copyright owner, but must also expressly grant the right of action under s.101A. The non-exclusive licensee then has the same rights and remedies as the copyright owner would have had.

In proceedings relating to copyright infringement, there are a number of presumptions laid down by the 1988 Act (in ss.27(4), 93A, 104, 105 and 106) that allow certain issues to be assumed and that shift the burden of proof to the other party.

Directive 2004/48/EC of the European Parliament and of the Council of 29 April 2004 on the enforcement of intellectual property rights ('the Enforcement Directive') is designed to harmonise sanctions and remedies across the EU and signal to Member States certain measures (such as the publication of judicial decisions and the development of professional codes of conduct) that would contribute to the fight against counterfeiting and piracy. The Directive includes procedures covering evidence and provisional measures such as injunctions and seizure. Remedies available to right holders include the destruction, recall or permanent removal from the market of illegal goods, as well as financial compensation, injunctions and damages. It also includes a right of information allowing judges to order people to reveal the names and addresses of those involved in distributing the illegal goods or services, together with details of the quantities and prices involved.

A proposed second Enforcement Directive (com(2005)276), which was revised in May 2006, states that Member States shall ensure that all intentional infringements of an intellectual property right on a commercial scale, and attempting, aiding or abetting and inciting such infringements, shall be treated as criminal offences. This is a further attempt to strengthen measures against counterfeiting and piracy, but has attracted fierce criticism from the software industry who are concerned that with so many patents whose validity is questionable, every software producer may potentially be committing a criminal offence if they are found to have infringed a valid patent.

Remedies are considered in more detail in Chapter 21.

16.10 Criminal Offences

Broadly speaking, most of the acts constituting infringement of copyright are also criminal offences if the requisite knowledge can be shown. Now that the New Copyright Regulations have introduced a new criminal offence of communicating a copyright work to the public in the course of a business or in circumstances prejudicial to the owner, service providers are also liable to prosecution. This is in addition to the fact that the New Copyright Regulations now give the High Court the power to grant injunctions against service providers where the service provider has actual knowledge of another person using their service to infringe copyright. Also, where an infringement constituting a criminal offence is committed by a company, the directors, managers, secretary and similar officers could also be guilty of an offence if the act was committed with that person's 'consent or connivance'. The presumptions referred to above do not apply in criminal proceedings (except s.27(4)) because the burden of proof in criminal proceedings is different from that in civil proceedings. Conviction for criminal offences under the Act can result in imprisonment or a fine or both. In addition, there can be an order for delivery up of infringing copies, which can be enforced by the Trading Standards Office. Trading Standards officers, HM Revenue & Customs and the police have rights under the Act (as amended by the Copyright, etc and Trade Marks (Offences and Enforcement) Act 2002) and other legislation to search for and seize infringing material and seek orders for delivery up and forfeiture of infringing material in connection with offences under the Act.

Summary

16.1 The copyright owner is the only person entitled to deal in the copyright work unless another person has a licence from the copyright owner. Anyone else copying, issuing copies to the public, performing etc. a substantial part of the work without the owner's authority infringes the copyright. 'Substantial' is judged qualitatively and not quantitatively.

16.2 Issuing copies of the work means making a work available to the public that was not previously in circulation anywhere in the EEA.

16.3 Any translation of a copyright work is an adaptation and amounts to infringement if done without the owner's authority.

16.4 The copyright owner's consent is needed before a copyright work can be rented out for profit.

16.5 Dealing in infringing goods (for example, importing) amounts to secondary infringement provided that the person dealing with the goods has the requisite knowledge.

Summary cont'd

16.6 Infringing copies include works legitimately made outside the United Kingdom but then imported into the United Kingdom, when making the works in the United Kingdom would have amounted to infringement or breach of an exclusive licence.

16.7 A range of remedies is available that includes damages, injunctions and delivery up or destruction of the copies.

16.8 The activities that fall under secondary infringement are also criminal offences.

Exercises

16.1 Consider whether the following are likely to lead to successful copyright infringement proceedings:

(a) Six bars in the refrain of a chart-topping song are identical to an extract from a piece of classical music composed in 1788.

(b) *A* Co. Ltd produce dining chairs of an unusual shape with African carvings on the back rest. These are available for sale in limited numbers at £2,000 each. *B* Co. Ltd start producing chairs of a similar shape but decorated with different art work and of generally inferior quality to be sold at £200 each.

(c) *C* Co. Ltd are the UK copyright owners of Wordplan 7, a word-processing program. It has come to their attention that *D* Co. Ltd are importing Wordplan 7 from India.

16.2 *E* is the Student Housing Officer for *F* University. As part of her job, she is required to provide information for new students about travelling and living in the locality.

Each summer, she spends time consulting rail and bus timetables, as well as investigating cheap but decent accommodation. When the information is collated, she writes a series of articles for the university's student journal with extracts from bus and rail timetables, adding useful hints on dealing with difficult landladies. The articles are usually published in *Fresher's Week* and are always an immediate success.

Last autumn, *G* collected the articles. She spent a few hours in the library extracting the main timetables and then added a list of cheap guest-houses obtained from the university telephone directories. She also listed a few cheap places to eat in town. The result was one long article on where to go in the area surrounding *F* University.

Advise *E*, who objects to *G*'s activities.

Chapter 17

Defences

Key words

▶ **Fair dealing for purposes of criticism or review** – will not infringe copyright if there is a sufficient acknowledgement, and the work has been made available to the public.

▶ **Fair dealing for purposes of reporting a current event** – will not infringe copyright if there is a sufficient acknowledgement, but does not apply to photographs.

▶ **Incidental inclusion** – casual, inessential, subordinate or merely background.

17.1 Introduction

In an action for infringement of copyright, there are a number of approaches that the defendant can adopt:

(a) challenge the existence of copyright or the claimant's ownership of copyright;
(b) deny the infringement;
(c) claim to have been entitled, because of a permission granted, to do the act in question, or argue that it is within one of the statutory fair dealing exemptions or claim public interest or EC competition law rights.

A claim of ignorance of the law, either as to the fact that copyright subsisted in the claimant's work or that the act committed constituted infringement of that copyright, will not work as a defence (*Mansell* v. *Valley Printing Co.* [1908] 2 Ch 441).

Ignorance of subsistence of copyright is, however, relevant as to damages. If the person charged with infringement can satisfy the court that he did not realise that copyright subsisted in the work that has been copied, then damages will not be awarded in respect of that period of ignorance. In the case of secondary infringement, as already discussed, an element of knowledge is required for the infringement to be actionable in the first place. The infringement only occurs if the person 'knows or has reason to believe' that he is dealing with an infringing copy of a copyright work.

17.2 Acts Permitted by Licence

An infringement is the doing of any of the acts restricted by copyright 'without the licence of the copyright owner'. Although assignments of copyright must be in writing signed by the copyright owner, there are no such formal requirements for the granting of licences of copyright (s.90). There are, however, special rights granted to an exclusive and non-exclusive licensee of copyright to pursue infringers, and to benefit from such rights the licensee must have been granted the licence in writing signed by the copyright owner (s.92 and s.101A). In the case of *Biotrading* v. *Biohit Ltd* and *Labsystems* v. *Biohit Ltd* [1998] FSR 109, the definition of an exclusive licensee for the purposes of s.92 was considered and the case made clear that all that was required was that somebody should be given the exclusive right to 'exercise a right'; therefore, in that case, the second claimant had been granted an exclusive right to import the products in question and was held by the court to be an exclusive licensee for the purposes of s.92 and entitled to bring an action for infringement in its own name.

A licence can be granted expressly in writing or orally or can, in certain cases, be implied (but as seen above, before the licensee takes court action, the licence will have to be recorded in writing, and an assignment of past rights of action will have to be entered into with the copyright owner if damages are to be recovered for any acts commited before the licence in writing was signed). In the case of *Film Investors Overseas Services SA & Another* v. *Home Video Channel Ltd* (*trading as the Adult Channel*) [1997] EMLR 347, an action for copyright infringement failed because the court found that the claimants knew, or strongly suspected, for several years that the defendants were carrying on the activity complained of and had, as a result, consented to or acquiesced in the activity.

Courts have implied licences of copyright in respect of commissioned copyright works for value. In a number of cases the courts have implied a limited licence to the commissioner to give effect to the obvious intention of the contract of commission. In *Cala Homes (South) Ltd* v. *Alfred McAlpine Homes East Ltd* [1995] FSR 1818, the Court found sufficient involvement by the commissioner in the drawing of plans to find joint ownership. The judge said that, had he not found sufficient involvement, he would have found an exclusive licence implied in favour of the commissioner. In the case of *Pasterfield* v. *Denham & Another* [1999] FSR 168, although the judge found a transfer of equitable ownership from the designer to the commissioner, he said that, had that not been his finding, he would have found an implied licence since the designer was aware of the commissioner's intentions to use the commissioned design in a promotional leaflet.

In *Griggs* v. *Evans* [2005] FSR 31 the court had to decide whether the designer of a new logo for Dr Martens footwear had retained the copyright in the logo for uses beyond use as point of sale material in the United Kingdom. The owners of Dr Martens footwear argued that there was an express or an implied term in their contract with the designer that they would own all the copyright in the new logo. These kinds of dispute are unfortunately all too common, and yet could easily be avoided by the parties entering into written contracts at the outset, setting out who will own the copyright in the designs to be created. In this case, the court found that it would never have been contemplated that the designer would retain the copyright in the logo and ordered the copyright to be assigned to the footwear company. The case sets out useful guidance as to when a licence will be implied and when an assignment of copyright will be implied.

The problem with implied licences and, to some extent, oral licences is establishing their exact terms. What is the duration and extent of the licence, to whom did it extend, were any royalties payable, in what circumstances could it be brought to an end by the licensor?

Provided that the defendant in an infringement action can prove to the satisfaction of the court that the allegedly infringing act was covered by a valid licence, the claim of infringement will fail.

17.3 Permitted Acts

The 1988 Act contains statutory permissions, or exceptions, to the exclusive rights of the copyright owner. Many of these have come about as a result of case decisions over the years that acknowledged the need for certain fair exceptions. A number of changes were implemented by the New Copyright Regulations to comply with the Copyright Directive.

Section 28A – making of temporary copies

One of the more important changes made by the New Copyright Regulations was a new permitted act for temporary copies. This amendment was seen as fundamental to the lawful functioning of the Internet, because in transmitting information over the Internet it is necessary for transient copies to be made on various computers. The new section provides that copyright in the various copyright works (other than a computer program or a database – these two types of work having been legislated for pursuant to two existing Directives) will not be infringed by the making of 'a temporary copy which is transient or incidental, which is an integral and essential part of a technological process and the sole purpose of which is to enable a transmission of the work in a network between third parties by an intermediary' (that is, over the Internet) or 'a lawful use of the work', provided that such copying has no independent economic significance.

Section 29 – research and private study

Anyone may make a copy of a literary, dramatic, musical or artistic work for the purpose of private study or for research for a non-commerical purpose provided that, in both cases, it is 'fair dealing' and, in respect of research, that it is accompanied by a sufficient acknowledgement (unless that would be impossible for reasons of practicality or otherwise). The New Copyright Regulations added specific references to acts relating to the observing, studying and testing of the functionality of a computer program which will not amount to fair dealing unless they fall within the acts permitted under s.50BA.

'Fair dealing' is not defined in the Act but case law suggests that the following will be relevant factors:

(a) whether the copying deprives the copyright owner of a sale which would otherwise have been made;
(b) the size or proportion of the piece copied; and
(c) whether the infringer will obtain a substantial financial benefit from the infringement.

Discussions of what constitutes fair dealing can be found in the cases of *Beloff* v. *Pressdram Ltd* [1973] RPC 765 and *Hubbard* v. *Vosper* [1972] 2 QB 84. *Hubbard* v. *Vosper* concerned a critical book about Scientology written and published by the defendant. This book included extracts from the claimant's books, bulletins and letters about Scientology. It was found by the Court of Appeal that, even though a substantial taking was shown, this could amount to 'fair dealing'. Fair dealing is a question of fact and impression. Lord Denning held that relevant factors to be considered could include the number and extent of extracts and the use made of the extracts. If the extracts are used as the basis for comment, review and criticism, that may be fair dealing. If they are used to convey the same information as the author, for a rival purpose, that may be unfair. Another relevant factor was the proportion of the copied part in relation to the comment added. The extent to which the work has been circulated will also be a relevant factor.

The section also exempts copying carried out by someone (other than the person who will be carrying out the research or study) on that person's behalf (including by a librarian) but makes clear that, in such cases, multiple copies are not permitted. Other forms of copying by librarians which are exempted are covered by ss.37–44.

Section 30 – criticism, review and news reporting

Reproduction of a copyright work for the purpose of criticism or review is permitted, provided that it is fair dealing, that there is a sufficient acknowledgment of the work and that the work has been made available to the public. Making available to the public can be by any means, including by means of an electronic retrieval system, by rental or lending, or by communicating the work to the public. However, unauthorised acts resulting in the making available will not count for the purposes of this permitted act. Fair dealing for the purposes of reporting a current event will not infringe the copyright in any work, other than a photograph, provided that there is a sufficient acknowledgement. However, with sound recordings, films or broadcasts, an acknowledgement will not be necessary if it would be impossible for reasons of practicality or otherwise. The exclusion of photographs must not be forgotten – this means that a newspaper, for example, should always obtain prior permission to use a photograph before going to press.

In *Newspaper Licensing Agency Ltd* v. *Marks & Spencer plc* [1999] RPC 536, Marks & Spencer's claim that it was entitled to distribute newspaper cuttings to its staff without a licence from the NLA, on the basis that it benefited from the defence in s.30(2) of reporting current events, failed. In that case Lightman J found that 'the daily programme of circulating and distributing cuttings of articles of interest to Marks & Spencer did not fall within the language of s.30(2), namely 'reporting current events'. Futhermore, the course followed by Marks & Spencer did not constitute 'fair dealing', since there was wholesale copying of material which went far beyond what was necessary to report current events. As discussed in Chapter 16, this decision was overturned on appeal on other grounds.

In *Fraser-Woodward Ltd* v. *BBC* [2005] EWHC 472 a photographer sued the BBC for unauthorised use of his photographs of Victoria Beckham in a programme called *Tabloid Tales*. The BBC successfully ran a fair dealing defence on the grounds that they used the photographs to criticise and review celebrity journalism. Some of the criticism related to the photographs themselves – namely, whether photographs taken of the Beckhams apparently off their guard were in fact prearranged with them – but the court held that the criticism could extend to the underlying philosophy or ideas of the work being criticised. In that case, the criticism was of a certain style of journalism.

Section 31 – incidental inclusion of copyright material

Incidental inclusion of a copyright work in an artistic work, sound recording, film or broadcast will not be an infringement and neither will the issue to the public, playing, showing or communicating to the public of the result of that incidental inclusion be an infringement. Incidental, but deliberate, inclusion of music will be an infringement. The wording of the 1988 Act suggests that, in the case of all other works, whether the incidental inclusion is deliberate or not is irrelevant.

The question of what comprises 'incidental inclusion' was considered in the case of *IPC Magazines Ltd* v. *MGN Ltd* [1998] FSR 431. This case concerned a television advertisement for the *Sunday Mirror* and a free women's supplement. That free supplement was compared with the claimant's magazine *Woman* and in the television advertisement the magazine cover of *Woman* was displayed. Richard McCombe QC said in this case that 'incidental' must be given its normal meaning (since it is not defined in the Act), which means casual, inessential, subordinate or merely background. He decided that the inclusion of the magazine cover of *Woman* in the *Sunday Mirror* advertisement had been an essential part of the advertisement for the *Sunday Mirror* free women's supplement.

In the case of *Football Association Premier League Ltd & Others* v. *Panini UK Ltd* [2003] EWCA Civ 995, the inclusion of Football Association badges and logos in photographs taken by a company for use on football cards for sticker albums was argued by the defendants to be 'incidental' and therefore allowed by virtue of s.31. The Court of Appeal held that the appearance of the badges and logos on the football cards was not incidental. In deciding whether the use was incidental, it was proper to ask why the work in question had been included, considering commercial and aesthetic reasons. Here, the use of the team and the logos in the stickers was not incidental.

Sections 31A–F (inclusive) – visual impairment

The New Copyright Regulations introduced various new provisions providing exceptions to copyright infringment concerning use in relation to the visually impaired.

Section 32 – things done for instruction or examination

Literary, artistic, dramatic and musical works may be copied or performed by a person giving or receiving instruction but not if done by reprographic process (for example, on a photocopier). The exception which most students would rely upon for photocopying relevant extracts and articles, is s.29 (but that requires fair dealing to be shown as well). Section 32 is aimed at allowing a teacher to reproduce a literary work by writing it up on a whiteboard or projector and allowing the students to transcribe from the whiteboard or direct from the literary work in question. The New Copyright Regulations introduced conditions that copies be accompanied by sufficient acknowledgement, unless it would be impossible to do so, and that the instruction was for a non-commercial purpose. If that literary, dramatic, musical or artistic works has been made available to the public, then it can be copied for instruction or preparation of instruction on the same terms as above, save that it must be fair dealing with the work, but there is no requirement that it be for a non-commerical purpose.

Films, sound recordings and broadcasts may be copied in a film or soundtrack (by the instructor or student) for the purpose of instruction on the subject of the making of films and/or soundtracks. In each case, the New Copyright Regulations introduced conditions of there being a sufficient acknowledgement (unless impossible) and the instruction being provided for a non-commercial purpose.

Anything done for the purpose of examination (for example, setting the questions and communicating them to the candidates) will not be a copyright infringement (although the Act specifically prohibits the photocopying of a musical work for use by an examination candidate to perform the work). The New Copyright Regulations introduced a requirement for sufficient acknowledgement to accompany the questions (unless impossible). If a copy of a copyright work made under this section is subsequently dealt in (for example, sold or hired), the subsequent act will be an infringement.

Section 33 – anthologies for educational use

It is permissible to include a short passage from a published literary or dramatic work (which is not intended for educational use) in a collection of similar works that is intended for use in an educational establishment provided that the collection consists mainly of material in which no copyright subsists and subject to limitations on the number of excerpts from works by the same author.

There must be sufficient acknowledgment of the copyright owner of the copied work.

Section 34 – playing, showing or performing in an educational establishment

Teachers and pupils (and anyone else at a school for the purpose of instruction) may perform musical, literary and dramatic works without permission. The performance must be before teachers and pupils and anyone else 'directly connected with the activities of the establishment' (governor of school or inspector) but specifically excludes performances before parents. It is for this reason that school plays open to the public (that is, parents and friends) require the licence of the owner of copyright in the play being performed.

This section also provides that the showing of films, sound recordings and broadcasts to teachers, pupils and persons directly connected with the activities of the establishment, for purposes of instruction, is not a performance in public and, therefore, not an infringement under s.19.

Section 35 – recordings by educational establishments

An educational establishment can make, or have made for it, a recording of a broadcast, but only for educational purposes. This exception does not apply to any broadcasts that are being licensed by a certified statutory licensing scheme. The New Copyright Regulations introduced the requirement of a sufficient acknowledgement and that the educational purposes are non-commercial.

Section 36 – reprographic copying by educational establishments

An educational establishment may make photocopies of published literary, dramatic and musical works for the purposes of instruction provided that no more than one per cent of any work is copied in any three-month period; the New Copyright Regulations introduced new conditions of sufficient acknowledgement (unless such acknowledgement would be impossible) and that the instruction is for a non-commercial purpose. If licences are available for copying of the works in question, this section will not apply.

Sections 37–44 (inclusive) – libraries and archives

The libraries and archives covered by these sections must fall within the statutory definition. A library in a company or firm will not be covered by all of these sections. The acts that a librarian may do under these sections without infringing copyright are broadly the following:

(a) provide a copy of an article from a periodical or a copy of a reasonable proportion of a published work (provided that the person to whom the copy is supplied satisfies the librarian that it will be used only for research for a non-commercial purpose or private study, a charge is made to cover cost of production, not more than one copy is made, and the librarian is satisfied that the request is not one of several related requests for such a copy);

(b) provide a copy of an article from a periodical or the whole or part of a published work to another library (provided that, in the case of a published work, the receiving library is not able to find the person who could grant the proper licence to make such a copy);

(c) make a copy of a published work to replace a missing or damaged permanent library copy in that or a separate collection (provided that it is not reasonably practicable to buy such a replacement or additional copy);

(d) make copies of previously unpublished works (subject to similar conditions as apply to (a) above) unless the copyright owner has prohibited copying and the librarian ought to have been aware of the fact; and

(e) make copies of a work where a copy of the work needs to be deposited in a library or archive as a condition of export of the original work.

Section 44A – legal deposit libraries

The Legal Deposit Libraries Act 2003 introduced provisions allowing for copying of a work from the Internet by a legal deposit library subject to certain conditions.

Sections 45–50 (inclusive) – public administration

Section 45 provides that anything done 'for the purposes of judicial proceedings' will not be copyright infringement; there is no 'fair dealing' requirement and multiple copies are not prohibited.

Section 47 permits copying with the authority of the appropriate person of any material that is open to inspection by statute provided that it is not intended to issue those copies to the public (although issuing copies to the public, purely for the purposes of facilitating the right of public inspection, is permitted).

Sections 50A–D (inclusive) – lawful users of computer programs and databases

These sections were added to the 1988 Act by the Copyright (Computer Programs) Regulations 1992 (SI 1992 No. 3233) and the Copyright and Rights in Databases Regulations 1997 (SI 1997 No. 3032). Sections 50A–C (introduced by SI 1992 No. 3233) essentially provide that a lawful acquirer of a computer program has certain rights to copy, adapt, decompile and make back-up copies of that program as is necessary for lawful use of that computer program. Certain of these rights cannot be excluded by contract between the licensor and licensee of the computer program and any clause attempting to exclude these provisions would be void.

Section 50BA was added by the New Copyright Regulations and provides that it is not an infringement of copyright in a computer program to observe, study or test the functioning of the program in order to determine the ideas and principles which underlie any element of the program provided that it is done so by performing lawful acts (that is, running, loading, storing etc. the program). Again, this right cannot be excluded by contract.

Section 50D (introduced by SI 1997 No. 3032) provides that it is not infringement of copyright in a database for a lawful user of any part of the database to do anything necessary for the purposes of access to or use of the contents of that database; again in such a situation any contractual clause which tries to prevent the act which would otherwise be an infringement of copyright is void.

Sections 51–53 (inclusive) – designs

The Copyright Act 1956 and the Design Copyright Act 1968 provided that a design that was capable of protection as a registered design that had been applied industrially, would not also be protected as an artistic copyright work after the period of 15 years from when the article in question was first offered for sale or hire. However, what these Acts did not deal with specifically was industrially applied designs which were not capable of registration – these designs, which did not satisfy the Registered Designs Act requirements of, say, aesthetic appeal, perhaps because they were purely functional, could still claim full-term copyright protection if there was an underlying two-dimensional artistic work. The result was some purely functional designs obtaining longer protection under copyright than more deserving, aesthetically appealing designs which were capable of registration, and so only benefited from a limited period of copyright protection.

Finally, in *British Leyland Motor Corp.* v. *Armstrong Patents Co. Ltd* [1986] RPC 279, which dealt with a claim by the owner of copyright in design drawings for car parts, the court felt moved to use the equitable concept of non-derogation from grant to allow reproduction of those copyright works as necessary for producing car parts to repair a car. The case highlighted the need for a change in the law. The result was a new right in designs, namely the unregistered design right (UDR) (see Chapter 21) created by the 1988 Act, that protects aspects of shape and configuration and was aimed at the protection of works of an industrial or functional nature. Before 1 August 1989, as already explained, an artistic work that was applied industrially was protected as a copyright work.

In the case of *Mars UK Ltd* v. *Teknowledge Ltd* [2000] FSR 138, the defendant had reverse engineered a 'discriminator' used in coin-operated machines which allowed the recalibration of such machines to accept different coinage. This discriminator was protected by confidential information, copyright and database right. The defendant claimed that it was entitled to reverse engineer the discriminator by virtue of a common law 'right to repair' or 'spare parts defence'. The court found that although a limited spare parts defence was set out in the 1988 Act in relation to design right, such a defence was not available in relation to copyright in computer programs or database rights.

Section 51 of the 1988 Act essentially provides that making an article that is shown in 'a design drawing' (that is, reproducing a two-dimensional work in three-dimensional form) is not an infringement of the copyright in the design drawing. Nor is it a copyright infringement to copy an article made to the design (that is, reproducing a three-dimensional article in three-dimensional form). It may, however, separately be an infringement of the unregistered design right (see Chapter 21). Furthermore, the section does not apply to designs for artistic works (for example, the design drawing for a sculpture), or for a typeface, where copyright can still be enforced. The complexity of the wording of the section has led to considerable difficulties, as demonstrated by the unsatisfactory result of the Court of Appeal decision in the *Lambretta* case. The section also excludes surface decoration from its provisions, but the issue which arose in the *Lambretta* case was deciding how the section applies to a design drawing which features some aspects of surface decoration, but also aspects of shape and configuration. The Court of Appeal (by majority) decided that the section would apply to the whole design drawing, even if it contained a mixture of two- and three-dimensional aspects. A more satisfactory result would have been for the section to have only applied to those aspects of shape and configuation.

An article made within the ambit of s.51 can also be issued or communicated to the public or included in a film without an infringement of the copyright occurring. Section 51 did not apply to pre-1989 design documents in respect of any allegedly infringing acts performed before 1 August 1989.

In *BBC Worldwide Ltd & Another* v. *Pally Screen Printing Ltd & Others* [1998] FSR 665, which concerned the Teletubby characters, the defendant had manufactured various garments with pictures of the Teletubbies displayed on them. In that case, it was found that these copies had been made from television programmes and children's comics and were, therefore, seen to be an indirect infringement of the three-dimensional Teletubby characters themselves. On an application for summary judgment, the judge found that there was an arguable defence under s.51 because the images used on the garments amounted to indirect copies of articles made to the Teletubbies designs.

Section 52 provides that (subject to some excepted works) if an artistic work (which may be three dimensional or two dimensional) is industrially produced, its copyright protection will be reduced to 25 years from the end of the year in which it was first marketed. It is possible that a copyright work will also have been registered as a registered design. If that is so, then the proper exercise of those registered design rights will form a defence against any claim of copyright infringement in respect of the same work (s.53). The overlap between copyright and the design rights is discussed in Chapter 21.

Sections 54 and 55 – typefaces

Typeface designs can be copyright artistic works. However, it is not an infringement to use a typeface in the ordinary course of typing, printing or typesetting, or to possess an article for such use, or to do anything with the work produced. Making, importing or dealing in articles designed to produce the typeface in question will not, however, be exempted.

Section 56 – works in electronic form

Section 56 allows the use of computer programs (or other works in electronic form – CD ROMs and so on) by a subsequent purchaser of the same copy of that work, without the need for the copyright owner's consent – but this is subject to any provisions prohibiting transfer or bringing the original licence to an end on transfer of the licence.

The rights that the purchaser acquires are the same rights that the original purchaser had, either by express or implied licence or by rule of law. Rule of law would include ss.50A–D of the 1988 Act.

Sections 57–75 (inclusive) – miscellaneous

There are exceptions relating to: reproduction of works of unknown authors; use of written or recorded speeches in reports of current events and broadcasts; the public performance and/or broadcasting of extracts read from published works; reproduction of abstracts to technical or scientific articles; recordings of folksongs; reproduction of any buildings, sculptures, public works of artistic craftsmanship in a graphic work, photograph or broadcast; advertising of an artistic work for sale; reproduction of part of an artistic work by the artist (when no longer owning copyright in the original copyright work); and reconstruction of a building.

The Secretary of State may order the lending to the public of copies of certain works, subject to payment of a reasonable fee (s.66). Copyright in a film will not be infringed if it was reasonable to assume that the copyright in it had expired and the identity of the key personnel could not be ascertained (s.66A).

Non-profit-making clubs and societies can play sound recordings in public without consent of the copyright owner (s.67). Incidental copying for the purpose of broadcasting is permitted, as is recording by the BBC for the purpose of supervision and control.

Section 70 is the one which permits you to record television and radio programmes so that you can watch or listen to them later, although it is more limited than many think, and has been amended by the New Copyright Regulations. The recording must now be made in 'domestic premises' for private and domestic use, and solely for the purpose of viewing it or listening to it at a more convenient time. In *Sony Music Entertainment (UK) Ltd & Others* v. *Easyinternetcafe Ltd* [2003] EWHC 62, Easyinternetcafe operated an Internet café where they offered a CD burning service to customers so that they could retain a copy of any material they had downloaded from the Internet while using the computers at the Internet café. Easyinternetcafe claimed they were not liable for any possible infringement because, among other things, the copies were made for the customers' private and domestic use to enable them to view the material at a more convenient time. The court held that there was no evidence to this effect and in any event the copying was carried out by Easyinternetcafe, which was a commercial entity charging for the CD burning service, and that the copying was certainly not for Easyinternetcafe's private and domestic use. It is also permissible to make a photograph from a broadcast image, again solely for private and domestic use and in domestic premises. Broadcasts, certain sound recordings and films may be played in public without infringement as long as the audience is not charged for viewing (s.72). Section 73 relating to the reception and retransmission of wireless broadcasts by cable has been amended by the New Copyright Regulations, and a new s.73(A) added relating to royalties. Broadcasts may be copied for the purpose of adding subtitles or other modifications to assist handicapped viewers and listeners, and reissued to the public without infringing rights in the broadcast (s.74). Recordings are also permitted for archiving purposes (s.75).

Hot Topic . . .

MUSIC FILE-SHARING ON THE INTERNET

As we have seen, some of the copyright infringements are primary infringements, where no knowledge is required to be proved, and others are secondary infringements, where it is necessary to show that the alleged infringer knew or had reason to believe that they were dealing with an infringing copy. This issue has been highlighted recently by the growing trend of music file-sharing on the Internet, and the accessibility of music downloads from Internet sites. Record companies first targeted the service providers who made available the software which enabled consumers to upload their sound recordings onto the Internet so that others could freely access and download them. Litigation in the United States against Napster led to the demise of Napster in its original form where music could be accessed free, and more recent litigation against Kazaar was also successful, even though their model was slightly different from the Napster model in that none of the music files were held by Kazaar on a central server. It is difficult to predict how a court would react to a similar case brought in the United Kingdom, as there are clearly policy reasons for protecting original sound recordings from unauthorised reproduction, but the wording of the 1988 Act does not spell out a clear infringement and an Amstrad-type defence may well be available to the service provider (where, in *CBS Songs Ltd* v. *Amstrad Consumer Electronics plc & Another* [1988] AC 1013, Amstrad successfully argued that their tape-to-tape cassette recorders could be used for lawful recording, and so their actions in selling them did not constitute authorising a copyright infringement).

However, the record companies have now started targeting the consumers themselves. The case of *Polydor Ltd and Others* v. *Woodhouse and Others* [2005] EWHC 3191 showed that neither innocence nor ignorance is a defence to a copyright infringement where illegal file-sharing is concerned. The facts involved several recording companies who had discovered that the defendant in question had P2P software on his computer and that music files (which were copies of the claimants' sound recordings and protected as copyright works) had then been placed into a shared file. The defendant admitted to owning the software and that his children were allowed access to the computer, but denied that he had committed any infringing act.

Section 16(1) of the 1988 Act states that: 'The owner of the copyright in a work has ... the exclusive right to ... communicate the work to the public.' Section 20 stipulates that such communication is '... an act restricted by the copyright in (a) a literary, dramatic, musical or artistic work, (b) a sound recording ...'. Therefore the unauthorised sharing of music on the Internet clearly falls within the Act, and the court found that the defendant was liable for those acts. He was the named account holder and had control over who used the computer and the software on it. He was therefore a primary infringer under the sections referred to above, and his alleged lack of knowledge of the infringing acts was irrelevant and provided him with no defence.

17.4 Public Interest Defence and the Human Rights Act 1998

There is no statutory public interest defence as such but it is a defence, along with claims of national security, which can be claimed successfully in certain limited cases and is recognised by s.171(3) of the Act. Here it is enough to mention that in a number of cases this argument has been successful, for example *Beloff* v. *Pressdram Ltd* [1973] RPC 765 and *Cambridge Nutrition Ltd* v. *BBC* [1990] 3 All ER 523, although in *Beloff*, the plaintiff's case failed because she did not own the copyright in the relevant work.

In *Hyde Park Residence Ltd* v. *Yelland* [2000] RPC 604, a newspaper, which had used security camera footage of Diana, Princess of Wales and Dodi Al Fayed taken the day before their fatal accident, failed in its argument that it was entitled to publish those photographs without permission, on the basis that such publication was in the public interest. In denying its application, the court said that although the stills were arguably of public interest, their publication was unnecessary as the information contained in the photographs could have been conveyed in a way that did not require infringement of copyright in the photographs.

In *Ashdown* v. *Telegraph Group Ltd* [2002] Ch D 149, Mr Ashdown MP claimed copyright infringement against the Telegraph Group when it published excerpts from confidential diaries and records in its newspaper. The Telegraph Group claimed various defences including under the Human Rights Act 1998 on the basis that Article 10 of the European Convention for the Protection of Human Rights and Fundamental Freedoms (which was implemented by the Human Rights Act) entitled the newspaper to protection for its right of freedom of expression. The Court of Appeal held that there could be rare circumstances where the right to freedom of expression might override copyright and that while these were not capable of precise categorisation or definition, s.171(3) did permit a public interest defence in such circumstances. In this case the publication was not justified by public interest considerations because the newspaper had published for essentially commercial purposes.

17.5 Competition or Euro Defence

The conflict between intellectual property rights (essentially monopoly rights) and rights of free competition is a tension which is common to all intellectual property rights. This issue is dealt with in Chapter 24.

Summary

17.1 A defendant may avoid liability for infringement by showing that his activities are exempt under the legislation or that he had permission. He may also claim that the claimant's exercise of his copyright is against the public interest or is anti-competitive.

17.2 The defendant may claim that his activities fall within a licence agreement. Such agreements need not be in writing and can be implied in certain circumstances.

17.3 The Copyright, Designs and Patents Act 1988 provides for a number of permitted acts.

17.4 Copies of copyright works may be made for a number of reasons provided there is fair dealing in the sense that the owner is acknowledged and the copying has not taken place to enrich the defendant.

17.5 The common law recognises the defence of public interest. The Human Rights Act 1998 is also a relevant consideration in copyright infringement cases.

17.6 A defence is available if the copyright owner's rights conflict with EC competition law.

Exercise

A and *B* became well known after they were captured by rebels and kept in a remote part of Eritrea for five years. On their release back to the United Kingdom, they were approached by *C* News, a daily newspaper, for a series of articles on their experiences. A fee of £25,000 each was agreed.

During the interviews *A* and *B* recounted their experiences to *D*, a reporter. Everything was recorded on her tape recorder. Afterwards *D* spent considerable time editing the recordings, entering details into her word processor and producing a number of articles based on the interviews. These were published by *C* News:

(a) *E* TV uses a substantial amount of the material from the articles as part of its news programme without acknowledging the source.

(b) *F* was also captured by the rebels. He knows that *A* and *B* were held for only two years. After that they had joined the rebels in looting campaigns. He writes an article for a competing newspaper disputing their story, making substantial use of the material in the articles published by *C* News.

(c) *G*, a research student engaged in a PhD thesis on rebel groups, uses material from the articles for her thesis. *H*, a political history teacher, photocopies the articles for his pupils.

Advise *E* TV, *F*, *G* and *H* of their legal liabilities and the defences available, if any.

Chapter 18

Ownership and Duration of Copyright, Moral Rights and Artist's Resale Right

Key words

- **Derogatory treatment** – 'addition to, deletion from or alteration to or adaptation' of a copyright work which distorts or mutilates the work or is in any way prejudicial to the honour or reputation of the author.
- **False attribution** – a false attribution of ownership, not merely something which was or might be understood by some or more people to be a false attribution.
- **Making by an industrial process** – more than 50 articles have been made, or any quantity has been made if the goods are made in lengths or pieces, but are not hand-made goods.

18.1 Ownership of Copyright

Copyright in a work is first owned by the author of that work. In the case of literary, dramatic, musical and artistic works the author is just who you would imagine it to be. In the case of other types of work, the author may be the producer (for sound recordings), the producer and principal director (for films), the person who made the arrangements necessary for the creation of the work (in the case of computer-generated works), the person making the broadcast, or the publisher (in the case of typographical arrangements). The first owner of copyright in films and sound recordings was, until 31 December 1996 when the Copyright and Related Rights Regulations 1996 came into force, the person who made the arrangements necessary for the creation of the work. The general rule about ownership of copyright vesting in the author is subject to one important statutory exception. If a literary, artistic, dramatic or musical work or a film is created by an employee in the course of his employment, that employee's employer will be the first owner of copyright in the work. This statutory exception did not apply to films until the Copyright and Related Rights Regulations 1996 came into force. The questions of who is an employee and what is meant by 'course of employment' are not answered in the statute, although s.263 states that reference to an employee or employment is to be read as a reference to employment under a contract of service or apprenticeship.

Whether a copyright work has been created by an employee in the course of employment will depend on the nature of his employment and the nature of the copyright work. In *Stephenson Jordan & Harrison Ltd* v. *MacDonald & Evans* [1952] RPC 10, a former employee of the claimant had written a book and purported to assign the copyright in it to his publishers. The book was made up partly of lectures that had been written and presented publically by him while he was working for the claimant and partly based on information acquired while on an assignment for a client of the claimant. The court held that the material based on public lectures did not fall within his contract of employment, but the work for the particular client did. The question of whether copyright in a drawing belongs to the author or his employer was considered in *Ultra Marketing (UK) Limited and Thomas Alexander Scott* v. *Universal Components Ltd* [2002] EWHC 2285. Although this was a 2002 decision, the issue was considered under the Copyright Act 1956 because one of the drawings under investigation was drawn in 1976. The judge's decision that copyright vested in Mr Scott rather than the company was based on a number of factors: (1) the company did not deal in the type of frames for which the drawing was a design; (2) Mr Scott was not being paid by the company at the relevant time; and (3) Mr Scott did not work on the drawings during the working day or at the company's premises. The test of whether an employee is employed to do the type of work which gives rise to a copyright work was used in the patent case of *Greater Glasgow Health Board's Application* [1996] RPC 207 (discussed in more detail in Chapter 5): was that type of work an integral part of what the employee was employed to do?

Under the Copyright Act 1956, there was another exception to the first owner rule. The commissioner for money or money's worth of a photograph, sound recording, engraving or portrait was treated as the first owner (1956 Act, ss.4(3) and 12(4)). Under the 1988 Act, commissioners of copyright works do not own the copyright in the resulting work. However, because the general intention in contracts of commission is that the commissioners should obtain some rights of use, if not ownership, case law has developed over time to give commissioners certain rights (see, for example, *Griggs* v. *Evans*, discussed in Chapter 17).

Joint ownership

In the case of *Cala Homes (South) Ltd* v. *Alfred McAlpine Homes East Ltd* [1995] FSR 1818, the court found that, as a result of the involvement of the commissioner in the creation of the work, there was joint ownership. The court added that if it had not held that the commissioner was a joint owner, it would have found an implied term that the drawings were made exclusively for the commissioner. However, in subsequent cases (*Fylde*

Microsystems Ltd v. *Key Radio Systems Ltd* [1998] FSR 449; *Robin Ray* v. *Classic FM plc* [1998] FSR 622; *Pierce* v. *Promco SA and Others* [1999] ITCLR 233; *Hadley & Others* v. *Kemp & Another* [1999] EMLR 589; and *Robert James Beckingham* v. *Robert Hodgens & Others* [2003] EMLR Civ 18), the court made it clear that it would only find joint ownership of copyright where there is a true contribution to the act of authorship of the work in question. Variously the judges in these cases said that in order for there to be joint ownership, the claimants would have to show that they had made 'a significant and original contribution to the creation of the work' and that the claimants had to have made a contribution 'which approximated to penmanship: a direct responsibility for what actually appeared on the page'; and that there was no requirement that before a work could be regarded as a work of joint authorship, there had to have been a joint intention to create a joint work.

Hot Topic . . .

PERFORMANCE AND CREATION

One interesting area concerning the issue of joint ownership is the difference between contributing to the underlying copyright work and contributing to the performance. For example, in the *Hadley* v. *Kemp* case referred to above, the lead singer and other musicians of the band Spandau Ballet sued another band member, Gary Kemp, for a share of the past royalties on the basis that they were co-writers of the songs. The court held that Gary Kemp had written all of the songs himself on a piano or guitar, and

had then presented the songs to the band in rehearsals. The rest of the band's contributions were matters of performance rather than composition, so they were not joint authors of the songs. Similarly in *Brighton* v. *Jones* [2005] FSR 16, as we saw in Chapter 14, the director of a play was not a joint author of the play because her suggestions made during rehearsals to changes in the script and how it would be performed amounted to contributions to the interpretation and theatrical presentation of the

dramatic work, rather than to its creation. Compare those decisions with *Sawkins* v. *Hyperion Records Ltd* [2005] EWCA Civ 565, also mentioned in Chapter 14, where a musicologist who had updated four existing music works by adding performance indications and some missing notes to the scores owned the copyright in the resulting scores as original musical works. And in *Beckingham* v. *Hodgens* [2003] EWCA Civ 143, a violinist was found to be a joint author of a song called Young At Heart as a result of the violin part which he played as a session musician at the recording of a new version of the song.

As a result of the uncertainty in this area, the question of ownership of copyright as between the commissioner and the author should always be provided for in any contract for a commission.

There are specific provisions in the 1988 Act on ownership of Crown copyright, parliamentary copyright and copyright of international organisations. Copyright in any works created by an officer of the Crown or under the direction or control of the House of Lords or House of Commons, or by an officer or employee of an international organisation will, generally speaking, vest in the relevant directing or controlling body (ss.163, 164 and 168).

18.2 Moral Rights

The moral rights of the author or creator of a copyright work, as distinct from the rights of ownership of the copyright, are: (a) the right to be identified as the author (paternity right); (b) the right to object to derogatory treatment of the work (integrity right); and (c) the right not to have a work falsely attributed. These rights may be waived in writing by the person entitled to the right, may be generally or specifically waived, conditionally or unconditionally waived, and a waiver may be expressed to be revocable at any time. Even though the 1988 Act requires a waiver to be in writing, the common law on waiver and estoppel still applies in relation to this area. The owner of the copyright in a work may not always be the same person as the owner of the moral rights in that work. Copyright is an economic-based right whereas moral rights protect the artistic rights of the creator.

These moral rights apply in respect of the whole or a substantial part of a copyright work, but in the case of the false attribution right and right to object to derogatory treatment, any part of a copyright work (even if not substantial) is protected.

There are now also moral rights for performers. These are discussed in Chapter 20.

18.3 Paternity Right

This is the right of the author of a literary, dramatic, musical or artistic work and the right of a director of a film to be identified as such whenever, generally speaking, the work is performed in public, issued or communicated to the public, or commercially exploited. For the right to exist, it must be asserted by the person entitled to the right. An assertion must be made in an assignment of the copyright in the work or in some other written document. An architect also has the right to be identified on his or her buildings. The right of paternity does not apply to computer programs, typefaces and computer-generated works. Where a third party has been licensed by the owner of copyright in cases where the work was created by an employee and the copyright vested in his employer by operation of law, then the employee (who will be the owner of any moral rights in that work) will not be entitled to exercise his moral rights against that third party (s.79).

There are also other specific exceptions to the enforcement of the paternity right in relation to publication in newspapers, magazines and so on (ss.79(5) and 79(6)), and in relation to any activities that broadly correspond to the copyright permitted acts (see Chapter 17).

18.4 Right to Object to Derogatory Treatment

This moral right (sometimes called the right of integrity) arises automatically and does not need to be asserted. It applies to the same copyright works as the paternity right. A 'derogatory treatment' is an 'addition to, deletion from or alteration to or adaptation' of a copyright work which distorts or mutilates the work or is in any way prejudicial to the honour or reputation of the author. A translation is not a 'treatment' for these purposes and neither is a change in the key or register of a musical work.

The same exceptions apply to this right as do to the paternity right (other than design of a typeface that is not specifically excepted here), plus a few more. Also, in relation to derogatory treatment of a building, the architect's rights are limited to having his or her name removed from it. The right does not apply in circumstances where the copyright in a work created by an individual is vested in the employer, the Crown, Parliament or an international organisation by operation of law, and the owner of the copyright has given his authority for the particular treatment of the work, unless the identity of the author was made known at the time of publication or any earlier publication, in which case a sufficient disclaimer is required.

18.5 False Attribution

The right not to have work falsely attributed is also an automatic moral right and applies to literary, artistic, musical and dramatic works and films. It is the right not to be falsely attributed as the author or the director of the work in question. It is also an infringement of this right falsely to attribute an artistic work as the unaltered work of the author when the work has been altered.

In *Clark (Alan)* v. *Associated Newspapers Ltd* [1998] 1 All ER 959, Lightman J said that for s.84 to be infringed, it had to be shown that there was, in relation to the work in question, a false attribution of ownership and not merely something which 'was or might be understood by some or more people to be a false attribution'.

18.6 Rights of Privacy in Photographs and Films

This specific right is to protect private commissioners of photographs and films (most typically, the wedding couple). Under the 1956 Act, a commissioner of photographs, who paid for the commission, was the owner of copyright in those photographs. Under the 1988 Act, all commissioned copyright works (including photographs) are owned by the author. This would have left the private consumer who commissions photographs of, essentially, private events (weddings, christenings, barmitzvahs) unprotected from commercial exploitation of those photos. Section 85 reinstates some protection by leaving the copyright with the photographer but giving the commissioner in these cases a moral right to prevent the photographs being issued to or communicated to the public, or exhibited in public.

18.7 Dealings in Copyright and Moral Rights

Copyright must be assigned in writing, signed by the assignor. Assignments may be made of limited rights (such as of certain of the exclusive rights only) and it is also possible to assign future copyright (in other words, copyright in works still to be created).

Moral rights cannot be assigned; they attach to the original author of a work and can only be asserted or waived by that person. Moral rights can, however, pass under a testamentary disposition (save for false attribution, which remains with the personal representatives of the deceased), and can be bequeathed independently of the ownership of copyright in the work to which they relate. If no specific independent disposition is made of the moral rights, they will automatically transfer with the copyright relating to the work in question. If the copyright work is bequeathed to two or more persons, any related moral rights will be split accordingly. If no disposition of the copyright in that work is made, the personal representatives will be entitled to exercise the moral rights.

Moral rights owned by more than one person are exercisable severally; in other words, each person who is entitled to assert, waive or exercise a moral right does so for themselves only (s.95(3)). Waiver of moral rights by one joint owner does not act as a waiver for the other owners. When passing by testamentary disposition, moral rights will bind the persons inheriting with any prior waivers or consents. Any damages recovered by a person inheriting moral rights will be treated as part of the estate of the original owner of the moral rights.

18.8 Duration of Copyright

For most works, copyright lasts for 70 years from the end of the year in which the author (who may be a different person from the first owner) dies. Until 1 January 1996, the period from death was 50 years but the Duration of Copyright and Rights in Performances Regulations 1995 (SI 1995 No. 3297) has brought the United Kingdom into line with the rest of Europe with the harmonised term of 70 years (being the period which already applied under German copyright law). This extension of the duration of copyright (which only applies to literary, dramatic, musical and artistic works and films) means that certain works, whose copyright had expired, are susceptible to copyright protection again. Moral rights relating to such copyright works are also revived by the Regulations. To deal with the obvious problems, there are transitional provisions covering works already published while outside copyright protection, including the right for such a work to be reproduced subject to payment of a reasonable royalty.

In the case of works of joint authorship, the duration of copyright protection runs from the death of the last of the authors to die. In the case of unknown authorship, the period runs from the end of the year in which the work was first made or, if during that period the work is made available to the public, the period of 70 years will run from the end of the year in which it was so made available. For a work to have been made available for the purposes of duration of copyright, it must have been made available with the permission of the copyright owner.

In the case of films, under the Copyright Act 1956 in general terms copyright lasted for 50 years from the end of the year in which the film was registered under the Cinematograph Films Act 1938 or, if later, released. However, the 1995 Regulations not only extended the 50-year period for film copyright to 70 years but also changed the rules governing duration of copyright in films. Copyright in such works now lasts for 70 years from the end of the year in which the last of the principal director, author of screenplay, author of dialogue or composer of music specific to the film dies. Special provisions apply in cases where one or more of the contributors is unknown. Where there is no-one falling within the category of persons by reference to whom duration of copyright is measured, copyright in a film will last for 70 years from the end of the year in which the film is made or, if later, released.

Copyright in computer-generated works still lasts for only 50 years from the end of the year in which the work is made and copyright in a sound recording lasts for 50 years from the end of the year in which it is made or, if during that period the sound recording is released, 50 years from the end of the year in which it is released (with the permission of the copyright owner). Generally speaking, copyright in broadcasts lasts for 50 years from the end of the year in which the broadcast is made. Copyright in typographic arrangements lasts for 25 years from the end of the year in which they are first published. There is an important section (s.52) which limits the duration of protection of artistic works which have been industrially exploited. This provides that at the end of 25 years from the end of the year in which articles made by an industrial process were first marketed, then articles of any design can be made to the design without infringing the copyright in it. The Copyright (Industrial Process and Excluded Articles) (No. 2) Order 1989 defines what amounts to making by an industrial process, which generally speaking means that either more than 50 articles have been made, or any quantity has been made if the goods are made in lengths or pieces, but are not hand-made goods. So for example, a fabric design which has been made in lengths would only be protected by copyright for 25 years from the end of the year in which the first length was made. The Order also excludes certain articles from the effects of s.52, such as works of sculpture, and printed matter primarily of a literary or artistic character (for example, greetings cards).

All of these provisions on duration of copyright are now expressly subject to provisions regarding duration as they apply to nationals of other countries, provided that the period of copyright will not extend beyond the period specified by the 1995 Regulations.

18.9 Duration of Moral Rights

The various moral rights last for as long as the copyright in the work to which they relate lasts, except for the false attribution right, which lasts until 20 years after the death of the person entitled to that right.

18.10 Artist's Resale Right

As a result of the approval of European Directive 2001/84/EC, the Artist's Resale Right Regulations 2006 came into force in the United Kingdom on 14 February 2006. The right, also known as *droit de suite*, is arguably the most important development in copyright law for artists and entitles the author of the original work of art to a royalty on resale.

The resale right applies so long as copyright subsists in the work and to any works of graphic or plastic art, such as pictures, paintings, photographs and sculptures, provided that the work is only produced in limited numbers (including one-offs). The obligation to pay the royalty applies only to those resales of €1,000 and over.

The right will not apply to the first sale of the work nor will it apply to works which fall outside the definition of works, referred to above and set out in the Regulations. Private resales between individuals are exempt from the obligation to pay a royalty and a sale for not more than €10,000 by a seller who acquired the work directly from the author less than three years before the resale is also exempt. Furthermore, resale rights are only exercisable by certain nationalities, notably to the exclusion of US nationals, and the Regulations do not extend to sales which precede 14 February 2006.

The royalty to be paid is based on the resale price itself, net of the tax payable on that resale. A percentage scale is set out in Schedule 1 to the Regulations, the highest being 4 per cent, but there is a limit on the total amount of royalties payable on any such resale to €12,500.

The royalty becomes payable upon completion of the sale, the seller and the buyer (or agent) being jointly responsible for payment, and may be withheld until evidence of entitlement to the royalty is produced. A collecting society will manage the collection of royalties.

Summary

18.1 Moral rights protect the artistic rights of the creator of the work, who may not always be the same person as the copyright owner.

18.2 In the case of original literary, dramatic, artistic or musical works, the copyright is owned by the creator unless the work was created by an employee in the course of employment.

18.3 When a literary, dramatic, musical or artistic work is commercially exploited or performed in public, the author has the right to be identified. This right must be asserted.

18.4 The author can object to his work being distorted or mutilated in a way that will affect his reputation. This is an automatic right.

18.5 It is also an automatic right not to have work falsely attributed.

18.6 The commissioner of photographs for private and domestic purposes is no longer the copyright owner since the 1988 Act, but has the right to prevent photographs being issued or exhibited in public.

18.7 Moral rights cannot be assigned but can be bequeathed to one or more persons.

18.8 The rights generally run for 70 years from the end of the year in which the author died, but for computer-generated works, sound recordings and broadcasts, the period runs to 50 years from the end of the year in which the work was made or released (whichever is later). The period for typographic arrangements is 25 years from the end of the year of first publication. Artistic works which have been industrially exploited will have their copyright protection period reduced to 25 years from the end of the year of first marketing.

18.9 An artist can now benefit from a royalty on every subsequent sale of one of his or her works, subject to various conditions.

Exercises

18.1 In 1987, students at *D* University organised a series of lectures and invited leading socialist politicians to speak. One of these was *A*. In part of his speech he said: 'If the budget permits, the next socialist government will ensure that each child over the age of six months will be entitled to free nursery education.' *A* delivered his speech without the use of notes. *B*, an enthusiastic student, attended the lecture and recorded *A*'s speech. *B*, who is now a journalist for a right-of-centre newspaper, writes a series of articles based on the recordings he took as a student. He quotes *A* as maintaining: 'Each child over the age of six months will be entitled to free nursery education!'

Advise *A*, who is now a member of a socialist cabinet that cannot afford to provide free nursery education.

18.2 *D*, a reporter from *C* News, recorded a verbatim account of *A*'s and *B*'s experiences following their release by rebels (see Exercise in Chapter 17). She spent considerable time working on a series of articles for *C* News. In her spare time, *D* also wrote a book on rebel groups using material she obtained from *A* and *B*.

Advise the following:

(a) *A* and *B* who are in the process of writing their memoirs and want to stop *D*'s publication;

(b) *C* News who wants to claim copyright in the book written by *D*.

Chapter 19

Database Rights

Key words

▶ **Database** – a collection of independent works, data or other materials which are arranged in a systematic or methodical way and are individually accessible by electronic or other means.

▶ **Extraction** – permanent or temporary transfer of the contents of a database to another medium by any means or in any form.

▶ **Maker** – the person who takes the initiative in obtaining, verifying or presenting the contents of the database and assumes the risk of investing in that obtaining, verification or presentation.

▶ **Reutilisation** – making the contents of the database available to the public by any means.

▶ **Substantial** – (in relation to any investment, extraction or reutilisation) substantial in terms of quantity or quality or a combination of both.

19.1 Introduction

For some time now, databases in their various forms have been protected as copyright works under the relevant copyright legislation. Under the 1988 Act, a database has always been treated as falling within the definition of a compilation, being a collection of materials or data from various sources, and was thus protected as a copyright work like any other literary work. However, this form of protection was for some time seen as inappropriate to many forms of databases where the true value lies not in the structure of the database itself but more in the information contained within that database. The result was that databases of limited originality were protected against copying for an unrealistically long period of time (70 years after death of the creator of the database or 50 years after creation of a computer-generated database), and yet the protection offered was only protection against copying of all or a substantial part of the database and did not prevent certain types of commercial use of the contents of the database.

Further, the treatment and protection of databases have developed along different lines in the various countries of the EU, and as databases have become more vital to business, it has become even more important that databases are given a consistent treatment throughout the EU to ensure the free movement of goods and services.

These problems led to an EU Directive (the European Parliament and

Council Directive on the legal protection of databases 96/9/EC) which was implemented into English law by the Copyright and Rights in Databases Regulations 1997 (SI 1997/3032). The Databases Regulations came into force on 1 January 1998 and, as well as creating a new database right, they amended provisions in the 1988 Act regarding copyright protection of databases. In consequence, certain databases can be protected by database rights and copyright in parallel. In addition, each of the independent works, data or materials comprised in the database might themselves attract separate copyright protection.

19.2 Subsistence and Duration

Database right

A database is defined as 'a collection of independent works, data or other materials which (a) are arranged in a systematic or methodical way and (b) are individually accessible by electronic or other means' (s.3A of the 1988 Act and Regulation 6). Database right comes into existence automatically as soon as a database meeting the relevant requirements has been created. Database right lasts for 15 years from the end of the year of creation of the database but if a database undergoes substantial change (including by the accumulation of possibly insubstantial changes) the 'new' database is protected for a further 15 years from the end of the year in which such change was made. Where a database is made available to the public during the 15-year period, database right in the database will expire 15 years from the end of the calendar year in which the database was first made available to the public (Regulation 17).

Database right will only subsist in a database if 'there has been a substantial investment in obtaining, verifying or presenting the contents of the database' (Regulation 13). Substantiality is said in the Regulations to be measured in terms of quantity or quality or a combination of both (Regulation 12). The substantial investment may be in any one of obtaining, verifying or presenting the contents of the database or any combination of those activities.

Database right will only subsist in a database if, when the database was made, the maker (or in the case of joint makers, one of the makers) was an EEA state national or habitually resident there or, in the case of a company or partnership, had the required link with an EEA state (Regulation 18). The residency requirements have been extended to include individuals habitually resident in, and companies and partnerships with the requisite link to, the Isle of Man.

The Databases Regulations apply retrospectively so that databases created between 1 January 1983 and 31 December 1997 will generally be protected by database rights for 15 years from 1 January 1998 (Regulation 30).

Copyright in databases

The Databases Regulations have withdrawn copyright protection from certain types of databases but a database will still be protected as a copyright work if it meets a new, stricter test, namely that the selection or arrangement of the database amounts to an intellectual creation of the author (s.3 of the 1988 Act as amended by Regulation 6). This phrase is clearly intended to exclude from copyright protection databases which are collected in a mundane way and arranged, say, alphabetically.

Databases created before 28 March 1996 (which was the publication date of the underlying Directive), which were protected by copyright before the Databases Regulations came into force, will continue to be protected as copyright works in accordance with the existing law even if they would not qualify for copyright protection under the Databases Regulations. However, databases created between 28 March 1996 and 31 December 1997, even if formerly protected by copyright, lost copyright protection with effect from 1 January 1998 if they did not meet the Databases Regulations' new 'intellectual creation' test (Regulation 29).

19.3 Ownership and Dealings

The rules concerning ownership of database right and of copyright in a database do not coincide, which means it is quite possible that, if both copyright and database right exist in a database, those rights will be owned by different people.

Database right

The first owner of the database right in a database is the maker of the database (Regulation 15). The 'maker' is defined in the Databases Regulations as 'the person who takes the initiative in obtaining, verifying or presenting the contents of the database and assumes the risk of investing in that obtaining, verification or presentation' (Regulation 14). As a result, there will be many situations where the initiator and the investor will be different people and these people will then be joint owners of the relevant database right. However, where a database is made by an employee in the course of his employment, the employer will be treated as the maker and, therefore, first owner of the database (Regulation 14(2)).

Copyright in databases

As explained in Chapter 18, copyright belongs to the author (except in the case of employees) and that is so even where a third party has invested heavily in the creation of the work by means of a commission.

Assignment and licensing

The provisions of the 1988 Act relating to assignment and licensing of copyright and the special rights accorded to exclusive licensees of copyright apply equally to database rights and exclusive licensees of database rights. There are special provisions in Schedule 2 of the Databases Regulations relating to licensing schemes operated by licensing bodies in relation to the grant of licences of various databases.

19.4 Infringement, Defences and Remedies

Database right

Database right entitles the owner of that right to prevent others from extracting or reutilising all or a substantial part of the database (Regulation 16). For these purposes 'extraction' is defined in the Regulations as the 'permanent or temporary transfer of the contents of a database to another medium by any means or in any form' and 'reutilisation' means 'making the contents of the database available to the public by any means'.

Repeated and systematic extraction or reutilisation of insubstantial parts of the database can also amount to infringement of the database right (Regulation 16(2)). However, if someone has been allowed to use a database which has been made available to the public, that person cannot be prevented from extracting and reutilising insubstantial parts of the database for any purpose (Regulation 19(2)). Where a database has been made available to the public, it is not an infringement of the database right for a lawful user of the database to extract a substantial part of the database for fair dealing purposes provided (a) such extraction is for the purpose of instruction or research and not for any commercial purpose and (b) the source is indicated (Regulation 20). There is, in certain circumstances, an exception for database right infringement in respect of the copying of work from the Internet by authorised deposit libraries (Regulation 20A). There is also a list of other permitted acts in Schedule 1 of the Databases Regulations.

Anything done after 1 January 1998 in relation to a database pursuant to an agreement entered into before that date will not generally constitute infringement of the database right.

If at any time it is not reasonably possible to establish the identity of the maker of the database and it is reasonable to assume that the database right has expired, it will not be an infringement of the database right to extract or reutilise a substantial part of the database (Regulation 21).

Copyright in databases

Copyright in a database is infringed by any of the activities which amount to infringement of other copyright works. An adaptation of a database, for the purposes of infringement of copyright by making an adaptation, means an arrangement or altered version of the database or any translation of it.

The general exceptions to copyright infringement of literary works apply to databases. It is also not an infringement of copyright in a database for a person, who has a right to use the database, to do any act which is necessary for access to and use of the database and any contractual provisions purporting to undermine this right will be void (s.50D of the 1988 Act – see Chapter 17).

Remedies

Remedies for infringement of copyright and database right are the same and are as set out in ss.96–102 of the 1988 Act. The presumptions laid down in the 1988 Act in relation to copyright works apply in almost identical terms to database rights (Regulation 22).

Hot Topic . . .

BRITISH HORSERACING BOARD DATABASE AND OTHER KEY CASES

British Horseracing Board Ltd & Others v. *William Hill Organisation Ltd* (Case C-203/02) was the first UK database right case and is the leading authority on the interpretation of the Databases Regulations.

The British Horseracing Board (BHB) maintains a database containing information on horses, riders, races and so on. BHB expends considerable time, effort and cost to maintain this database up to date and accurate. BHB licensed the database to a number of information service providers who in turn were allowed to transmit the data to their subscribers. William Hill was licensed through one of BHB's licensees to use the database information in its betting shops. However, William Hill also used that information in its online betting business (for which it was not licensed). BHB sued, seeking an injunction. The High Court judge decided that William Hill's use of BHB's racing information infringed BHB's database right because it took advantage of the investment BHB had made in obtaining, verifying and presenting the contents.

William Hill appealed this decision claiming, among other things, that in giving his judgment the judge had misinterpreted the Database Directive thus giving a too wide definition of database right and what it protects. The Court of Appeal felt that this point must be referred to the ECJ for interpretation, so the appeal was stayed pending a reference to the ECJ.

The UK Court of Appeal referred several questions to the ECJ. Surprising many commentators, and going against the opinion of Advocate General Stix-Hackl, the ECJ gave a narrow interpretation of the scope of the database right, resulting in no database right subsisting in databases such as that of the BHB. The ECJ said that investment in obtaining the contents of the database had to be investment in seeking out already existing independent data and compiling it into a database; and that investment in verification of the contents of the database meant checking and correcting the already existing data. Investment in the creation of the data in the first place does not count, nor does verifying its correctness as part of the creation process. The ECJ also said that although William Hill had extracted and reutilised a part of the database, it was not a substantial part of the database, because the data had not been the subject of the required investment in obtaining, verifying or presenting it. Moreover, even though William Hill had repeatedly and systematically extracted and reutilised insubstantial parts of the database, there would be no infringement because the cumulative effect of these acts did not reconstitute the whole or a substantial part of the database.

At the same time as giving judgment in the BHB case, the ECJ gave judgment in three cases involving database rights in lists of football fixtures. The fixtures lists were created by the football leagues in England and Scotland, a process that involved selecting the dates, times and teams that would play, and were licensed to the claimant, Fixtures Marketing Limited ('Fixtures'). Fixtures sued three entities (*Fixtures Marketing Ltd* v. *Organismos prognostikon agonon podosfairou*, Case C-444/02; *Fixtures Marketing Ltd* v. *Svenska Spel AB*, Case C-338/02; *Fixtures Marketing Ltd* v. *Oy Veikkaus Ab*, Case C-46/02) for use of the fixtures information on a website (in the first case mentioned) and on pools coupons (in the latter two cases).

In judgments that reflected those in the BHB case, the ECJ held that no database rights subsisted in the fixture lists because the investment that the leagues had made was as part of the creation of the data in the first place, not as part of a separate process of obtaining, verifying or presenting that data. In the first case, the ECJ also gave its opinion as to what constituted a relevant database, stating that the collection must have a fixed basis, it must include some means (for example, an index, table of contents, or particular method of classification) to allow retrieval of the individual data elements and that the individual data elements must be separable without the value (whether informative, literary, artistic, musical or other) of their contents being affected.

Summary

19.1 A database will only be protected as a copyright work if the selection or arrangement of the database amounts to an intellectual creation of the author.

19.2 The database right lasts for 15 years from the end of the year of creation of the database, or the end of the year of first marketing where applicable, and protects against unauthorised extraction or reutilisation of all or substantial parts of the database.

19.3 The investment in a database must be in seeking out already existing independent data and compiling it into a database, rather than in creating that data.

Exercise

Consider the protection available to the following:

(a) an alphabetical list of names and addresses of customers of a mail order business;
(b) a comprehensive audit of all IT systems used by a business and compiled by its IT manager;
(c) an index for a medical journal;
(d) a Directory of Solicitors practising in England and Wales.

Chapter 20

Performance Rights

Key words

▶ **Derogatory treament** – (in relation to live broadcasts and sound recordings of performances) any distortion, mutilation or other modification that is prejudicial to the performer's reputation.

▶ **Infringing article** – (in relation to a performer's moral rights) a sound recording of a qualifying performance which has been subjected to a derogatory treatment.

▶ **Performer's property rights** – the Reproduction Right, the Distribution Right, Rental and Lending Right and the Making Available Right.

20.1 Introduction

Copyright protects the results of artistic, literary, musical and dramatic effort. It requires the existence of a work that has been recorded in some form. So, if someone speaks a poem, without it having been written down or recorded in some other fixed form, no copyright will arise to protect the poem.

There is, however, clearly 'work' worthy of protection in any live performance, as distinct from any underlying copyright works that are being performed. Live performances are regularly recorded or transmitted in one form or another and, arguably, it should be the performer or performers who decide by whom and for what purpose such recordings and transmissions are made. This is particularly so where the performer has made a significant contribution to the work. However, because many performers are in a relatively weak bargaining position, these rights need to be entrenched in statute law as automatically arising and not depending on contract.

Before the 1988 Copyright, Designs and Patents Act, a number of specific legislative measures had been implemented, starting with the Dramatic and Musical Performers' Protection Act 1925 and culminating with the Performers' Protection Act 1972. The position under statute law in the early 1980s was that performers' rights were protected through criminal measures, which gave the performers no means of private redress or compensation beyond those that a performer was able to negotiate in any contract. The state of the law also left certain categories of performers unprotected (namely, variety and circus artists) and gave no recognition to those to whom recording rights had been granted. During the 1980s, this area of the law developed through case decisions. In *Rickless* v. *United Artists Corp.* [1988] QB 40 the court confirmed that performers and their successors should have a civil right of action to protect performers' rights.

The 1988 Act substantially improved the position of performers and those who have entered into exclusive recording contracts with performers, giving civil rights of action against persons doing certain acts in relation to a live performance (including recording that performance) without consent. The position of performers was further improved by the introduction of additional rights under the Copyright and Related Rights Regulations 1996 (SI 1996 No. 2967) which implemented European Directive 92/100 (the Rental and Lending Directive) and, more recently, the New Copyright Regulations. These regulations came into effect on 1 December 1996 and 31 October 2003 respectively, and include certain property rights which bring the performers' rights closer in line with copyright protection. The performers' pre-existing rights are now classified as 'non-property rights' under the 1988 Act. These rights are subject to exclusions which are similar to the permitted acts allowed in respect of copyright works. Finally, the Performances (Moral Rights, etc) Regulations 2006, which entered into force on 1 February 2006, create moral rights for performers, which together with the Copyright Directive, implement the UK obligations in relation to performances under the WIPO Performances and Phonograms Treaty.

20.2 Performers and Persons Having Recording Rights

The 1988 Act defines those performances that give rise to performers' rights and recording rights as being dramatic performance (including dance and mime), musical performance, readings and recitations of literary works and variety act performances or similar presentations. This definition is broad enough to cover the variety acts and circus acts that were not protected under previous statutes, and would undoubtedly include comedy acts. There are still areas of doubt and potential dispute that one can imagine being argued in future cases. For instance, certain sports or Olympic events could arguably fall within dramatic performance (for example, floor exercises, gymnastics and ice skating).

To be a qualifying performance, and thus be protected under the 1988 Act, the performance must be a live performance and must take place in a qualifying country, or must be performed by a qualifying person (generally an individual who is a citizen of or a resident in a qualifying country, or a legal body, for example a company, constituted under the laws of a qualifying country and having an established and real place of business in a qualifying country).

If these preconditions are met, then the 1988 Act automatically grants certain rights to the performer and any person having the right to make a film or sound recording directly from the live performance, or from a broadcast, or from another recording of the performance.

For a person to come within the definition of a person having recording rights in a performance, that person must be a qualifying person who has been granted exclusive recording rights by the performer. The 1988 Act defines exclusive recording rights as the right to record a performance for commercial exploitation to the exclusion of everyone including the performer. These rights can be assigned. If the person who has been granted the exclusive recording rights is not a qualifying person, but their licensee or assignee of the rights is a qualifying person, then the licensee or assignee will be the person with the recording rights under the 1988 Act.

The rights conferred by the 1988 Act protect performances that took place before August 1989, but the infringing acts under the Act must have taken place after that date to be actionable.

The rights of performers and those with recording rights exist separately from any copyright or moral rights arising in respect of the works that are performed or the works that result from the exercise of recording rights (that is, in any sound recordings or films of the performance). This means that a performer, or person with recording rights, can be guilty of copyright infringement if he or she has not obtained the necessary licences from the owner of copyright in a song, or piece of music, or dramatic work. It also means that the rights in a final sound recording of a performance will possibly belong to a different person from the person who was granted the recording rights.

20.3 Nature of Performance and Recording Rights

The performer's non-property rights are infringed by anyone who, without his or her consent, records a live performance; broadcasts live or makes a recording directly from a broadcast of the whole or a substantial part of the qualifying performance. These non-property rights of the performer give rise to a right to take action for breach of statutory duty. Such rights cannot be assigned but can be transmitted on the death of the performer. In addition, the performer will be entitled to 'equitable remuneration' where a commercially published sound recording is played in public or communicated to the public (other than by making available through an on-demand service). This right to equitable remuneration may not be assigned by the performer, except to a collecting society to enforce the right on behalf of the performer.

A performer's non-property rights are also infringed by anyone who, without his or her consent, shows or plays in public, or communicates to the public the whole or a substantial part of a recording of a qualifying performance knowing, or having reason to believe, that the recording was made without the performer's consent, or who imports into the United Kingdom (other than for domestic or private use), or possesses or deals in a business with, an illicit recording, believing, or having reason to believe, that the recording is illicit.

The performer's property rights may also be infringed by certain acts done in respect of recordings of a performance. The legislation gives the performer property rights in relation to recordings of qualifying performances. The four property rights given are the right to copy recordings of a performance (the 'Reproduction Right'), the right to issue copies of a recording to the public (the 'Distribution Right'), the right to rent and lend copies of the recording to the public (the 'Rental and Lending Right') and the right to authorise and prohibit the making available to the public of a recording of a qualifying performance (the 'Making Available Right').

The performer's Reproduction and Distribution Rights will be infringed by anyone who, without his or her consent, copies (which includes indirect and transient copying), or issues to the public copies of, the whole or any substantial part of a recording of a qualifying performance. There will be no infringement of the Distribution Right where copies of the recording are issued to the public if the copy of the recording has been first put into circulation in the EEA with the performer's consent. These property rights may be assigned (as with copyright) and the assignment may be partial or total. The assignment will not be effective unless it is in writing and signed by or on behalf of the assignor.

The performer's Rental and Lending Rights and the Making Available Right are also property rights, and may be assigned. Where a performer assigns his Rental Right in relation to a sound recording or a film to the producer of the sound recording or film, he retains an equitable right to remuneration. Again, this equitable right to remuneration may not be assigned by the performer, except to a collecting society to enable it to enforce the performer's right on his or her behalf.

The rights of a person having recording rights are infringed by anyone who, without that person's consent or the consent of the performer, makes a recording of the whole or a substantial part of the performance. Similarly those rights will also be infringed by anyone who, without the consent of the person having recording rights in the performance, or (where the recording is of a qualifying performance) without the consent of the performer, shows or plays in public, or communicates to the public the whole or a substantial part of a recording of the performance, or imports into the United Kingdom (other than for private use), or, in the course of business, possesses or deals in a recording of the performance. The infringement relies on the infringer knowing or having reason to believe that the recording was made without the consent of the performer or the person or persons having exclusive recording rights in respect of the performance, or, in the case of importing, possessing or dealing with, that the recording was an illicit recording. The performer's rights (and the rights of a person with recording rights) last for 50 years from the end of the year of performance or for 50 years from the end of the year of release, if that occurs within the first period. This could mean that the term of protection may be extended where a release of a performance does not take place within the same year as a performance ('release' means first published, played or shown in public or communicated to the public, with authority).

20.4 Moral Rights

Hot Topic . . .
NEW MORAL RIGHTS

The Performances (Moral Rights, etc) Regulations 2006 created moral rights for performers in relation to the whole or a substantial part of their performances, thus aligning rights in performances with copyright.

A performer now has a right to be identified as such where a person produces or puts in public, broadcasts, communicates to the public a sound recording of, or issues to the public copies of a recording of a qualifying performance. The Regulations prescribe the manner in which the performer is to be identified in relation to live performances, live broadcasts and sound recordings. The right to be identified must be asserted by the performer in order to be binding – this is generally done by an instrument in writing by or on behalf of the performer. The Regulations prescribe a number of exceptions to the performer's right to be identified (for example, where it is not reasonably practicable to identify the author or where the performance is given for the purposes of reporting current events).

A performer also has the right to object to derogatory treatment in relation to live broadcasts and in relation to sound recordings which are played in public or communicated to the public. A 'derogatory treatment' is any distortion, mutilation or other modification that is prejudicial to the performer's reputation. As with the right to be identified, there are a number of exceptions to the right to object to derogatory treatment (for example, modifications consistent with normal editorial or production practice). The right is also infringed by a person who possesses in the course of business or deals in an article which he knows or has reason to believe is an 'infringing article'. An 'infringing article' is a sound recording of a qualifying performance which has been subjected to a derogatory treatment.

These moral rights last for the duration of the performer's rights in the performance. As with copyright, a performer's moral rights can be waived in writing but cannot be assigned.

The new right only applies to performances after 1 February 2006.

20.5 Defences and Exceptions

Most of the infringing acts in respect of the non-property rights, which give rise to a civil right of action by a performer or a person having recording rights, depend on some degree of knowledge or constructive knowledge on the part of the infringer. In cases concerning a performer's recording rights under s.182 where knowledge is not required, if the infringer can show that at the time of the infringing act he believed that the consent of the relevant person had been given, then damages will not be awarded against the infringer. Where a property right of the performer is infringed, knowledge or constructive knowledge on the part of the infringer, again, is not required before infringement can be said to have taken place. However, there is no corresponding provision restricting damages or remedies where an infringer can show that, at the time of the infringing act, he believed that the consent of the relevant person had been given (as with non-property rights).

Consent can be given to do certain acts (that is, to record or to broadcast) in respect of a specific performance or any particular type of performance or performances generally, and may be given for past or future performances. A person with recording rights will be bound by any consent given by the performer who granted the exclusive recording contract (regardless of knowledge of the consent). In relation to the non-property rights, if a performer or a person having recording rights has given consent in respect of any of the acts requiring consent, then anyone acquiring rights from the performer or person having recording rights takes those rights subject to the consent (regardless of whether they are aware of the consent). It is, therefore, important in all cases where such rights are assigned or granted that the person acquiring the rights obtains full contractual warranties from the grantor or assignor so that, if it turns out that consents have previously been granted, the person acquiring the rights can make a contractual claim against the grantor or assignor.

Where a performer (or assignee) with property rights has granted a licence in relation to any of the acts requiring the performer's licence, then this licence will be binding on any successor in title to the interest in the rights, apart from a *bona fide* purchaser for value without notice of the licence.

In the case of the infringements involving importing, possessing or dealing in illicit recordings, if the infringer can show that he acquired the recordings in circumstances where he did not know, and did not have reason to believe, they were illicit, then the only remedy to be awarded against him will be damages not exceeding a reasonable payment in respect of the infringing act.

A recording that is made for 'private purposes' is not an 'illicit recording'.

In addition, there are a number of specific acts that may be done in respect of performances and recordings, without infringing the rights of the performer or the person having recording rights. These acts are set out in Schedule 2 to the 1988 Act and are broadly parallel to the permitted acts in respect of copyright works. The Copyright Tribunal has jurisdiction in respect of certain matters relating to the exploitation of the various non-property and property rights of performers or other persons entitled to record or to exploit recordings of performances.

20.6 Criminal Offences

In addition to the civil infringements of performance and recording rights which are now actionable under the 1988 Copyright Act and the 1996 and 2003 Regulations, there are a number of criminal offences in the 1988 Act arising out of certain acts involving illicit recordings. It is a criminal offence for a person, without sufficient consent, to do any of the following in respect of a recording which he knows or has reason to believe is an illicit recording:

(a) make for sale or hire;
(b) import into the United Kingdom (except for private and domestic use);
(c) possess such recordings in order to commit an infringing act or deal in such recordings in the course of a business.

Furthermore, it is a criminal offence for a person to infringe a performer's Making Available Right, either in the course of business or otherwise in a way which is prejudicial to the owner of that right, if he knows or has a reason to believe that he is infringing the right in the recording.

It is also a criminal offence to cause a recording of a performance (made without sufficient consent) to be shown or played in public, or communicated to the public, knowing or having reason to believe that the rights of the performer or the person having recording rights will be infringed by such act.

If any of these acts would be exempted from civil action by the permitted acts in Schedule 2 of the 1988 Act, then they will not be a criminal offence.

Other criminal offences under this part of the 1988 Act include falsely holding oneself out as able to give consent in relation to a performance (without having reasonable grounds for believing that such authority exists), and being a director, manager, secretary or similar officer of a body corporate convicted of a criminal offence who has consented to or connived in an offence.

There are specific provisions under the Act as to what can be done with illicit recordings that are delivered up or seized, and the time limit for making applications to the court for destruction or forfeiture of recordings which have been delivered up or seized.

The criminal offences committed under this part of the Act are punishable by fines and/or imprisonment depending on whether the conviction is summary or on an indictment.

20.7 Remedies and Penalties

Infringement of a performer's property rights will entitle the holder of those rights to sue for damages, injunctions, an account of profits and any other remedy available for infringement of any other property right.

Rather than specifying the remedies available to the holders of performers' non-property and recording rights, the 1988 Act provides that infringement of a performer's non-property rights and of a person's recording rights are actionable by those persons as a breach of statutory duty. Breach of statutory duty entitles a person to claim damages for losses suffered and/or for injunctive relief.

In addition, the Act provides for delivery up, upon an order of the court, of illicit recordings that are in a person's possession in the course of a business. This order may be applied for by the performer or person with recording rights as part of the civil action for breach of statutory duty, or it may be instigated by the relevant authorities as part of a criminal action. The performer or person with recording rights is also entitled to seize and detain illicit recordings if they are exposed for immediate sale or hire. The right may only be exercised if notice has been given to a local police station, access to the place where seizure will take place is available to the public, the illicit recordings are not at a person's permanent or regular place of business, no force is used, and, at the time of seizure, a notice is left containing the prescribed information about who seized the goods, on whose authority and on what grounds.

Summary

20.1 Performers and persons with recording rights have similar protection to the rights of copyright owners particularly since the 1996 and 2003 Regulations, and the 2006 Moral Rights Regulations.

20.2 The rights of performers are, however, more akin to those of copyright owners, as they protect the artistic creation, whereas the rights of the person with a recording right are purely economic rights created by contract. In order to have full protection for its rights, the holder of recording rights will need the contractual warranties of the performer as well as the rights granted by the Copyright, Designs and Patents Act 1988.

Summary cont'd

20.3 There are also particular practical threats to performers' rights posed by developing digital technology. The advances in this area mean that works of performers may be copied, many times over, with little reduction in quality. The 1996 and 2003 Regulations have gone some way towards addressing this issue.

Exercise

On 17 March 1997 *A* University Students' Union engaged the legendary Cameroonian poet *Z* to recite her work at one of their functions. *Z*, who composes her work with audience participation, improvised a number of new poems. The entire reading was taped by *Y*.

Y subsequently played the tape at a number of Students' Union functions. On each occasion he was paid a fee, which he donated to the Afro-Caribbean Society.

Z has a publishing contract with *X* Ltd, who are based in Paris. They have already published two collections of her poems, the first winning a literary prize, the second selling a total of 7 million copies worldwide.

On 1 May 1997, *Z* committed to paper the poems she had constructed at the Students' Union function on 17 March 1997 for *X* Ltd to publish.

Y's activities have come to the attention of *Z* and *X*, both of whom would like to put a stop to them.

Advise *Z* and *X*.

Chapter 21

United Kingdom Unregistered Design Right

Key words

- ▶ **Commission** – a commission for money or money's worth.
- ▶ **Design** – the design of any aspect of the shape or configuration (whether internal or external) of the whole or part of an article.
- ▶ **Original** – a design is not original if it is commonplace in the design field in question at the time of its creation.
- ▶ **Reproduction of a design** – (by making articles to the design) copying the design so as to produce articles exactly or substantially to that design.

21.1 Introduction

Until the Copyright, Designs and Patents Act 1988, protection for designs, whether artistic or functional, was dealt with by copyright and registered designs (and, to a lesser extent, patents). The duration of copyright protection was felt inappropriate for functional and commercially exploited articles and this was addressed to a certain extent by the Design Copyright Act 1968 (see Chapter 17). The registered design system was seen as a little too stringent and too formalistic to be of real commercial use to an industrial concern that produces thousands of designs requiring some level of protection.

The need for a change in the law in this area was highlighted by the decision in *British Leyland Motor Corp.* v. *Armstrong Patents Co. Ltd* [1986] RPC 279, which was discussed in Chapter 17, and the decision in *LB (Plastics)* v. *Swish Products* [1979] FSR 145. Following heavy lobbying, the issue was finally addressed in the Copyright, Designs and Patents Act 1988 by the creation of a new, hybrid design right known as unregistered design right.

The position has been confused somewhat by the introduction of the unregistered Community design right. References in this chapter to unregistered design are references to the United Kingdom unregistered design right under the 1988 Act. All references to the unregistered Community design right will be expressed in full.

21.2 What Design Right Protects

Design right arises automatically, like copyright, and subsists in the shape and configuration of the whole or part of an article, the design of which is original. Originality is dealt with in detail below.

An 'article' is not defined in the Act. However, there is case law which has described an article as applying equally to living and formerly living things as well as to inanimate things (see *Ocular Sciences Ltd and Another* v. *Aspect Vision Care Ltd* [1997] RPC 289 where the human eye was held to be an 'article'). Provided that the subsistence criteria are met, design right will subsist in any three-dimensional article (that is, an article which has aspects of shape and configuration), whether that design is functional or decorative.

Exclusions from design right protection

There are various exclusions which prevent design right from arising in certain articles which are designed to interface with other articles so that one or other article can perform the function which it was designed to perform or match the appearance of other articles. Design right is also excluded in the case of designs which are methods or principles of construction of an article.

'Must fit'

Design right will not subsist in features of shape or configuration which enable the article to be connected to, or placed in, around or against, another article so that either article may perform its function (the so-called 'must fit' or 'interface' exclusion). The way in which this section is worded means that the exclusion will apply to designs which feature the characteristics described, even if they also bear other characteristics, such as performing a decorative function. This means that it is also irrelevant that the designer could have found alternative ways of designing an article to achieve the interface (see *Ocular Sciences Ltd and Another* v. *Aspect Vision Care Ltd* [1997] RPC 289; *Ultraframe* v. *Fielding* [2003] RPC 435; and *Dyson Ltd* v. *Qualtex (UK) Ltd* [2006] EWCA Civ 166). In the *Ocular Sciences* case, the parts of a contact lens that were shaped to fit a human eye were excluded from design right protection, even though there were other possible shapes of contact lens, since all of them had parts which had to be shaped in a particular way so that they interfaced with an eye.

The ability to rely upon design right in not only the whole of an article but also the individual parts of an article can cause this exclusion to arise in relation to different parts of the *same* article. In the case of *Baby Dan AS* v. *Brevi SRL* [1999] FSR 377, for example, a stair gate designed to prevent young children from going up or down stairs was the subject of scrutiny under this section of the Act. The claimant in the case had relied upon design right in the whole of the stair gate as well as in individual parts of the stair gate which it claimed the defendant had copied. The defendant argued that design right could not subsist in various aspects of the stair gate because it was designed to fit against a wall or banisters and because its numerous component parts were designed to interface with each other to enable the stair gate to work. The court agreed that certain aspects of the design were designed to interface with a wall or banisters and held that design right did not subsist in those aspects of the design. However, the court rejected the argument that numerous parts of the design could be eliminated on the basis that those parts were designed to interface with each other. If this were the way the law applied, no design right would subsist in articles which were made up of component parts because they all have to fit together.

The claimant in that case had claimed design right protection in the *whole* of its design. It was therefore the *whole* of the stair gate which constituted the 'article' for the purposes of applying the exclusion to design right protection. It was only appropriate to consider excluding design right protection in individual parts of the design where design right protection was claimed in such parts of the stair gate *individually*, since then each of those parts (however such parts were defined for the purposes of the claim) would be a separate 'article' which was designed to interface with another 'article' (another part of the design).

'Must match'

Design right does not subsist in features of shape or configuration of an article that are dependent on the appearance of another article of which the article is intended by the designer to form an integral part (the so-called 'must match' exclusion).

A typical example of a design which will fall within the exclusion is the design of a replacement body panel for a car, as its appearance must match the rest of the car, so that the car's appearance returns to how it was before the panel was damaged. This is intended to prevent a monopoly arising in favour of the manufacturer of a product for the provision of spare parts for their product. However, this does not mean that a manufacturer can never prevent a competitor from supplying spare parts for its products, because the exclusion will not apply where an alternative design can be used which is consistent with the design of the main article. See, for example, the case of *Dyson* v. *Qualtex*, referred to above, in which the Court of Appeal upheld the trial judge's refusal to exclude design right protection in parts of the design of a vacuum cleaner where he considered on the evidence before him that it was not necessary to reproduce the features of certain parts in order to provide suitable replacement parts.

The same issues will arise in relation to the application of this exclusion from protection as arise in relation to the 'must fit' exception in the case of connecting parts of a product when it is sought to enforce design right in respect of those parts individually.

Hot Topic . . .

THE PROTECTION OF SPARE PARTS

The Court of Appeal in *Dyson Ltd* v. *Qualtex (UK) Ltd* [2006] EWCA Civ 166 has recently confirmed that there are effective rights to prevent manufacturers from producing copy spare parts. Spare parts manufacturers should therefore ensure that the designs of their spare parts are sufficiently different from the original parts if a design right infringement is to be avoided.

The first instance decision in this case provides a useful overview of much of the law relating to unregistered design, because Qualtex argued virtually every defence available to them under the design legislation and, on appeal, the Court of Appeal had to reconsider each defence and in particular the wording of the so-

called 'must fit' and 'must match' exceptions set out in s.213.

The case concerned the supply by Qualtex of spare parts for Dyson vacuum cleaners. Dyson had succeeded in proving before the trial judge that the identical spare parts which Qualtex had produced by copying Dyson's parts infringed their United Kingdom unregistered design right in the design of the Dyson parts. Qualtex were unsuccessful on almost every point. Undeterred, they appealed to the Court of Appeal, but Qualtex were again unsuccessful on almost every point.

Lord Justice Jacob described the wording of s.213 as 'full of uncertainty', 'posing near impossible factual questions' and

'obscure', and said that a judge's comment in another case that the wording left much to be desired was 'considerably understated'.

This case confirms that, unlike certain other countries such as the USA, original equipment manufacturers can prevent the sale of copy spare parts for their products, even if that spare part is only a small part of the product.

The whole issue of how to treat spare parts was one of the main sticking points when the new Community design rights were being discussed, and the resulting position under the Directive and the Regulation is something of a fudge. This resulted in particular in the introduction of a distinction between the protection of internal and external parts of a 'complex product' – a distinction which does not apply to United Kingdom unregistered design right.

Method or principle of construction

As noted above, design right does not subsist in a design for something which is a method or principle of construction – for example, the concept of a dovetail joint in the construction of a drawer.

Surface decoration

Surface decoration is also specifically excluded. The effect of the section is that all designs for features of an article which decorate the surface of that article should be protected by copyright or Community design right, rather than United Kingdom unregistered design right. Surface decoration has been defined as not only covering decorative additions to the surface of an article, such as embroidery or a painted pattern applied to the surface of an article, but also to design features which quite literally decorate the surface, even though they might be applied in the manufacture of the article. For example, in the case of *Mark Wilkinson Furniture Ltd* v. *Woodcraft Designs (Radcliffe) Ltd* [1998] FSR 63, it was held that decorative grooves cut into and decorative cock beading attached to the door panels of kitchen units would amount to surface decoration since they were there to decorate the surface of the doors and did not amount to aspects of shape or configuration of the kitchen units.

Can copyright and design right both subsist in a design?

Where a design falls to be protected under both the copyright and design right provisions of the 1988 Act because it fulfils the criteria for both types of protection, both rights will subsist. In many cases, the copyright will not be enforceable because of the operation of Section 51 – see Chapter 17 where this is discussed in more detail. However, where it does arise because, for example, an article which is potentially protected by design right is also a sculpture and therefore an artistic work protected by copyright, s.236 prevents the designer from enforcing the design right in the design. In other words, copyright takes precedence. However, this does not prevent a claim of infringement of both design right and copyright being made in infringement proceedings should one of the claims fails.

21.3 Criteria for the Subsistence of Design Right

There are two criteria which must be fulfilled for design right to arise. Firstly, a design must be 'original'. This means that it has not been copied from another design – that is, it is the result of the independent skill and labour of the designer. Secondly, a design must not be 'commonplace' in the design field in question at the time the design was created. This means that it is necessary to look at the relevant design field at the time the design was created in order to confirm that there were no other identical or very similar designs. This includes old designs which are still present in the marketplace (see *Scholes Windows Ltd* v. *Magnet Ltd* [2002] FSR 10).

The relevant design field is an issue which the courts have had to consider in several cases. The tendency is for the courts to prefer a fairly broad definition of the relevant design field. For example, in the *Scholes Windows* case, it was held that the relevant design field to be considered was the field of window designs generally and not a special, narrower category of 'uPVC windows'.

21.4 How Design Right Arises

As mentioned above, design right is an automatic right, and arises as soon as a design is created by either producing design drawings or making a first prototype recording or embodying the design.

There is also a qualification criterion which must be fulfilled. This can be fulfilled in one of three ways.

The first is that the creator of the design must be a 'qualifying individual' (s.218 of the 1988 Act), the same principle which arises in relation to copyright. The rules on qualification and the countries to which design right protection extend are, however, different from the copyright provisions and are set out in s.217. Design right is not granted to citizens of all the countries to which copyright protection is granted. Since there are some countries which do not have an unregistered design right system, the United Kingdom has no reciprocal protection arrangements with them. This means that a US citizen, for example, cannot have design right protection for a design under the first qualification criterion.

In the case of joint designers, the design qualifies for protection as long as one of the joint designers is a qualifying person, but only that person is entitled to design right.

The second criterion is where a design has been commissioned or created by an employee, when the design will qualify for design right protection if the commissioner or employer is a qualifying person (s.219).

The third criterion is the 'qualification by reference to first marketing' in s.220. This is that the design was first marketed in the EEC or another country with reciprocal protection by a qualifying person who is exclusively authorised to put the articles on the market in the United Kingdom (for example, they have an exclusive licence for the United Kingdom).

21.5 Who Owns Design Right?

The first owner of design right will be one of four people: the creator; the creator's employer; the person who commissioned the design; or the person who first marketed the articles under s.220.

If the creator of a design created the design in the course of their employment, their employer will automatically be the owner of the design right. The meaning of 'in the course of employment' has been considered in several cases in which a variety of different circumstances have been considered by the Courts as potentially being 'in the course of employment'. The cases vary as to what is treated as being 'in the course of employment'.

If someone creates a design during working hours and the creation of that design falls within that person's job description, the design will usually be deemed to be the employer's property. However, if an employee creates a design outside normal hours of work but using the employer's resources, it is questionable whether the design is the property of the employer or the designer. The position is even less clear in the case of an employee who is not employed as a designer, but who creates a design during working hours. It seems logical that if the designer uses his employer's resources, the employer should own the design right in the design. Where the employee has not used his employer's resources, however, the answer might be different.

What is clear is that an employee who creates a design in his own time using his own resources will own the design right in the design, even though he might be employed as a designer at other times.

A commission arises where someone engages a designer to create a design in return for valuable consideration. The consideration need not be money, but it has to represent something of value. However, commissioning someone to design and manufacture a product in return for an agreement to buy the finished products from that person may not amount to sufficient consideration for a commission to arise (See 'Commissioned designs – Who owns them?' by Clark, *Copyright World*, May 2002, for a review of the cases on this issue).

21.6 Duration of Design Right

Design right lasts for a maximum of 15 years from the end of the year of creation of the design. However, in the case of a design which is commercially exploited, the design right period is reduced to ten years from the end of the year in which the design is first made available for sale. In the *Dyson* case, the Court of Appeal approved the trial judge's finding that a design is not made available for sale when products made to the design are advertised, or even when orders are taken for those products, but only when products are actually delivered pursuant to orders which have been taken. In addition, during the last five years of protection, anyone can copy the design, subject to taking a licence from the design right owner and paying a reasonable royalty. This is known as a 'Licence of Right'. This has consequences for the remedies available for the infringement of the design right in a design which is within the licence of right period (see section 21.8 below).

If someone offers to take a licence of right during the last five-year period, the design right owner cannot refuse to grant the licence. If the terms of the licence cannot be agreed between the parties, they will be determined by the Comptroller of Patents at the Patent Office.

21.7 Infringement

Design right is infringed when a design is copied so as to produce articles 'exactly or substantially' to the design. An 'infringing article' is defined accordingly in s.228. An article will also be treated as an infringing article if it has been made outside the United Kingdom (and is therefore not technically an infringing article), but is subsequently imported into the United Kingdom and it would have been an infringement to make the article in the United Kingdom (s.228(3)).

Design right is not a monopoly right and it is therefore necessary to show, as with copyright, that copying has taken place before an infringement will be established. Copying might be inferred by demonstrating that the person accused of copying the design has had the opportunity to copy the design and that there is a substantial similarity between the alleged infringing article and the design said to have been copied. Copying can also take place subconsciously – that is, a design is reproduced exactly or substantially by subconscious recollection of an earlier design in which design right subsists.

It is also irrelevant whether design right is infringed directly by copying the original design or indirectly by copying some other representation of the design (such as a photograph in a magazine), including another infringing article. The acts of infringement for which someone can be liable are divided into 'primary' and 'secondary' acts. Primary infringement covers: manufacturing or authorising the manufacture of; or making of a design document to enable the manufacture of an infringing article. Secondary infringement covers: the importing for commercial purposes; offering or exposing for sale or hire in the course of a business; selling, letting or hiring in the course of a business; or possessing for commercial purposes an infringing article.

Acts done in relation to an article for 'commercial purposes' are defined in s.263(3) as being done with a view to the article being sold or hired in the course of a business. Therefore mere use in the course of a business is not enough (for example, the use of an infringing chair design in a hotel lobby).

The difference between primary and secondary infringement is that for primary infringement, there is no need to show that the infringer knew that the article being made was an infringing copy. For the acts of secondary infringement, a claimant must show that the defendant knew or had reason to believe that the article with which they were dealing was an infringing article. See Chapter 16 for a discussion of when a defendant will be deemed to have the requisite knowledge.

In order to be actionable in the United Kingdom, the act of infringement has to take place in the United Kingdom. It will not be possible to take action against someone for authorising the manufacture of potentially infringing articles from the United Kingdom if the manufacture of those articles takes place outside the United Kingdom. This of course is increasingly prevalent with the increase in articles being made in the Far East. It will therefore be necessary to find an alternative act of infringement committed by that person, such as importing the infringing articles into the United Kingdom.

More than one person can be liable for the same acts of infringement of design right in a design. This can arise where two or more persons are said to be acting towards a 'common purpose' of carrying out acts which prove to be an infringement of the design right owner's rights (see *Unilever plc* v. *Gillette (UK) Ltd* [1989] RPC 583 D). Directors can be made liable for the infringing acts of companies in which they are involved. Whether they are held liable depends upon the extent of their involvement in the particular acts complained of. In *Re Mitsubishi Corporation* (10 June 2005), an interim injunction application to prevent the infringement of a trade mark, the court permitted the sole director of a company to be joined to the action and was made a party to the injunction order on the basis that he was the sole director of the company and it was clear that any tort committed by the defendant company must have been committed on his instructions. In *MCA Records* v. *Charly Records* [2002] FSR 26, a copyright case, the court held that a director could be liable for the acts of the company of which he was a director where he did not commit the infringing act himself, if he had procured or induced the company to do those acts, or if he had joined with the company in concerted action to see that those acts were done. It was necessary to show some personal involvement in the release of the infringing product.

21.8 Remedies for Infringement

The following are the usual remedies available for the infringement of design right:

(1) an injunction preventing the continuation or further commission of infringing acts;
(2) damages for the design right owner's lost profits or an account of the profits made by the infringer;
(3) delivery up or destruction of infringing articles in the possession or control of the infringer;
(4) disclosure of the identity of the supplier of the infringing articles, where relevant;
(5) interest and costs.

An injunction is a final order preventing the infringer from continuing to commit the infringing acts complained of. Failure to comply with the order can be a contempt of court, punishable by imprisonment or a fine, depending upon the severity of the breach.

Where a design is subject to a Licence of Right and the infringer undertakes to take a licence in the course of court proceedings, the court will not order an injunction (s.239(a) of the 1988 Act).

Damages and accounts of profits

Section 229 provides for damages or an account of profits.

In the case of infringing articles which are commercially exploited, the basis of a damages award is usually the loss of profit which would have been made by the design right owner on the same quantity of sales of its own products that it would have sold had the copies not been on the market. Lost profits are assessed by working out what the design right owner's profit less 'direct expenses' of producing and selling that quantity of products would have been (see *Gerber Garment Technology Inc* v. *Lectra Systems Ltd* [1997] RPC 443 CA). Direct expenses are all the expenses which are attributable only to the production and sale of the actual products in question. It is therefore irrelevant to consider, for example, what the design right owner's general overheads of running its business would be. The obvious direct expense for a wholesaler of a product is the cost of buying stock. With regard to other relevant direct expenses, if the design right owner had to employ extra staff in order to handle the copied products specifically because they could not be handled using existing resources, this would constitute an additional or 'direct' expense which would be deductible in arriving at a lost profit figure. Similarly, if the design right owner would have had to make special deliveries of its products which it would have sold had the infringer not sold its copy products in order to fulfil orders because those orders could not be fitted in with other deliveries to customers buying its products, this would be a deductible expense.

However, it cannot always be shown that the claimant would have sold one of its original articles had the copies not been on the market, for example where the copies were much cheaper than the originals. The claimant's damages on those sales by the defendant will be equivalent to a reasonable royalty, as if the parties had a licence agreement between them.

In the case of an account of profits, because it is the profit which the infringer made which is being considered, it will be relevant to deduct an appropriate proportion of the infringer's general business overheads ('indirect expenses'), as well as any other expenses which have the effect of reducing its profit on the infringing articles sold, albeit in the appropriate proportion to the infringer's overall business (see *Celanese International Corp.*

v. *BP Chemicals Ltd* [1999] RPC 203). An account of profits is a discretionary remedy, but it is available in most cases as an alternative to damages. It can be useful in a case where the infringer's profit is much greater than the profit which the design right owner would have made, where the royalty method of assessing damages applies, or where the infringer is able to rely upon the innocence defence. Under s.233, if an alleged infringer can prove that it was not aware that design right subsisted in the design alleged to have been copied, it will escape liability for damages. This does not, however, prevent the design right owner from seeking an account of profits or any of the other remedies. See also the Intellectual Property (Enforcement, etc) Regulations 2006.

In addition, someone accused of infringing design right by committing an act of secondary infringement will not be ordered to pay the design right owner damages in relation to any articles sold which he did not know or have reason to believe were infringing articles at the time he acquired them. The design right owner may be entitled to an injunction to prevent the infringer from acquiring any more of the infringing items, but the infringer will be allowed to sell off its remaining stock of the infringing products, subject to paying the design right owner a reasonable royalty.

Damages where a licence of right is available

Where a design is within the licence of right period of design right, it will usually only be possible to obtain damages equal to up to twice the amount of a reasonable royalty based on the numbers of infringing articles which the infringer has sold during that period (s.239(1)(c)). This provision only applies if in proceedings for infringement of design right, the alleged infringer undertakes to the design right owner at any time before trial to take a licence of right in the event that the design right owner is successful in its claim. If the alleged infringer does not give such an undertaking, the design right owner will be able to claim damages in full.

This does not affect the damages available for infringing acts committed prior to the licence of right period. In addition, if the infringer wishes to sell off its remaining stock of infringing articles, it will have to agree the terms of a licence of right with the design right owner.

The royalty payable will be a reasonable market royalty which will need to be assessed using evidence of comparable licences granted by the design right owner, where possible, or other, similar licences if the design right owner has not itself granted any. If this is not possible, the assessment will be as described below under the subsection *'Licences of right'*, since the approach will be the same as if a royalty rate were being assessed outside the context of litigation.

Additional damages

Under s.229, the court has the power to award additional damages if the infringement was flagrant or the infringer benefited substantially from the infringement. However, such damages are very rarely awarded.

Delivery up/destruction

Delivery up is an equitable remedy and is therefore subject to the discretion of the court. The court will not order infringing articles to be delivered up to the design right owner under s.230 unless it is also prepared to make an order for the disposal of those articles under s.231.

The court will not order someone to deliver up infringing articles where the design is subject to a licence of right and the infringer undertakes to take a licence.

There is a limitation period of 6 years from the date the infringing article was made on the entitlement to seek delivery up, subject to limited exceptions.

Disclosure of names of suppliers/importers/others

Under the principle set out in the case of *Norwich Pharmacal* v. *Commissioners of Customs and Excise* [1973] FSR 365, the successful claimant in an action is entitled to the disclosure of the names of all other parties which have committed an infringing act in respect of the same articles, from manufacturers to importers. The rationale for this is that it is inequitable for the infringer to withhold information about an infringement of an intellectual property right.

It is possible to obtain such information in an application to the court for pre-action disclosure where the rights' owner seeks to obtain information from a party which is not an infringer itself, but which is in possession of such information. This is to enable the rights' owner to pursue the party which is infringing its rights. The costs of such an application, including the defendant's costs, will usually have to be borne by the party seeking the information. The remedy is an equitable one and therefore within the discretion of the court.

Costs and interest

A successful claimant or defendant is also entitled to seek payment of its legal costs incurred in the proceedings, together with interest on those costs from the date of the judgment on liability. A successful claimant will also be entitled to payment of interest on the damages awarded or payment ordered under an account of profits. Interest runs from the date of the infringing act(s).

Limitation period

The limitation period for making a claim for infringement of design right is 6 years from each act of infringement committed. Where design right is being infringed on a continual basis, each new act of infringement will have its own corresponding limitation period.

Licences of right

Failing agreement, the terms of the licence would be determined by the Comptroller of Patents, who would also determine the royalty rate payable on the basis of evidence put forward by each party. In the absence of any evidence of a typical royalty which the design right owner would expect to receive (often the design right owner will not have such evidence because it does not license its designs), one formula which the courts can apply is to calculate what 25 per cent of the licensee's 'available profits' are on sales of the infringing product. This principle is set out in the *Gerber Garment Technology* v. *Lectra Systems* case referred to above.

'Available profits' are the licensee's gross profits on sales of the products in question less the direct expenses incurred in buying, advertising, distributing and selling (see above for the meaning of 'direct expenses'). The licensee's general overheads are not taken into account. The royalty often ranges from between about 3 per cent and 10 per cent of the licensee's selling price for its product.

21.9 Who Can Enforce Design Right?

Design right is enforceable by the design right owner or an exclusive licensee of the design right owner.

Where an exclusive licensee of the design right owner seeks to enforce design right, it is necessary to join the design right owner to the court proceedings as either a claimant or a defendant. In the latter case, the design right owner will have no liability for costs to any party to the proceedings. This approach would be the usual approach to adopt if the terms of the licence provided for the licensee to take action to protect the licensed rights or if the design right owner simply did not wish to become involved in the proceedings.

A non-exclusive licensee will need the design right owner to enforce the licensed design right on its behalf or to enter into an agreement with the licensee granting the licensee the right to issue and conduct proceedings in the licensee's own name. Suitable indemnity provisions should be included in the agreement to protect the design right owner.

21.10 Relationship with Other Rights

Copyright

As has been noted already, although both copyright and design right can subsist in a design, it is not possible to enforce design right in a design in which copyright also subsists as a result of s.236.

Unregistered Community design right

The position with the unregistered Community design right is different from the position with copyright, in that United Kingdom design right and unregistered Community design right can both subsist and be enforced in a design. This can cause problems because of the different ownership provisions which apply in relation to commissioned designs. Under United Kingdom design right, the commissioner owns the design right. There are no such provisions under unregistered Community design right law, which means that the designer will own the unregistered Community design right.

The unregistered Community design right also gives its owner greater powers of enforcement against infringements of the design because of the possibility of infringement of the right through mere use of an infringing article and the absence of a distinction between primary and secondary infringement. The list of infringing acts under design right law is more limited and, in order to prove infringement in the case of acts of secondary infringement, it is also necessary to prove that the alleged infringer knew or had reason to believe that acts were an infringement of design right.

21.11 Groundless Threats

The recipient of a groundless threat of court proceedings for the infringement of United Kingdom design right, unregistered Community design right and registered United Kingdom and Community design right is entitled to sue for the damage which it suffered as a result of the threat, in addition to an injunction against the making of further threats and a declaration that the threats are unjustifiable. For example, if the recipient of such a threat ceased sales of the allegedly infringing products upon receipt of the threat and thereby lost the profits on the sales which it would otherwise have made, it is entitled to sue the person making the threat to claim compensation for that loss.

There is an exception to this rule in relation to allegations of infringement by the manufacture or importation of infringing products only, which cannot give rise to a groundless threat.

It is up to the person making the threats to show that the acts alleged to be infringing did constitute (or, if done, would have constituted) an infringement of the relevant right. A threat will be considered to be groundless if the maker of the threat, for example, had no reasonable grounds for making it, such as when the rights alleged to subsist in the design in question do not in fact subsist, the person making the threats does not own the rights claimed or the allegedly infringing design is found not to infringe the rights.

Note that solicitors themselves can be liable for making a groundless threat, by writing a letter making the claims on behalf of their client.

Summary

21.1 Unregistered United Kingdom design right arises automatically in the whole and/or part of a qualifying design.

21.2 It protects the shape and configuration, but not surface decoration, of any original article which is not commonplace.

21.3 It usually lasts for 10 years from the end of the year in which articles made to the design were first marketed.

21.4 Licences of right are available in the last 5 years of protection.

21.5 An article will infringe design right if it is made to substantially the same design.

Exercise

A, a United Kingdom company, commissioned B, an Australian citizen, to create a new table design, and paid B a design fee for doing so. Articles made to the design were first marketed in the United Kingdom in 2001. C, a competitor of A, saw that the table was very successful for A and sent a photograph of the table to its Hong Kong manufacturers to copy. A has just discovered that C is selling copies of the table and wants all sales stopped immediately. Advise A accordingly.

Chapter 22

Unregistered Community Design Right

Key words

▶ **Design** – the appearance of the whole or a part of a product resulting from the features of, in particular, the lines, contours, colours, shape, texture and/or materials of the product itself and/or its ornamentation.

▶ **Identical** – includes designs with features which differ only in immaterial differences.

▶ **Individual character** – the overall impression the design produces on the informed user differs from the overall impression produced on such a user by any other design which has been made available to the public.

▶ **New** – no identical design has been made available to the public before the date on which the design for which protection is claimed has first been made available to the public.

22.1 Introduction

The unregistered Community design right is a right created by Council Regulation (EC) No. 6/2002 of 12 December 2001 on Community designs (the 'Regulation'). The Regulation also creates the registered Community design right, many of the provisions of which are the same as the unregistered Community design right provisions, including in particular the criteria for subsistence and many of the infringement provisions. The registered Community design right is dealt with in Chapter 23. Both rights apply throughout the European Union.

22.2 What the Unregistered Community Design Right Protects

Unregistered Community design right subsists in a design. A 'design' is defined as 'the appearance of the whole or a part of a product resulting from the features of, in particular, the lines, contours, colours, shape, texture and/or materials of the product itself and/or its ornamentation' (Article 3(a)).

A 'product' means 'any industrial or handicraft item, including *inter alia* parts intended to be assembled into a complex product, packaging, get-up, graphic symbols and typographic typefaces, but excluding computer programs' (Article 3(b)).

A 'complex product' means 'a product which is composed of multiple components which can be replaced permitting disassembly and re-assembly of the product' (Article 3(c)).

22.3 Criteria for the Subsistence of Unregistered Community Design Right

In order for a design to qualify for protection as a Community design, it must be 'new' and have 'individual character' (Article 4). Provided that the subsistence criteria are met, unregistered Community design right will subsist in any two- or three-dimensional design, whether that design is functional or decorative. There are, however, exclusions from protection based upon aspects of technical function, interface and appearance of a design which are similar to (but not the same as) those which apply to United Kingdom design right. These are considered further below.

A design is 'new' if no identical design has previously been made available to the public. Another design will be identical if it differs only in immaterial details from the design seeking protection. It is therefore only necessary for there to be one such previous design in the marketplace for novelty to be destroyed.

A design has 'individual character' if it creates a different overall impression on the 'informed user' from any design previously made available to the public. The 'informed user' is someone who has some knowledge of the design field in question but who is not necessarily an expert. This was considered in *Woodhouse UK plc* v. *Architectural Lighting Systems* [2005] ECPCC (Designs) 25, in which 'informed' was held to imply some notion of familiarity beyond the knowledge of the average consumer, and to require some knowledge of market trends and availability of products and some knowledge of basic technical considerations. It was held not to require any familiarity with the underlying technology, eye appeal being held to be the more important consideration. It is also necessary to take into consideration the nature of the product to which the design is applied or in which it is incorporated, and in particular the industrial sector to which it belongs and the degree of freedom of the designer in developing the design, in deciding whether a design has individual character.

Complex products

For designs for component parts of complex products, there are additional requirements that the part remains visible during normal end use of the product and that the visible features of the component part fulfil the novelty and individual character criteria.

Making available to the public

A design is considered to have been made available to the public if it has been disclosed, for example, by publication, exhibition or use in the course of trade. There is an exception to this rule where such disclosure could not reasonably have become known in the normal course of business to the circles specialised in the sector concerned, operating within the Community. A design will not be considered to have been disclosed if it is disclosed to a third person under explicit or implicit conditions of confidentiality.

Exclusions from unregistered Community design right protection

There are exclusions which prevent unregistered Community design right from arising in certain products which are designed to enable them to interface with other products so that one or other product can perform the function which it was designed to perform, and in products whose designs are only attributable to the function which they have to perform. Therefore, features of a design which are excluded from protection for one of these reasons are not to be taken into account in assessing whether other features of the design fulfil the requirements for protection.

As noted above, protection is also excluded for component parts or features of a part which are not visible during normal use of a product or which do not fulfil the novelty and individual character requirements. Again, such features are not taken into account in assessing whether other features of the design fulfil the requirements for protection.

The so-called 'must-fit' exclusion states that a Community design shall not subsist in features of appearance of a product which must necessarily be reproduced in their exact form and dimensions in order to permit the product in which the design is incorporated or to which it is applied to be mechanically connected to or placed in, around or against another product so that either product may perform its function (Article 8). The way in which Article 8 is worded, in particular the use of the words 'necessarily' and 'exact form . . .', means that the exclusion will probably not apply where there are alternative ways of designing those features to achieve the same function.

The ability to rely upon unregistered Community design right in not only the whole of a product but also the individual parts of a product can cause the exclusion to arise in relation to different parts of the *same* product in the same way as considered in relation to United Kingdom design right, although the same result will probably not be obtained where there are alternative ways of designing interface features. This problem will not arise where it is the whole product which is relied upon in its entirety.

There is no direct equivalent to the so-called 'must match' exception which applies to United Kingdom design right.

Community design can subsist in a design serving the purpose of allowing the multiple assembly or connection of mutually interchangeable products within a modular system, for example, a Lego brick.

A Community design will not subsist in features of appearance of a product which are solely dictated by its technical function. This exception denies protection to aspects of products the appearance of which is dictated *solely* by the function which the product has to perform. Accordingly, designs which also have an aesthetic appeal in addition to their functional purpose will still attract protection.

22.4 How Unregistered Community Design Right Arises

Unregistered Community design right is an automatic right which arises as soon as a product the design of which meets the subsistence criteria is disclosed by being made available to the public.

There are no further qualification provisions other than that the product must be made available to the public. In contrast to the position under United Kingdom design right, therefore, it is possible for a citizen of a country which does not benefit from United Kingdom design right protection (for example, the USA) to obtain protection under the unregistered Community design right.

22.5 Who Owns Unregistered Community Design Right?

The first owner of unregistered Community design right will be the designer or the designer's employer.

If the designer of a product created the design in the course of employment, the employer will automatically be the owner of the unregistered Community design right in the product. The meaning of 'in the course of employment' has already been considered in relation to United Kingdom design right. The same principles are likely to apply to unregistered Community design right.

There are no provisions dealing with commissioned works. There is therefore a potential conflict with United Kingdom design right law if both rights fall to be considered in relation to the same design. The position under unregistered Community design right in relation to commissioned works is that the right is owned by the designer, whereas the commissioner will own the United Kingdom unregistered design right. As with copyright in relation to commissioned works, there is still the possibility of an equitable right to the unregistered Community design right arising in favour of the commissioner, if, for example, both parties agreed that the commissioner would own the rights.

If two or more people jointly develop a design, the right to the Community design vests in them jointly.

22.6 Duration of Unregistered Community Design Right

Unregistered Community design right lasts for three years from the date on which the product in which a design has been incorporated or to which a design has been applied is first made available to the public within the Community.

22.7 Infringement

Unregistered Community design right is infringed when a product which does not produce a different overall impression on the informed user (referred to below as an 'infringing product') is used. You will recognise this as the same test as for subsistence of the right.

'Use' has a broad definition in the Regulation and includes making, offering, putting on the market, importing, exporting, stocking for any of those purposes, or otherwise using an infringing product.

Unregistered Community design right is not a monopoly right and it is therefore necessary to show that copying has taken place before an infringement will be established. As with copyright and United Kingdom design right, copying might be inferred by demonstrating that the person accused of copying the design has had the opportunity to copy the design and that there is a substantial similarity between the alleged infringing article and the design said to have been copied.

However, unlike under copyright or United Kingdom design right law, there is no requirement to prove knowledge on the part of the infringer. In this respect, liability for infringement is strict. This will have an important effect on retailers who, before the introduction of the Community design, were able to avoid infringement by showing that they did not know or have reason to believe that the article which they were selling was a copy. Since that defence does not apply with the Community design, it is essential for retailers to obtain indemnities from their suppliers so that they can recoup any damages which they may have to pay for stocking a copy.

Place where the acts of infringement take place

An infringement of unregistered Community design right is actionable in any Member State of the EU in which the infringement occurs. The usual rules on jurisdiction apply to determine where proceedings for infringement should be commenced.

Limitation on the enforcement of the rights conferred by a Community design

Article 20 of the Regulation provides that the rights conferred by the Community design do not extend to the following acts:

(a) acts done privately and for non-commercial purposes;
(b) acts done for experimental purposes;
(c) acts of reproduction for the purpose of making citations or of teaching, provided that such acts are compatible with fair trade practice and do not unduly prejudice the normal exploitation of the design, and that mention is made of the source.

There are also exclusions relating to equipment on ships and aircraft registered in a third country when these temporarily enter the territory of the Community, the importation in the Community of spare parts and accessories for the purpose of repairing such craft and the execution of repairs on such craft.

Article 21 of the Regulation creates a limitation on the enforcement of the Community design right in respect of a product in which a protected design is incorporated or to which it is applied, which has been put on the market in the Community by the holder of the Community design or with his consent. It is not therefore an infringement of the Community design right to buy such a product in the EU and to use it, including, for example, by incorporating it into another product which is subsequently sold.

22.8 Remedies for Infringement

These are set out in Article 89(1)(a)–(c). The court has the power to make the following orders:

(a) an order prohibiting the defendant from proceeding with the acts which have infringed or would infringe the Community design;
(b) an order to seize the infringing products;
(c) an order to seize materials and implements predominantly used in order to manufacture the infringing goods, if their owner knew the effect for which such use was intended or if such effect would have been obvious in the circumstances.

Article 89(1)(d) provides that the national law of the Member State in which the acts of infringement or threatened infringement are committed applies in relation to other remedies available for the infringement of the unregistered Community design right. The remedies for infringement and the limitations on those remedies will therefore be similar to those for infringement of United Kingdom design right, which were discussed in Chapter 21.

Article 90 provides for applications for interim relief, such as an interim injunction.

The limitation period for making a claim for infringement of unregistered Community design right is 6 years from each act of infringement committed. Where unregistered Community design right is being infringed on a continual basis, each new act of infringement will have its own corresponding limitation period.

22.9 Licences of Right

Licences of right are not available under unregistered Community design right in light of the very short period of protection afforded by the right.

22.10 Dealing with the Unregistered Community Design Right

As with other intellectual property rights, the unregistered Community design right may be assigned or licensed.

Article 32 provides that licences may be granted for the whole or part of the Community and that a licence may be exclusive or non-exclusive.

Unless the licence provides otherwise, the licensee may bring proceedings for infringement only if the right holder consents, although the holder of an exclusive licence may bring proceedings if the licensor does not bring infringement proceedings within an appropriate period, having been given notice by the licensee to do so.

A licensee is entitled to intervene in an infringement action brought by the licensor for the purpose of obtaining compensation for damage which it has suffered.

22.11 Relationship with Other Rights

Both copyright and unregistered Community design right can subsist in a design and are both enforceable, which contrasts with the position under United Kingdom design right. However, the Regulation gives Member States the option of making alternative provisions about the co-existence of copyright and unregistered Community design right, so the position might not be the same in all countries.

In the United Kingdom, both unregistered Community design right and United Kingdom design right can also subsist and be enforced in a design. As noted in Chapter 21, this can cause problems because of the different ownership provisions which apply in relation to commissioned designs.

22.12 Groundless Threats

Refer to Chapter 21 in relation to the rules on groundless threats, which now also apply to the unregistered Community design right.

Summary

22.1 Unregistered Community Design will subsist in the whole and/or part of any new design with individual character.

22.2 Design includes any aspect of lines, contours, colours, shape, texture and/or materials of the product itself and/or its ornamentation.

22.3 The right arises automatically and lasts for 3 years from the date on which it was made available to the public.

22.4 The right can be infringed by using the design, and there is no knowledge requirement for liability to arise (as there is for secondary infringements of copyright and United Kingdom design right).

Exercises

22.1 Who can own an unregistered Community design?

22.2 When will the right first come into existence?

22.3 Who can infringe an unregistered Community design, and how?

Chapter 23

United Kingdom and Community Registered Designs

Key words

▶ See Chapter 22.

Introduction

Copyright and unregistered design right are both concerned with the protection of aspects of design. Copyright was always available to protect artistic designs (whether in two-dimensional form as graphic works or photographs, or in three-dimensional form as sculpture, works of architecture or works of artistic craftsmanship). Until the Copyright, Designs and Patents Act 1988 ('the 1988 Act'), the low level of artistic quality required for protection of two-dimensional works, and the possibility of infringement of a two-dimensional work by a three-dimensional representation, meant that functional articles could be protected by copyright existing in underlying design drawings. After August 1989, this form of protection for functional designs and other aspects of shape or configuration was replaced by United Kingdom unregistered design right (and more recently the unregistered Community design as an additional right).

Registered designs, which have existed since the Registered Designs Act 1949 (RDA), have always been available as a supplement to copyright protection. The 1988 Act made some minor changes to the RDA. However, since then, more substantive changes have been made to the RDA in order to implement the European Directive 98/71/EC on the legal protection of designs – this Directive aimed to harmonise the requirements for registered design protection across Member States. Accordingly, each Member State should apply the same law to their own national registered design.

However, in addition to national registered designs, Council Regulation of 12 December 2001 on Community Designs (6/2002/EC) ('the Regulation') also introduced a single, EU-wide design registration, called the Community Registered Design. This is operated by the Office for Harmonisation in the

Internal Market (OHIM) in Alicante, Spain. The beauty of this new right is that the subsistence requirements and infringement provisions are virtually identical to those that apply to the national design registrations (unlike, for example, the differing provisions which apply to national and Community trade marks). References to the RDA are to that Act as amended by the 1988 Act and by the Registered Design Regulations 2001 which came into force on 9 December 2001. References to the 'old RDA' are to the RDA before its amendment by the Registered Design Regulations 2001.

The main advantages of a registered design over the unregistered rights are:

(1) there is no need to prove copying for an infringement of a registered design – the registered design owner has a monopoly in that design; and
(2) the registered design can last for up to 25 years, whereas unregistered Community design only lasts for 3 years, and unregistered United Kingdom design right usually only lasts for 10 years, with licences of right being available in the last 5 years.

This chapter therefore considers the registered design rights which exist in the United Kingdom and through the EU at the Community level. Owing to the harmonisation of United Kingdom registered design law with Community registered design law, most of this chapter will refer only to the Community registered design but, in most cases, the same will apply to the United Kingdom registered design.

23.2 The United Kingdom Registered Design

The territorial scope of the United Kingdom registered design is obviously limited to the United Kingdom. The amendment to the RDA also affected registered designs which were in existence prior to the amendments coming into force insofar as enforcement of the right is concerned. The test for infringement of an earlier registered design is now the same as the test for infringement of a design registered under the harmonised system.

Applications for the United Kingdom registered design are made to the Patent Office in the United Kingdom on payment of a fee.

23.3 The Registered Community Design

As in the case of the unregistered Community design right, the registered Community design right is a right created by the Regulation. Many of the rules on registered Community designs are therefore the same as the unregistered Community design right provisions, including, in particular, the criteria for subsistence and many of the infringement provisions. These were considered in Chapter 22. Both rights apply throughout the European Union.

The registered Community design right is not an automatic right and therefore an application for registration must be filed, together with payment of a fee.

A registered Community design can be used to protect the aspects of shape, configuration, contours and lines of a design, its texture, ornamentation, colours and even packaging. It can also protect logos, motifs and typefaces, either as stand-alone designs or as decoration on a product or its packaging.

Since it is the design itself which is protected by the registration, once registered, it can be applied to any number of different products.

23.4 What are the Criteria for Registration?

Designs can be registered if they are 'new', which means that they do not differ only in immaterial details from another design already in the marketplace and have 'individual character', which means that they create a different overall impression from other designs on the 'informed user' of such a design (see the definition of this term in Chapter 21). Novelty and individual character also have the same meanings as in relation to the unregistered Community design right.

The same exclusions for functional designs and interface design features apply as they do for unregistered Community design right, discussed in Chapter 22.

A design can be marketed for up to 12 months prior to filing an application in order to test the success of the product in the marketplace without prejudicing the registrability of the design – that is, its novelty will not be affected by the fact that it had already been disclosed, provided that period is less than 12 months prior to the date of application.

23.5 What does the Registered Design Cover and for How Long?

The registered Community design allows one registration to be filed for all 25 Member States of the EU with the Community designs office. The United Kingdom registered design obviously only covers the United Kingdom, as noted above. It is also possible to file a registered Community design application for a series of designs in one application for a lower fee than the cost of multiple, separate applications, provided that all the designs are for the same type of product (for example, all lighting designs). It is therefore possible for designers to protect a complete new collection of products in one application. This makes the registered Community design very cost-effective in protecting a wide range of products – for example, a range of cutlery which features a certain handle design.

The duration of a registered design is 25 years, renewable every 5 years on payment of a renewal fee to the relevant registered designs office (the Patent Office in the United Kingdom and OHIM for the registered Community design).

23.6 What Protection does the Registered Design Give?

A registered design will be infringed if a design which does not create a different overall impression on the informed user (the same test as for subsistence) is used without the authorisation of the registered design owner. As in the case of the unregistered Community design right, 'use' includes making, offering for sale, selling, importing and exporting to and from the EU infringing products and stocking such products for the above purposes. It is not necessary to show that a registered design has been copied or that the alleged infringer knew that they were infringing – the registered design creates a monopoly right in this respect.

23.7 Who has the Right to Register a Design?

The position for registered Community designs is the same as with the unregistered Community design right. The person entitled to apply for the registered Community design will therefore be either the designer(s) or their employer.

In relation to the United Kingdom registered design, any application to register a design must be made by the owner of the design who can be the author of the design in accordance with s.2 of the RDA, or the owner as a result of assignment, transmission or operation of law. Where unregistered design right subsists in a design which is intended to be registered, the application for registration must be made by the owner of the unregistered United Kingdom design right.

23.8 Dealing with Registered Community Designs

As with other intellectual property rights, registered Community designs may be assigned or licensed. The provisions are the same for the registered Community design as in relation to the unregistered Community design right considered in Chapter 22, save for the following, additional provisions.

Article 28 provides that a transfer of a registered Community design must be entered in the register and published at the request of one of the parties and that until the transfer has been entered in the register, the assignee of the registered Community design may not enforce the rights under the registered Community design.

The grant or transfer of a licence must, at the request of one of the parties, be entered in the register and published.

23.9 Dealing with United Kingdom Registered Designs

The RDA does not specify the formalities for assigning, licensing, charging or otherwise dealing in registered designs. However, these dispositions are clearly permitted since s.19(1) RDA says that the person who becomes entitled to a registered design or to an interest in a registered design (such as a licence) shall apply to the Registrar to record him on the Register (subject to provision of proof of title).

As a result of the possible interrelationship between registered designs and unregistered design right, the Registrar will not record any disposition in an interest in a registered design unless he is satisfied that the person claiming an interest has acquired an interest in the corresponding unregistered design right (s.19(3A)). In particular, where a person owns a registered design and the unregistered design right in that design, any assignment of the unregistered design right will be presumed to be an assignment of the registered design also, unless the contrary intention is expressed or implied (s.19(3B)).

A registered design may be given as security, as is the case with other proprietary rights.

Hot Topic . . .

THE FUTURE OF THE UK REGISTERED DESIGN

The introduction of the registered Community design has proved something of a nemesis for the United Kingdom's national registered design system.

In the first two years since the registered Community design right became available, nearly 25,000 applications were received by OHIM with businesses from the United Kingdom coming in behind Germany and Italy as making the highest number of applications. No doubt one of the key reasons that the registered Community design has proved so popular is the relatively low cost of making an application (€350 for a design as at May 2006) for protection that covers the whole of the EU and provides a right that is directly enforceable in all Member States. For designers and companies who operate in several Member States rather than just the United Kingdom, this cost is likely to compare favourably to making individual applications at national design registries.

The trend towards applying for registered Community design rights reflects the same trend in relation to Community Trade Marks. In the face of this competition, and no doubt falling revenues of the United Kingdom Patent Office, a regulatory reform order has been proposed which would: (a) end the power of the United Kingdom registrar to refuse to register a design on the ground that it lacks novelty or individual character; (b) allow multiple designs to be registered in a single application; (c) end the withdrawal of some registered designs from public inspection; and (d) facilitate the restoration of lapsed design registrations. The proposal is, as of May 2006, being scrutinised by Parliament. The proposed changes are an attempt to make the national United Kingdom registered design system a more attractive prospect for designers and therefore more competitive with the registered Community design. Whether this strategy will yield results is doubted, as the considerable cost-savings and far wider coverage offered by the Community system are likely to be the deciding factors for most businesses.

23.10   Remedies and Limitations on Enforcement of Registered Designs

There is an exclusion in Article 22 of the Regulation in favour of any third person who can establish prior use (that is, use before the date of application of the registered design or the date of priority if claimed). That third party has to show that they have in good faith commenced use within the Community, or have made serious and effective preparations to that end, of a design which is covered by the scope of protection of a registered Community design, which has not been copied from the registered design. The exception creates a limited right to continue exploiting the design. This right cannot be licensed, but it can be transferred with the business in the course of which the prior use was made or preparations for use commenced.

The same limitations also apply as they did with unregistered Community design right where the use is undertaken privately and for non-commercial purposes etc. – see Chapter 22.

As a result of the Intellectual Property (Enforcement, etc) Regulations 2006 ('the Enforcement Regulations') the RDA now provides for similar remedies as are available for other intellectual property rights. A defendant, who can show that, at the date of the infringing act, he did not know and had no reasonable grounds for supposing that the design was registered, will not have damages or an account of profits awarded against him (see s.24B). The defendant will not be deemed to know, or have had reasonable grounds for believing, the design to be registered, even if the word 'registered' or a similar marking was displayed on an article bearing the design, unless the word or marking was accompanied by the registration number of the design. Obviously, a prudent person would carry out a search of the United Kingdom Register, even if only the word 'registered' was displayed, but this section of the RDA suggests that failure to do that would not deprive the defendant of a defence to a damages award. Section 24B of the RDA provides that the court may still grant an injunction in the case of an innocent defendant. Even before the Enforcement Regulations amended the RDA, the approach of the courts was to make awards in registered design infringement cases akin to the remedies granted in respect of the infringement of other intellectual property rights.

Unlike trade marks, patents and registered Community designs, United Kingdom registered designs only offer protection against acts committed after the date of the registration certificate (not the date of filing the application).

The remedies for infringement of the registered Community design are the same as for the infringement of the unregistered Community design right (see Chapter 22). There is no express provision in the Regulation equivalent to s.24B RDA for innocent infringement of the right. However, Article 89 provides for 'any order imposing other sanctions appropriate under the circumstances which are provided by the law of the Member State in which the acts of infringement or threatened infringement are committed'.

23.11 Who can Enforce a Registered Design?

Until 2006 the owner of a United Kingdom registered design was the only person entitled to enforce the right in a registered design. Unlike the situation under the Patents Act and the 1988 Act, exclusive licensees of registered designs did not have a right to sue for infringement (for example, see *Isaac Oren* v. *Red Box Toy Factory* [1999] FSR 785, a case decided under the old United Kingdom law). However, as a result of the Enforcement Regulations, exclusive licensees of registered designs now have the same rights against (i) subsequent owners of the registered design as against the person granting the licence; and (ii) infringers of the registered design as the owner of the registered design has. The provisions for bringing an action in respect of the infringement of a registered design if you are an exclusive licensee (see s.24F) are the same as the provisions for an exclusive licensee of a copyright work.

The licensee of a registered Community design may bring proceedings in its own name for infringement of a Community design, but only if the right holder consents (or the licence agreement provides for the licensee to do so). However, an exclusive licensee may bring an action for infringement in its own name, if the right holder, having been given notice to do so, does not himself bring infringement proceedings within an appropriate period (see Article 32(3) of the Regulation).

A licensee of a registered Community design is also able, for the purpose of obtaining compensation for damage suffered by him, to intervene in an infringement action brought by the right holder.

23.12 Groundless Threats

Refer to Chapter 21 in relation to the rules on groundless threats which also apply to the registered design. These provisions are contained in Community Design Regulations 2005 (SI 2005 No. 2339) in relation to the registered Community design and s.26 of the RDA in relation to the United Kingdom registered design. Groundless threats provisions are no stranger to the United Kingdom registered design and unregistered design right, which have had them for some time. They came into force for the registered Community design and unregistered Community design right on 1 October 2005.

The case of *Carflow Products (UK) Ltd* v. *Linwood Securities (Birmingham) Ltd and Others* [1998] FSR 691 is worth noting for the application of the groundless threats provisions under the old United Kingdom registered design system (the groundless threats provisions referred to above remain the same). The defendant claimed for losses arising out of the threats section as a result of the second defendant (Argos) cancelling all orders of the alleged infringing product. This claim was not successful as the judge in that case found that, although a threats letter had been sent to Argos, it was not until the writ was issued that Argos made the decision to withdraw the infringing product from sale. Once the writ had been issued, the court said that the correspondence containing the threats 'was little more than historical interest'.

23.13 Deferment of Publication of a Registered Community Design Application

Article 50 of the Regulation provides the opportunity to defer the publication of a registered Community design for up to 30 months from the date of filing (or any earlier priority filing date) in case the normal publication following registration could destroy or jeopardise the success of a commercial operation involving the design.

23.14 Cancellation Procedure

Under the old RDA, once registered, a registered design could be cancelled: (a) on the application of the proprietor without cause or (b) on the application of any person interested on grounds that the registration should never have been granted or (c) if the design had a corresponding copyright in subsistence and that copyright had expired. These applications for cancellation would take effect, respectively, (a) immediately, (b) with effect from registration and (c) on expiry of the corresponding copyright. These provisions are still relevant for United Kingdom registered designs granted pursuant to the old RDA.

In relation to all new applications, the provisions for cancellation as far as the United Kingdom registered design are concerned were harmonised with Community registered design law by the 2001 Regulations.

A registered design may be cancelled at any time on the application of the proprietor or it may be declared invalid on the application of an interested party or person holding conflicting rights on broadly the following grounds: (1) failure of the application to meet the legal requirements for registration;

(2) the applicant not being the proper applicant; and (3) objections by holders of earlier rights or earlier distinctive signs. A cancellation will be effective from the date of the registry's decision (or such other date as the registry directs); a declaration of invalidity will result in the registration being treated as invalid from the registration date (or such other date as the registry directs).

23.15 International Provisions

A registered design is a national right providing protection for the design in question only within the country of registration or, in the case of the registered Community design, a right which applies throughout the EU. However, as already explained, an application will fail if the design is not new and does not have individual character, and this is an international test.

The Paris Convention provides rights of priority in respect of registered design applications, in the same way as it does for patents and trade marks. If an application for a registered design has been filed in a Convention country, further applications for the same or substantially similar design may be filed in other Convention countries within six months of that first application. Those subsequent Convention applications may claim as their priority date the application date of the first application in a Convention country. Since all such applications will be treated as having been filed on the same date, they will not fail the novelty or individual character tests merely because of the existence of corresponding international registrations or applications.

23.16 Criminal Offences in Relation to UK Registered Designs

It is a criminal offence to mark an article in a way which suggests that the design applied to it is a registered design when it is not or once the registered design has expired (see s.35 RDA). The penalty for such an offence is a fine. There are specific provisions which enable the Secretary of State to prevent publication and registration of a design if it is considered to be prejudicial to the defence of the realm, and which prohibit an applicant from filing corresponding applications for such a design outside the United Kingdom. Failure to comply with any directions given in connection with that provision or filing an application for a design which has been blocked pursuant to that section is a criminal offence punishable by imprisonment and/or a fine. It is also a criminal offence to falsify, or procure falsification of, an entry on the Register of Designs or any documents purporting to be a record of Register entries (s.34). This is punishable by imprisonment and/or a fine.

As with most criminal offences involving intellectual property rights, officers who have consented to or connived in the commission of an offence by a corporate body will also be guilty of a criminal offence (s.35A).

However, unlike with copyright and trade marks, there are no criminal provisions for an infringer of any of the registered or unregistered design rights.

23.17 Parallel Actions under National and Community Registered Design Laws

Article 95 of the Regulation provides that the court first seized in respect of an action involving the same cause of action and the same parties will have jurisdiction, the later court having to decline jurisdiction or stay any proceedings issued before it if the court's jurisdiction is disputed.

Summary

23.1 The Registered Community Design provides one design registration which gives protection throughout all 25 Member States of the EU.

23.2 The right lasts for an initial period of 5 years, but can be renewed up to a maximum period of 25 years.

23.3 The same tests for subsistence and infringement apply as with the unregistered Community design, save that there is no need to prove copying since the Registered Community Design is a monopoly right.

23.4 There is a 12-month grace period within which a valid application can still be filed even though the design has been made available to the public in the preceding 12 months.

23.5 Unlike the old United Kingdom registered design system, the right protects the design irrespective of the nature of the goods on which it is used.

Exercise

A designs a new clock in his spare time, based on a design he saw in a museum in Peru 10 years ago. He discusses it with his boss at the watch manufacturer where he works, and they decide that they should put the watch into production.
Advise *A* as to:

(1) how to protect the new design;
(2) whether the design will be new; and
(3) how to protect his own interests in the design while allowing his employer to exploit it.

Part IV

Competition

Chapter 24

Intellectual Property and Competition Law

Key words

▶ **Exhaustion of rights** – where products incorporating intellectual property rights are put into circulation within the EEA with the owner's consent, those rights are exhausted and the owner cannot prevent the free movement of those products.

24.1 Introduction

Intellectual property rights are essentially the creation of total or qualified monopolies. The ownership of an intellectual property right entitles the owner to prevent third parties from exploiting the intellectual property in question, in some cases, for an unlimited period. Having the exclusive right to exploit a particular form of intellectual property also gives the owner the potential to license others for a fee to exploit the same intellectual property.

In contrast, competition policy is all about freedom, and works against monopolies. There is a natural tension between the ownership and exercise of intellectual property rights and competition law. The approach of the United Kingdom and the EC competition laws to this tension has been quite different in the past, but as a result of recent changes in the law, the United Kingdom position is moving closer to the EC's position.

24.2 United Kingdom Competition Law and Intellectual Property

Competition law in the United Kingdom has recently undergone a fundamental change. Previously there were three statutes regulating competition in the United Kingdom: the Fair Trading Act 1973 (dealing with mergers and monopolies); the Restrictive Trade Practices Act 1976 (dealing with restrictive trading agreements); and the Competition Act 1980 (dealing with anti-competitive practices). The Competition Act 1980 was little used in practice and lacked effective sanctions. The Restrictive Trade Practices Act 1976 was considered to be unduly formalistic in its approach to regulating competition and to catch, unnecessarily, many innocuous agreements. The Restrictive Trade Practices Act 1976 and much of the

Competition Act 1980 have been repealed by the Competition Act 1998 which came into force on 1 March 2000. Parts of the Fair Trading Act 1973 remain in force, but most of the merger control provisions in the Fair Trading Act have been replaced or amended by the Enterprise Act 2002. The Enterprise Act has also replaced or amended legislation relating to the functions and procedures of the United Kingdom competition authorities (primarily the Office of Fair Trading and the Competition Commission), market investigations and appeals. In addition, the Enterprise Act 2002 introduced new legislation relating to the criminalisation of cartels, disqualification of directors for infringements of competition law and 'super-complaints'.

The Competition Act 1998 effectively implements the EC competition law framework (see below) into United Kingdom national law. This means that:

(a) agreements which have as their object or effect the distortion of competition in the United Kingdom and
(b) any abuse of a dominant position in the United Kingdom

will be outlawed by that Act.

Where these agreements or abuses involve intellectual property rights they will be treated in the same way as any other commercial agreement. There are no specific exemptions in relation to intellectual property licences or other agreements or arrangements involving intellectual property.

24.3 EC Competition Law and Intellectual Property

The principles of EC competition law are set down by various Articles of the Treaty of Rome. The relevant Articles are:

Article 28 – 'quantitative restrictions on imports and all measures having equivalent effect shall . . . be prohibited between Member States';

Article 29 – 'quantitative restrictions on exports and all measures having equivalent effect shall be prohibited';

Article 30 – 'The provisions of Article 28 . . . shall not preclude prohibitions or restrictions on imports, exports or goods in transit justified on grounds of . . . the protection of industrial and commercial property';

Article 81(1) – prohibits agreements, arrangements and concerted practices which may affect trade between Member States and which have as their object or effect the prevention, restriction or distortion of competition within the common market;

Article 82 – prohibits any abuse of a dominant position within the whole or a substantial part of the common market; and

Article 295 – 'This treaty shall in no way prejudice the rules in Member States governing the system of property ownership'.

Intellectual property rights can be used to prevent the free movement of goods, can be the subject of an agreement that has an anti-competitive effect or can give someone a position of market dominance which might be abused. For this reason, the exploitation of intellectual property rights is affected by competition law.

24.4 Intellectual Property and Free Movement of Goods

The use of intellectual property rights, which are essentially national rights, as a means of preventing free circulation of goods or services in the EEA, is prohibited by Articles 28 and 29. However, Article 30 provides a get-out where restrictions can be justified on certain specified grounds and Article 295 gives recognition to the rights of proprietors of intellectual property rights and the right to enjoy the essential right conferred by the intellectual property right. This means that if someone owns an intellectual property right, they should have the right to be the first person to put a product into circulation that reproduces or incorporates that intellectual property and to sue infringers. However, once the owner has put those products into circulation in the EEA, in EC competition law terms, they have exhausted that right and cannot use it to prevent free circulation of those goods. This concept as it applies to trade marks is now enshrined in United Kingdom law by s.12 of the Trade Marks Act 1994.

Put simply, if the owner of a trade mark in France manufactures and sells products under that trade mark in France, he cannot then use his corresponding trade mark rights in Italy or Germany to prevent the French goods being resold in Italy or Germany. By putting the goods on the market under the trade mark somewhere in the EEA, the owner has exhausted his rights in the trade mark. The owner can still, however, prevent a third party applying his trade mark to any other goods. This concept of exhaustion of rights has given rise to a line of interesting cases concerning what happens when a trade mark is owned by different proprietors in different countries.

In the case of *Van Zuylen Freres* v. *HAG* [1974] ECR 731 (commonly referred to as HAG I), the HAG coffee business, which had originally been owned by a German enterprise, was divided as a result of the Belgian subsidiary having its assets sequestrated in 1944 for being enemy property. Eventually those assets were sold off and in 1971 the trade mark previously held by the Belgian subsidiary was bought by Van Zuylen. Van Zuylen then sued the German HAG company for infringement of its trade mark when the German company started to sell coffee under the HAG name in Luxembourg. The ECJ held that Van Zuylen could not use its trade mark rights to prevent the import of goods to which the trade mark had been legitimately applied.

This decision was distinguished in the decision in *CNL-Sucal NV SA* v. *HAG GF AG* [1990] 1 ECR 3711 (HAG II), which involved the German trade mark owner bringing an action to prevent the importation of coffee marked by the Benelux trade mark owner. The ECJ said that, because a trade mark is intended to guarantee the identity of the origin, and hence the quality of the goods, a trade mark owner could only have exhausted his rights in respect of trade marks that were in his ownership or under some form of common control. Where marks were of common origin, but the owner voluntarily split the ownership without exercising any quality control, that owner had given up any right to seek protection against importation of goods marked with that mark. The split of ownership in the case of the HAG marks had not been voluntary because of the sequestration.

In the later case of *IHT Internationale Heiztechnik GmbH* v. *Ideal Standard GmbH* [1994] 3 CMLR 857, the voluntary splitting of ownership of a trade mark was seen as allowing each of the subsequent owners to exercise their trade mark rights to prevent imports of products bearing their trade mark. This principle will only be followed where the transaction that splits ownership of the trade marks is an arm's-length commercial transaction and is not aimed at partitioning the EC.

One special exception to the exhaustion of rights doctrine, particularly in the area of trade marks, relates to repackaged and relabelled goods. As the underlying purpose of a trade mark is seen as guaranteeing the origin and quality of the goods, there can be situations where the originally marked goods might, on reselling, have their quality interfered with by the reseller. This can happen when goods need to be repackaged or relabelled to meet language or regulatory requirements of the importing country. This issue has been considered most frequently in the field of pharmaceuticals, where repackaging for regulatory purposes is most likely to happen and where such repackaging could have an impact on the products themselves.

In a series of 1996 decisions before the ECJ (*Bristol-Myers Squibb* v. *Paranova, Eurim-Pharm* v. *Beiersdorf* and *MPA Pharma* v. *Rhone-Poulenc* [1996] FSR 225), it was confirmed that a trade mark owner could not use his rights to prevent importation of products that had been put into circulation in the EC with his consent unless, as a result of relabelling or repackaging, the quality of the goods might be adversely affected. In these cases, the court considered that alteration only to the outer packaging would not impair the goods unless the quality of the replacement outer packaging was such as to undermine the good reputation of the trade mark owner. Also, if during repackaging the goods have been exposed to inappropriate storage conditions (such as high temperature or humidity) or if in any translated or reproduced instructions there are any errors or omissions, this too could impact adversely on the trade mark owner. The list is not exhaustive and it seems that the ECJ is prepared to consider any sensible objection on the grounds that it impairs the quality and reputation of the goods and, hence, the trade mark. In *Glaxo* v. *Dowelhurst* (Case C-143/00) [2002] FSR 61, the ECJ confirmed that, although repackaging is *prima facie* harmful to the trade mark owner's rights, the trade mark owner cannot rely on those rights to prevent repackaging if it is objectively necessary to avoid artificially partitioning the market within the EEA. Repackaging, rather than relabelling by overstickering the original packaging, will be objectively necessary if a significant proportion of consumers would object to relabelled products. The ECJ also confirmed that the parallel importer must give prior notice to the trade mark owner of any intended repackaging. The United Kingdom High Court followed the ECJ in a second judgment on 6 February 2003 and held that, on the facts, repackaged products did infringe the United Kingdom trade marks, but relabelled (overstickered) products did not.

Another ECJ case considered the position where the trade mark owner uses slightly different trade marks for the same product in different Member States, so that the mark used on the repackaging differs from that on the original packaging (*Pharmacia and Upjohn* v. *Paranova* (Case C-379/97) [2000] FSR 621).

In *Phytheron International SA* v. *Jean Bourdon SA* (Case C-352/95) ECJ, 20 March 1997 [1997] FSR 936, the owner of a French trade mark relating to health products refused to allow the products bearing the trade mark to be imported into France from Germany (being the EU country into which they had been sold from Turkey). This refusal was based on French trade mark law. The seller of the products argued that the French law on this point was in breach of EU competition law and the case was referred to the ECJ. The ECJ decided the case on the basis, not of the Treaty of Rome, but on the EU Trade Marks Directive and the provision preventing a trade mark owner from using his trade mark rights to stop the importation of goods to which the trade marks had been applied by or with his consent (unless the goods had been subsequently impaired). The position regarding goods imported into the United Kingdom from outside Europe has been far less clear. There have, however, been a string of recent cases on this issue starting with *Silhouette International Schmied GmbH and Co. KG* v. *Hartlauer Handelsgesellschaft mbH* [1998] FSR 729. In that case, Silhouette objected to the sale in Austria of grey market 'Silhouette' glasses. The glasses were old models which had been offered for sale in Eastern Europe but were then reimported into Austria. Silhouette argued that the sale of the glasses in Austria amounted to an infringement of the registered trade mark there since it had not consented to the sale of those glasses in Austria. The ECJ held that individual EEA Member States could not provide in their national laws that trade mark owners were automatically deemed to have consented to the sale of genuine grey market goods imported from outside the EEA. At the time, this case was thought to mean that trade mark owners could prevent the sale into Europe of grey market goods which had been imported from outside the EEA. The position was clarified in *Sebago Inc. and Ancienne Maison Dubois et Fils SA* v. *GB Unic SA* [1999] 2 CMLR 1317. In that case, Sebago and its Belgium distributor objected to the sale in Belgium of Sebago shoes which had been imported from El Salvador without Sebago's consent. The defendant argued that consent could be implied because the shoes were identical to others which were sold in Belgium through Sebago's authorised distributor. The ECJ disagreed. It held that a trade mark owner cannot be deemed to have consented to the parallel importation of its branded goods from outside the EEA just because it had itself sold the same type of goods within the EEA.

Both these cases originated from actions in countries other than the United Kingdom. The United Kingdom High Court seemed to be taking a slightly different view as was shown in the case of *Zino Davidoff SA* v. *A&G Imports* [1999] RPC 631. This concerned the sale of a fragrance which had been imported into the United Kingdom from Singapore. The High Court in the United Kingdom held that Davidoff could not prevent the sale of these goods in the United Kingdom if it had not expressly prohibited the sale of those goods in the United Kingdom when it first put the goods on the market. The fragrance had been sold to Davidoff's distributor in Singapore without any such restriction and, therefore, the court held that Davidoff could not now prevent the parallel importation into the United Kingdom. This case was referred to the ECJ for a further ruling and came up for consideration with the joined cases brought by Levi Strauss against Tesco and Costco (*Zino Davidoff SA* v. *A&G Imports Ltd, Levi Strauss & Co.* v. *Costco Wholesale UK Ltd, Levi Strauss & Co.* v. *Tesco Stores Ltd* [2002] Ch 109). The ECJ's decision in these cases shifted the position on parallel imports back in favour of the trade mark proprietor. It held that: (1) implied consent of the trade mark proprietor who has placed his goods on the market outside the EEA to the subsequent marketing of those products within the EEA can only be found if the facts show that the trade mark proprietor has renounced his right to oppose such marketing; (2) the burden of proof is on the parallel importer to prove such consent by the trade mark proprietor; (3) just because the trade mark proprietor has not informed all subsequent purchasers of his opposition to subsequent marketing, and the goods do not have any statement on them prohibiting sale in the EEA, and there is no contractual restriction imposed on the purchaser of the goods from the trade mark proprietor on resale in the EEA, implied consent from the trade mark proprietor to sale in the EEA cannot be inferred; and (4) it does not matter that the parallel importer is not aware of the trade mark proprietor's objections to resale of the products in the EEA.

The issue of copyright in packaging of parallel imported goods was considered in the case of *Parfums Christian Dior SA* v. *Evora BV* (Case C-337/95) [1998] 1 CMLR 737. In this case, Evora (through its subsidiary chemist business) advertised for sale certain Christian Dior perfume products which it had obtained through parallel imports. The advertising included leaflets comprising photographs of the perfume bottles and associated packaging. Christian Dior sued for infringement of its trade marks and copyright claiming that the advertising leaflets contained unauthorised reproductions of the Dior trade marks and of the copyright works comprised in the perfume bottles and packaging. The court decided that the EU Trade Mark Directive specifically allowed use of trade marks in connection with the resale of goods in the EU which had been put onto the EU market by the trade mark owner, and in relation to copyright, similar principles applied as a result of the impact of Articles 30 and 36 (now Articles 28 and 30) of the Treaty of Rome on free movement of goods. See also the case of *Norwegian Government* v. *Astra Norge AS* (Case E-1/98) Advisory Opinion of the ECJ, 24 November 1998 [1998] 1 CMLR 860. However, there is a distinction between copyright works which are reproduced in a physical form (where exhaustion of rights applies in the same way as in relation to trade marks) and copyright works whose value is realised in performance or broadcast of the work (where each separate performance or broadcast requires authorisation and, therefore, any one particular broadcast or performance does not exhaust rights in the copyright work). For decisions on the latter issue see *Ministère Public* v. *Tournier Civil Party Verney* (Case C-395/87) [1991] FSR 465 and *Warner Brothers Inc. & Another* v. *Christiansen* (Case C-158/86) [1988] ECR 2605.

The ECJ has also considered the application of Articles 28 and 30 to patents. In *Merck & Co. Inc.* v. *Primecrown* (Joined cases C-267/95 and C-268/95) [1997] FSR 237 the patent owner had marketed the patented drugs in Spain and Portugal (once they had joined the EC) at a time when no patent protection was available for drugs in those countries. The ECJ held that the products had been put into circulation in the EC by the patent owner (or with his consent) and as a result he had exhausted his rights in the patent. The absence of patent protection in Spain and Portugal was irrelevant. This position was confirmed in *Sandvik Aktiebolag* v. *K. R. Pfiffner*

(UK) Ltd [2000] FSR 17, where the proprietor of a patented product had consented to its marketing in countries in the EC where it had not obtained patent protection.

Although exhaustion of rights has not been considered in case law in the area of designs, the new Council Regulation on the Community Designs and the Directive on the legal protection of designs both include specific provision on the exhaustion of rights doctrine, and consequently this is mirrored in the Registered Designs Act 1949 as amended by the Registered Design Regulations 2001.

24.5 Licensing and Article 81

Article 81(1) of the Treaty of Rome prohibits agreements, arrangements and concerted practices that have as their object or effect the prevention, restriction or distortion of competition and that may affect trade between Member States. Intellectual property licences (particularly exclusive licences) are likely to fall within the ambit of Article 81(1). The consequence is that the agreement (or possibly just the anti-competitive provisions) will be void under Article 81(2), and the parties might be subject to fines of up to 10 per cent of worldwide turnover. It was previously possible to apply to the European Commisson for an individual exemption under Article 81(3). Regulation 1/2003 (the Modernisation Regulation) which came into force on 1 May 2004, abolished the system under which parties notified the European Commission of their agreements to gain an exemption. Parties to agreements are now required to assess their own agreements and establish whether an agreement that falls within Article 81(1) satisfies the criteria in Article 81(3). If the arrangements can be justified on the basis that they contribute to improving the production or distribution of goods, or they promote technical or economic progress, and they allow consumers a fair share of resulting benefit, the arrangements may not be caught by Article 81(1).

Licensing intellectual property rights is the way in which technological advances are exploited, in most cases, for the ultimate benefit of the consumer. Competition authorities recognise this. Consequently, the European Commission has the power to enact Regulations (which have direct effect in all EC countries) which disapply Article 81(1) from certain categories of agreement. These Regulations are known as Block Exemption Regulations.

24.6 Block Exemption Regulations

Although there are Block Exemption Regulations relating to vertical agreements (Regulation 2790/99), specialisation agreements (Regulation

417/85) and research and development agreements (Regulation 418/85) which are relevant to certain arrangements involving intellectual property rights, there is currently only one block exemption specifically relating to intellectual property licences. This is the Technology Transfer Block Exemption ('TTBE') (Regulation 772/2004), which covers licences of patents and/or know-how. The Regulation came into force with effect from 1 May 2004 and replaced the earlier Technology Transfer Block Exemption (Regulation 240/96) which was viewed as inflexible. At the same time the European Commission issued a Notice entitled 'Guidelines on the Application of Article 81 of the EC Treaty to Technology Transfer Agreements' which is not binding on the Community Courts.

The new TTBE represents a very significant change to the EC rules. It has introduced new market share limitations for the first time in relation to technology licensing arrangements. These are calculated by reference to the previous year's sales data for the relevant technology and product markets. The TTBE distinguishes between competitors and non-competitors: actual or potential competitors cannot rely on the block exemption in respect of certain clauses if they have a combined market share above 20 per cent, and the market share threshold for non-competitors is 30 per cent for each party. There are stricter rules for agreements between competitors as they are seen as more likely to have serious anti-competitive effects. The distinction between the treatment of competitors and non-competitors is carried through into separate lists of 'hardcore restrictions' for competitors and non-competitors. Any inclusion of a hardcore restriction will prevent the entire agreement from benefiting from the TTBE. The TTBE also lists restrictions which are not block exempted and which require individual assessment of their anti-competitive and pro-competitive effects. If an agreement contains any of these restrictions the rest of the agreement can still be covered by the block exemption, if the restriction can be severed from the agreement. The European Commission and the national competition authorities in each Member State of the EU will be able to withdraw the benefit of the block exemption if the effect of an agreement will be to restrict access to the market for other technologies or for other potential licensees, or where the licensed technology is not exploited.

The TTBE also applies to software copyright and designs and may apply to trade mark licences provided that the licence does not constitute the primary object of the agreement, and the licence is directly related to the application of the licensed technology. However, there are no equivalent Regulations for licences of other types of copyright or trade marks. This is unsatisfactory because the European Commission and the ECJ have made it clear that such licences can fall foul of Article 81(1) and, arguably, licences of trade marks and copyright are more widespread than patent or know-how licences.

In the area of copyright licensing, a distinction is made between 'non-performance copyrights' (that is, copyright embodied in a physical product) and 'performance copyrights'. Agreements relating to the licensing and exploitation of performance copyrights are treated more favourably under Article 81(1), probably because in these days of satellite and other forms of transmission, a licence agreement is the only way of controlling the exploitation of such copyrights outside the licensed territory. The decision of *Coditel SA* v. *Ciné Vog Films SA (No. 2)* [1982] ECR 3381 is instructive on the type of restrictions which will be held to fall within Article 81(1).

In relation to trade mark licensing, *Re the Agreements of Davide Campari-Milano SpA* [1978] FSR 528 and *Moosehead/Whitbread Commission Decision* (90/186/EEC) [1991] 4 CMLR 391 are helpful for guidance on what kinds of restrictions can fall within Article 81(1). In the *Campari* case, provisions requiring the licensee to comply with the licensor's manufacturing instructions and to buy secret raw materials from the licensor were held not contrary to Article 81(1), as they were necessary to maintain the quality of the goods and hence the goodwill of the trade mark. Similarly in *Moosehead*, quality control restrictions were held not to fall within Article 81(1). However, *Moosehead* also contained restrictions on passive selling outside the licensed territory and this is what brought the arrangement within Article 81(1). As it happened, an exemption was granted because the arrangements overall did not eliminate competition in respect of the goods in question in the Common Market.

Hot Topic . . .

INTELLECTUAL PROPERTY AND ARTICLE 82

Article 82 of the Treaty of Rome prohibits activities that constitute an abuse of a dominant position and that have a potential effect on trade between the countries of the EEA. Like Article 81(1), an offender can be subject to fines of up to 10 per cent of worldwide turnover. An infringement may also enable third parties to claim damages or injunctive relief in national courts.

Article 82 is aimed not only at concerted activities between two or more parties but also at the activities of a single entity. In order to hold a dominant position, a party must have a dominant share of the relevant product market within a substantial part of the EEA; this has been held, in a number of cases, to mean one country or even a regional area of a country. The definition of the relevant product market is crucial

to deciding the market share, and the Commission has defined 'product markets' very narrowly in some cases.

There is no exact percentage share above which dominance is proved. Whether a share of 40 per cent is dominant will depend on a number of factors: what are the shares held by other participants in the relevant product market?; what are the barriers to entry? (If the other participants do not own the vital intellectual property rights of which the 40 per cent holder is owner or exclusive licensee, then the 40 per cent company will probably be dominant.)

Dominance alone is not prohibited by Article 82. Once dominance is established, abuse of that dominance must be shown. The list of activities that are an abuse is non-exhaustive. The most common examples are discriminatory pricing, predatory pricing (that is, setting prices low to get rid of the competition with a view to then increasing prices), discount and rebate schemes to tie in customers, refusal to supply and tie-in sales.

It has always been considered that ownership of intellectual property rights could, of itself, constitute dominance so that abuse of that ownership (for example, by refusing to grant licences or charging excessive licence fees) could give rise to a breach of Article 82. Until the case of *RTE and ITP* v. *Commission* [1995] 4 CMLR 718 (Magill), however, this had not been confirmed. In that case, the ECJ decided that the refusal to license a third party to reproduce programme schedules breached Article 82, because the ownership of copyright in the weekly programme schedules gave an effective monopoly over a class of information and hence their refusal to supply prevented an unfulfilled consumer need being met. This is

not to say that ownership of any intellectual property right will put the owner in a dominant position – the distinguishing factor in the Magill case was that, by owning copyright in the television programme listings, RTE had an effective monopoly over a category of information. Whilst the ECJ said that intellectual property rights would only breach Article 82 in exceptional circumstances, it found that the exceptional circumstances in that case included the fact that the refusal to grant a licence amounted to preventing a new product from coming on the market for which there was a proven consumer demand (see also *Volvo AB* v. *Erik Veng (UK) Ltd* (Case C-238/87) [1988] ECR 6211 and *IMS Health* (Case C-418/01) [2004] CMLR 28).

In *Attheraces Ltd* v. *British Horseracing Board Ltd* [2005] EWHC 3015 the United Kingdom court held that Attheraces Ltd had a dominant position in the market for the supply of pre-race data to those in the horse racing industry who needed the information to provide their services to their customers. They had abused that dominant position by threatening to cut off the supply of the information without justification and by proposing excessive and unfair prices.

Then, of course, there is the *Microsoft* case (Commission Decision of 24 March 2004, Case COMP/C-3/37.792 – Microsoft), who were fined 497 million euros by the European Commission in March 2004 for two alleged abuses under Article 82. The first related to their tying in of their Media Player product to their operating system, and the other related to their work group server operating system. In relation to the latter, Microsoft were found to have abused their dominant position in relation to operating systems (they had 90 per cent of the market) in order to leverage their position in relation to work group server operating systems. The case was brought as a result of Microsoft's refusal to supply interoperability information to a competitor, Sun Microsystems, relying on their intellectual property rights. Sun had wanted the information in order to develop their own software for work group server operating systems that would run on Windows. Microsoft was forced to disclose this information to its competitors in order to promote innovation in the market. Microsoft's appeal to the Court of First Instance was heard in April 2006 and a decision is awaited.

In the meantime, the European Commission is currently undertaking a policy review under Article 82.

Summary

24.1 Ownership and exercise of intellectual property rights conflict with competition policies.

24.2 In the United Kingdom, competition law has now been reformed by the Competition Act 1998 and is now based on the principles of EC competition law.

Summary cont'd

24.3 The principles of EC competition law can be found in Articles 28–30, 81, 82 and 295 of the Treaty of Rome.

24.4 Once the owner of an intellectual property right has freely put products on to the market in one part of the EEA, he cannot use his rights in another part of the EEA to prevent resale of the goods in question unless, in the case of repackaged goods, the quality of the goods has been adversely affected.

24.5 Agreements that distort competition in the EEA are controlled by Article 81.

24.6 Where consumers are likely to benefit, the competition authorities can make provision for automatic exemption from Article 81(1) under a Block Exemption Regulation. To date there is only one Block Exemption relating specifically to intellectual property licensing – the Technology Transfer Block Exemption.

24.7 Article 82 controls activities that amount to an abuse of a dominant position.

Exercises

24.1 How does ownership of an intellectual property right conflict with competition?

24.2 Outline the laws and bodies in place that are used to promote competition in the United Kingdom. Are they adequate?

24.3 How might an owner of intellectual property abuse his rights so as to distort competition in the EEA? Discuss whether EC competition law is adequate to control such abuse.

24.4 Is there a proper balance in protecting the fruits of creative endeavour and maintaining an effective competition policy?

24.5 Consider the courts' developing attitude towards parallel imports.

Part V

Intellectual Property and the Internet

Chapter 25

The Internet

Key words

▶ **Framing** – where one website frames a page from another, without the URL of the other site being shown.
▶ **Linking** – connecting one website to another through the use of hypertext links.

25.1 Introduction

The Internet has become an established medium for communication and the carrying on of business. Because goods and services are advertised, sold and, in some cases, delivered over the Internet, all those intellectual property issues which arise in the course of traditional forms of advertising and trade arise in the Internet environment.

As the Internet was a completely new channel which gave rise to forms of business not previously envisaged, there had been a feeling at the outset that intellectual property would be treated differently in this new environment. Although it is true that some changes have been and will continue to be made to existing laws to iron out some of the extreme consequences of a strict application of existing intellectual property laws to the Internet environment, in broad terms the same rules that apply 'offline' apply 'online' in relation to ownership, use and infringement of intellectual property rights. This is probably one of the main reasons why, despite the growing body of English case law on intellectual property and the Internet, most of the decisions to date have been unsurprising in their results.

25.2 Copyright and the Internet

The Internet, as its name suggests, is an international network of computers enabling communication worldwide between anyone connected to that network. In order for a computer to access any material which is transmitted over the Internet, it is necessary for that computer to produce a copy of the material in question even though such a copy may only be transitory. If the material in question is a copyright work, such copying would in theory require the permission of the copyright owner (but see now s.28A of the 1988 Act, for example).

Because the Internet has grown so suddenly and was, at least, initially spearheaded by many newly formed start-up companies and individuals who may not have previously operated established businesses, the need for licences of any copyright materials being reproduced by these Internet businesses was sometimes overlooked. The design of a website, all contents of that website displayed when accessed, and the software used to create and needed to access the website are all copyright works in which the copyright will be owned by somebody. When users visit a website, they are producing a copy of all the relevant website pages on their own computer in order to view that website. Going one step further, if a user then downloads and prints any part of the website it is making a copy which requires the licence of the copyright owner. One further step that is often taken is to create a link from one site to another which will generally involve producing a copy of an element of the other website. Again, a licence to reproduce relevant copyright works is needed. However, the general practice on the Internet has been not to seek a licence and to presume an implied licence from the operator of the website. This licence can easily be presumed in the case of access to a website, and to downloading and printing off certain parts of a website (although one can imagine that such a licence could not necessarily be implied in relation to all parts of a website). The uncertainty in this area has been alleviated by the Copyright and Related Rights Regulations 2003 (SI 2003 No. 2498) ('Copyright Regulations').

A website providing a link to material on another website so that that material appeared on the first website would be caught by the new definitions of broadcasts and on-demand services which cover all Internet transmissions.

25.3 The Copyright Directive

The copyright issues arising out of the Internet prompted discussion at the European level, which resulted in the Directive of the European Parliament and the Council of the European Union 2001/29/EC on the harmonisation of certain aspects of copyright and related rights in the information society. As its title suggests, the main aim of the Directive was to harmonise the laws of Member States in relation to the protection of copyright works in the electronic environment. Because of the conflicting concerns of two strong lobby groups, the telecommunications companies and the rights holders, the Directive took a long time to get approval; it received final approval on 22 June 2001 with an implementation deadline of 22 December 2002. After extensive consultation, the Copyright Regulations came into force in the United Kingdom on 31 October 2003. The Regulations amended the wording of the 1988 Act, and the effects of these changes have been covered in the relevant earlier chapters of this book.

25.4 Trade Marks and the Internet

Whenever goods or services are being advertised or traded over the Internet, the same issues that arise in relation to traditional trading in connection with trade marks arise in this context. However, one specific area of concern that has arisen out of the Internet in connection with trade marks is in relation to domain names. These are the Internet addresses registered by users of the Internet to enable e-mails to be sent to them or their websites to be located. It is usual for an organisation with an established trading name to wish their domain name to incorporate all or part of its trading name which is likely, therefore, to be a trade mark. However, the registration process for domain names is far less regulated than that applying to the registration of trade marks. In particular, it is possible for a number of domain names to co-exist for the same goods or services which comprise essentially the same word or trade name provided that at least one character is different; so, for instance, website.com, web-site.com and web_site.com could all co-exist as domain names for the same type of business, although to the casual observer there is very little difference between them. This problem should be alleviated by the fact that there is now a new range of top-level domain names available for use. These top-level domain names include .aero, .biz, .coop, .info, .name, .museum and .pro. The intention is to enable businesses to register a domain name which may comprise the same trading name as another business but to identify it as being in a particular business area, thus distinguishing those businesses using the same trading name but in different business fields and hopefully avoiding the problem of competing businesses seeking to register the exact same domain name. There are two major dispute resolution procedures which can be used as an alternative to litigation in relation to domain name disputes. These are the Internet Corporation for Assigned Names and Numbers (ICANN) Uniform Domain Name Dispute Resolution Policy (UDRP), which is administered by WIPO and others, and the dispute procedure which is operated by Nominet, the United Kingdom domain name registration authority. The ICANN UDRP can be used in disputes involving domain names in the .com, .org and .net top-level domains including the list of domains referred to above, as well as several country-specific domain names (for example, .nu, .tv, .ws), while Nominet deals with disputes involving domain names in the .uk top-level domain.

A particular problem that arose in relation to domain names has been the practice of 'cyber squatting'. This practice involved an individual or organisation that did not have rights in a particularly well-known trade name, registering a domain name comprising that trade name in advance of the legitimate owner of that trading name. The 'cyber squatter' then approached the legitimate trader seeking large sums of money for transfer of the registered domain name. Although the legitimate trade mark owner might be able to avoid paying for the cyber squatter's domain name by registering a domain name with a small variation, most large trading organisations would prefer to know that any domain name incorporating any part of their trade mark was owned by them rather than an uncontrolled third party. In the area of domain names, one of the most well-known cases is *British Telecommunications plc v. One in a Million Ltd and Others, Virgin Enterprises Ltd v. One in a Million Ltd, J. Sainsbury plc v. One in a Million Ltd, Marks & Spencer plc v. One in a Million Ltd, Ladbroke Group plc v. One in a Million Ltd* [1999] FSR 1. In that case, the defendant had specialised in registering domain names which contained the names or brands of well-known businesses without the brand owner's consent and offering them for sale. Among the brands concerned were Marks & Spencer, Sainsbury, Virgin and British Telecom, and all of these companies sued the defendant alleging passing off and trade mark infringement. The court in that case found for the claimants on both claims. First, although the court acknowledged that the mere creation of an 'instrument of deception' (in this case, the domain names containing the claimants' well-known brand names) was not passing off, the subsequent offering for sale of those names with the implied potential damage arising out of the brand owner not buying those names, did amount to passing off. In relation to trade mark infringement, the court found that the defendant's use of the claimants' well-known trade marks which had a reputation in the United Kingdom was detrimental to the marks and was enough to amount to infringement under s.10(3) of the Trade Marks Act. However, in other domain name cases, the courts have been prepared to accept that several people might have legitimate claims to the same domain name. In *MBNA America Bank NA, MBNA International Bank Ltd v. Stephen Freeman* [2001] EBLR 13, the claimant was not awarded an interim injunction to prevent the defendant from using a website which he had set up using the letters MBNA for dissimilar services (banner advertisements on websites), because there was no likelihood of confusion. He was, however, restrained from selling the domain name prior to the trial without the leave of the court. In *French Connection Ltd v. Sutton* [2000] ETMR 341, the owners of the well-known brands did not succeed in their application for an interim injunction for passing off against an individual who had registered the domain name FCUK.com and tried to sell it to the claimant. The judge was not convinced of the claimant's goodwill in the FCUK mark, or that people would be confused. Following similar logic, in the case of *easyJet Airline Co. Ltd v. Dainty (t/a Easy Realestate)* [2002] FSR 6, easyJet, the airline (which had expanded its brand into other areas such as Internet cafés and car rental), was able to get an injunction against the defendant who had registered Easyrealestate.co.uk as a domain name. However, easyJet had been successful in this case because the court found that the use of the 'easy' name by the defendant, together with the get-up of its website which was very similar to the easyJet get-up, constituted passing off. The judge said that easyJet did not have the exclusive right to use the word 'easy' in combination with any other word. This is similar to the position in the offline world where use of a commonly used word as a brand name will create hurdles for a brand owner seeking some exclusivity of its brand name. In *Phones 4U Ltd* v. *Phone4U.co.uk Internet Ltd* [2005] EWHC 334, the claimant again failed to prevent the defendant from using domain names incorporating 'phones4u' even though both businesses sold telephones. The Court found that the claimant's reputation in Phones4u only extended to its retail shops, and that it was made sufficiently clear on the defendant's website when a purchase was about to be made that it was not the claimant's site. However, this decision was overturned by the Court of Appeal as we were going to press – [2006] EWCA Civ 244.

Hot Topic . . .
INTERNET LINKS

A practice on the Internet which has raised trade mark issues is linking. Linking involves the creation of hypertext links from one website to another. A simple link will take the user to the homepage of the other website; a deeplink will take the user to a page other than the homepage. In both instances the link is often created using a word which is the trade mark or trading name of the operator of the linked-to website. If such use is without authority, this can result in a claim for trade mark infringement and/or passing off. A similar activity is framing, which is where one website frames a page from another, without the URL of the other site being shown. This can lead to a claim in passing off where there is a risk of the user being confused as to the origin of the framed page. There has been a United Kingdom case on trade mark infringements and metatags. A metatag is a word which is used as a keyword for search engines. Use of the word in a website will ensure that the website address is thrown up by certain search engines when a user conducts a particular search incorporating that keyword. If the keyword selected is someone else's trade mark or trading name, an action for trade mark infringement and/or passing off may arise.

In *Reed Executive plc & Another* v. *Reed Business Information Ltd & Others* [2004] EWCA Civ 159, the defendant, who was in a similar business field to the claimant, used the word 'Reed' as a metatag on its website so that search engines would direct users to the defendant's site when the word 'Reed' was used as search parameters. The Court of Appeal held that there was no trade mark or passing off infringement by using the word 'Reed' as a metatag (but see also the earlier case of *Roadtech Computer Systems Ltd* v. *Mandata (Management and Data Services) Ltd* [2000] ETMR 970).

25.5 | Patents and the Internet

Although not a problem which has yet arisen in the United Kingdom, a few years ago there were a number of claims threatened by US companies for infringement of patents that they claimed to have obtained in relation to processes used for online trading. One example of this was amazon.com that obtained a preliminary injunction in the USA to protect its patented express lane shopping technology against infringement. This injunction was obtained against barnesandnoble.com which had been using a version of one-click technology which Amazon claimed infringed its patent. However, following challenges raised by Barnes and Noble as to the validity of Amazon's one-click technology patent, the preliminary injunction was discharged. BT also failed in its attempt to sue Prodigy Communications, a US ISP, for infringement of BT's patent which BT claimed gave it a monopoly over hyperlinking. The BT patent covered a system allowing multiple users to access data stored on a central computer from remote terminals – the US court decided that Prodigy's activities were not caught by the patent.

An interesting point concerning patents and the Internet arose in the case of *Menashe Business Mercantile Ltd* v. *William Hill Organisation Ltd* [2003] 1 All ER 279 CA. In this case, Menashe held a European patent with effect in the United Kingdom for an invention called 'interactive computerised gaming system with remote control'. This system claimed 'a gaming system for playing an interactive casino game comprising a host computer, at least one terminal computer forming the player station, communication means for connecting the terminal computer to the host computer and ... characterised in that the terminal computer is situated at a location remote from the host computer'. William Hill claimed that there was no infringement of the United Kingdom patent since the host computer used in the operation of this system was located outside the United Kingdom. The court held that as far as users were concerned, they would be operating their terminals and benefiting from the system in the United Kingdom and, as such, the patented system was being used in the United Kingdom.

It is worth noting that in the USA a method of doing business can be patented whereas, under English law, such methods are specifically excluded under s.1(2) of the Patents Act. However, as discussed earlier, there are ways of constructing a patent specification so that software which achieves a new technical effect can obtain patent protection (especially if applied for through the European patent route). This, together with possible changes resulting from the discussions between the European Commission and the European Parliament in order to decide on a future course of action (see Chapter 3) could result in many similar claims for infringement of software patents relating to innovative Internet applications arising in the United Kingdom courts before too long.

25.6 Confidential Information and the Internet

In the case of *Sir Elton John & Others* v. *Countess Joulebine & Others*, LTL 20/2/2001, Countess Joulebine operated a website on which users were encouraged to post juicy bits of gossip. A counsel's advice relating to a case involving Sir Elton John was posted on the site anonymously. Countess Joulebine created a link from the homepage to the advice so that users could access it more easily. Sir Elton John obtained an injunction and sued for breach of confidence. Joulebine claimed she did not realise the advice was posted in breach of confidence and thought it might be a prank. The judge decided that Joulebine ought to have known that the advice was likely to have been posted in breach of confidence and therefore, as soon as she became aware of its existence on her website, she should have removed it (and certainly should not have created a link to the homepage). In reaching his decision the judge referred to established authorities on breach of confidence.

Summary

25.1 In the Internet environment, broadly the same rules apply to intellectual property as apply in the 'offline' environment.

25.2 This has been confirmed in relation to trade marks and passing off by cases such as *British Telecommunications plc & Others* v. *One in a Million*.

25.3 The Copyright Regulations have updated the law in relation to copyright in the Internet environment.

Exercise

Consider the changes introduced by the New Copyright Regulations. Do they represent a fundamental change in United Kingdom copyright law?

Bibliography

Bainbridge, *Intellectual Property Law*, 5th edn, Longman.

Bentley and Sherman, *Intellectual Property Law*, 2nd edn, OUP.

Clark, 'What is a Work of Artistic Craftmanship?', *Copyright World*, November 2000.

Clark, 'Commissioned Designs – Who Owns Them?', *Copyright World*, May 2002.

Cornish and Llewelyn, *Intellectual Property Law*, 5th edn, Sweet & Maxwell.

Garnett, Davies and Harbottle, *Copinger and Skone James on Copyright*, 15th edn.

Holyoak and Torremans, *Intellectual Property*, 2nd edn, Butterworths.

Howe, *Russell-Clarke and Howe on Industrial Designs*, 7th edn.

Laddie, Prescott, Vitoria, Speck and Lane, *The Modern Law of Copyright and Designs*, 3rd edn.

Index